THE HYPERNATURALS™

VOLUME THREE

BOOM!
STUDIOS

ROSS RICHIE CEO & Founder • JACK CUMMINS President • MARK SMYLIE Chief Creative Officer • MATT GAGNON Editor-in-Chief • FILIP SABLIK VP of Publishing & Marketing • STEPHEN CHRISTY VP of Development
LANCE KREITER VP of Licensing & Merchandising • PHIL BARBARO VP of Finance • BRYCE CARLSON Managing Editor • MEL CAYLO Marketing Manager • SCOTT NEWMAN Production Design Manager • DAFNA PLEBAN Editor • SHANNON WATTERS Editor
ERIC HARBURN Editor • REBECCA TAYLOR Editor • CHRIS ROSA Assistant Editor • ALEX GALER Assistant Editor • WHITNEY LEOPARD Assistant Editor • JASMINE AMIRI Assistant Editor • STEPHANIE GONZAGA Graphic Designer
MIKE LOPEZ Production Designer • HANNAH NANCE PARTLOW Production Designer • DEVIN FUNCHES E-Commerce & Inventory Coordinator • BRIANNA HART Executive Assistant • AARON FERRARA Operations Assistant • JOSE MEZA Sales Assistant

THE HYPERNATURALS

WRITTEN BY
DAN ABNETT & ANDY LANNING

ART BY
TOM DERENICK
ANDRES GUINALDO WITH INKS BY BIT

COLORS BY
STEPHEN DOWNER

LETTERS BY
ED DUKESHIRE

COVER BY
FRANCESCO MATTINA

EDITOR
DAFNA PLEBAN

MANAGING EDITOR
BRYCE CARLSON

TRADE DESIGN BY
MIKE LOPEZ

QUANTINUUM CONTENT DESIGNS BY
STEPHANIE GONZAGA
MIKE LOPEZ

CREATED BY
ABNETT, LANNING & WALKER

CHAPTER NINE

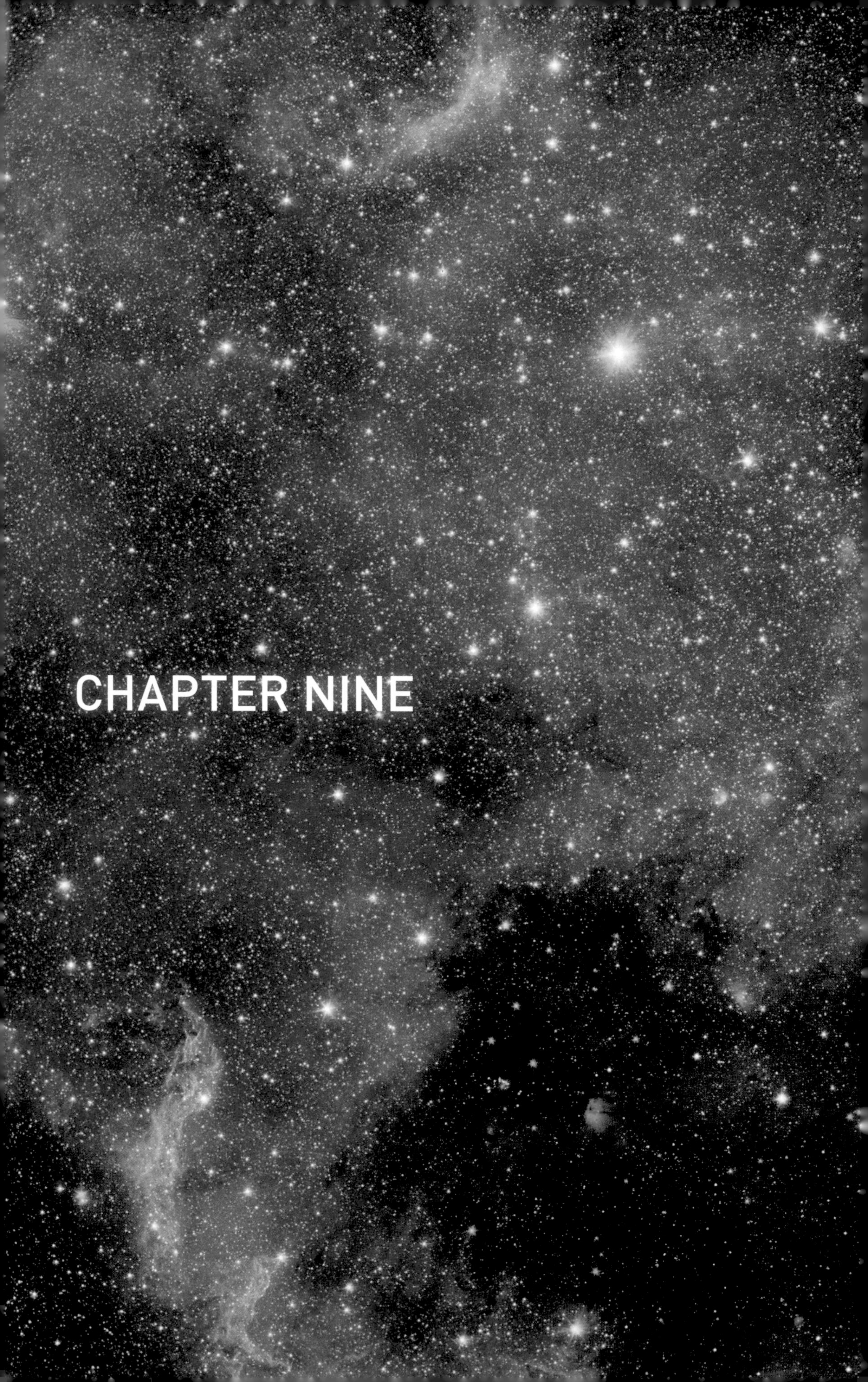

• **You have selected Q-Data link.**

• It is the 13th of January in the year **100 A.Q.**
   • Touch here to select an alternative to the **Anno Quantinuum** calendar system.
   • Touch here to load local weather reports for your **current cosmic location.**
   • Touch here to access **Q-Data newsflows** from planets near your current cosmic location.
   • Touch here for latest **Quantum Trip** transit times.

• Q-Data entry: The Quantinuum

• The Quantinuum is the name for the **human galactic culture**, and also for the **artificial intelligence** that controls its function.

• The Quantinuum was created 100 years ago at the start of the **Nanocene Era**. The Nanocene began when the Quantinuum AI achieved Singularity and refashioned human galactic culture. Succeeding the **Holocene Era**, the Nanocene is the next progression of human evolution and...

(to read this entry in full, touch here)

• You have selected live feed newsflow.

• Artificial stars ignited to light **Dark Nebula** prior to colonisation, **Colonial Resource** reports
• **Princess Alqua Farqua Laik** attends groundbreaking ceremony at the site of the **42 Baronus** space needle
• Confirmed reports of an incident at the museum world **Repository [33 Tarsus Red]**. **Hypernaturals** on scene
• Confirmed reports of break-out at **Tartarus Omni-max prison**
• Death reported of actor **Bretley Krecker**, famous for his award winning lead roles in the forties classics **Last Year In Aldebaran** and **Every Trip You Take**, as well as his beloved twenty year stint in **A.I. Law** as hard-hitting cyber-attorney **Rudy Twist**
• **Hypernaturals Central, San Diego**, refuses to comment on a connection between the attack **on Repository** and the ongoing investigation into the disappearance of the **Centennial Year Iteration** of the Team, lost during an emergency response mission to **28 Kosov** three days ago

• The Hypernaturals are the Quantinuum's foremost champions. Famous across the entirety of human galactic culture, the team members are selected on the basis of their **hypernatural powers** and their strength of character, and serve for five-year terms. In honor of the start of the twenty-first term, the line-up of the team's so-called "Centennial Year Iteration" has recently been announced amid huge publicity and--

...BREAKING NEWS... reports say the incident at the Quantinuum Archive and Museum World Repository involves Hypernaturals versus unregistered hyper-gifted individuals action and significant damage to the facility...

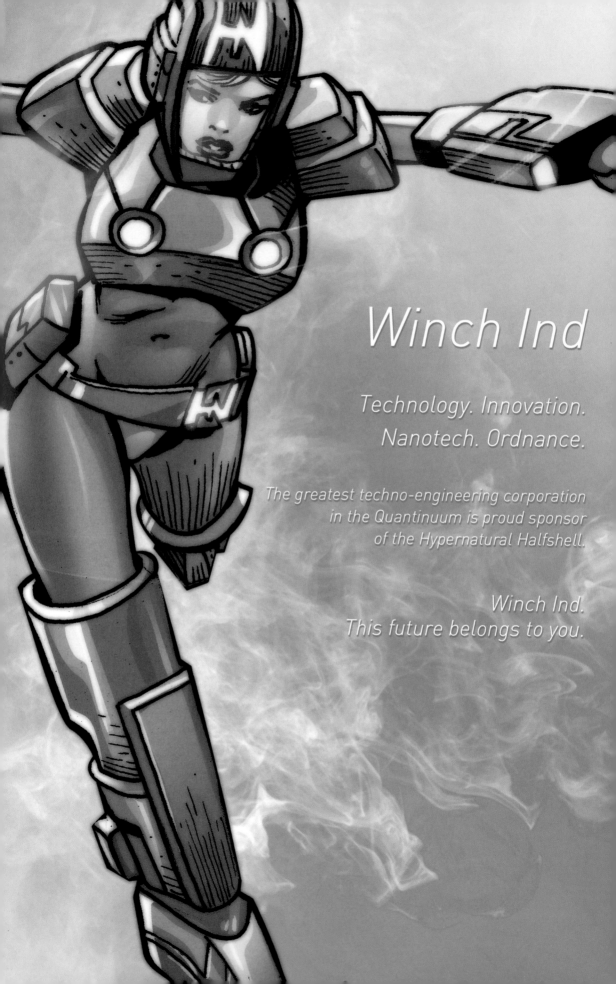

Winch Ind

Technology. Innovation.
Nanotech. Ordnance.

The greatest techno-engineering corporation
in the Quantinuum is proud sponsor
of the Hypernatural Halfshell.

Winch Ind.
This future belongs to you.

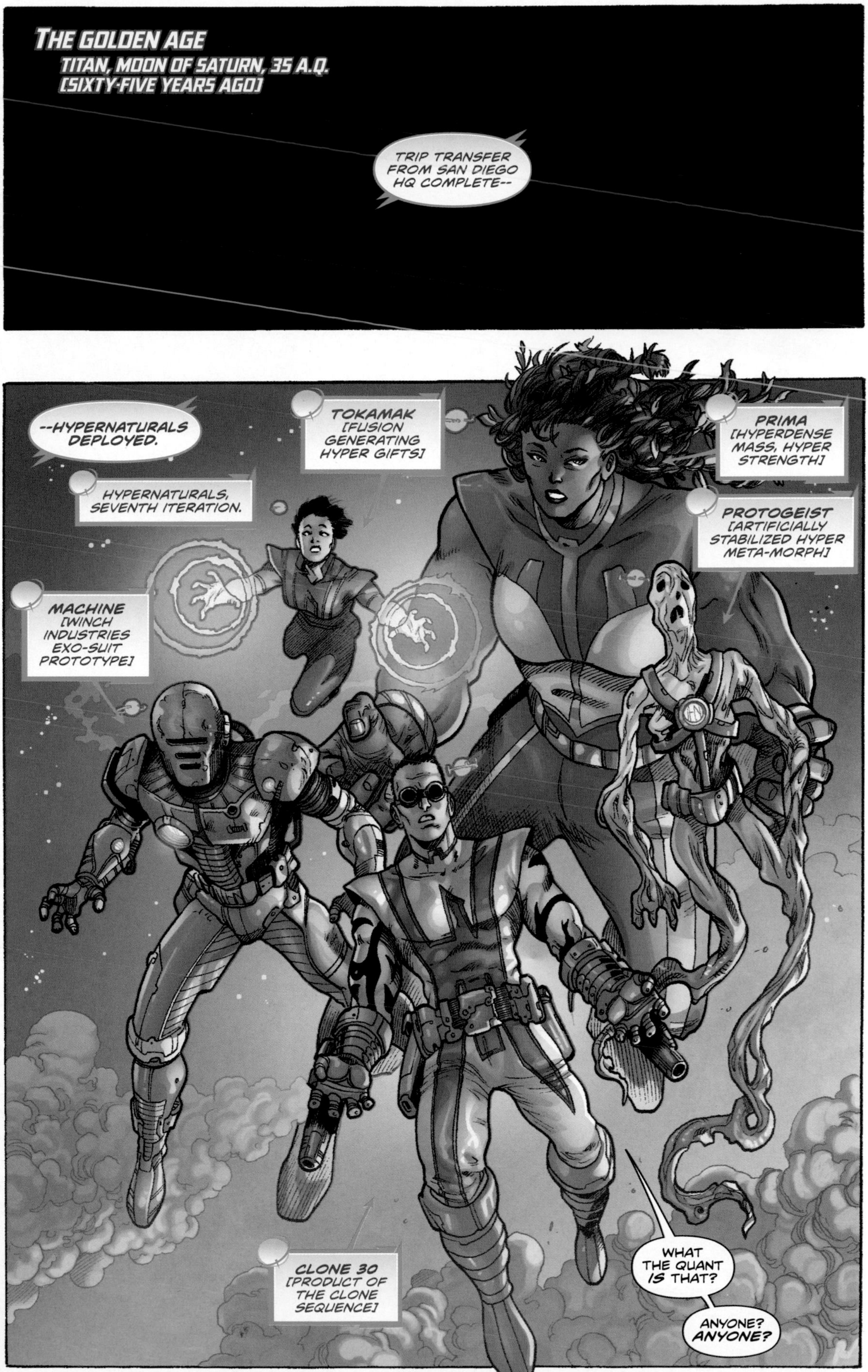
THE GOLDEN AGE
TITAN, MOON OF SATURN, 35 A.Q.
[SIXTY-FIVE YEARS AGO]
TRIP TRANSFER FROM SAN DIEGO HQ COMPLETE--
--HYPERNATURALS DEPLOYED.
HYPERNATURALS, SEVENTH ITERATION.
TOKAMAK [FUSION GENERATING HYPER GIFTS]
PRIMA [HYPERDENSE MASS, HYPER STRENGTH]
PROTOGEIST [ARTIFICIALLY STABILIZED HYPER META-MORPH]
MACHINE [WINCH INDUSTRIES EXO-SUIT PROTOTYPE]
CLONE 30 [PRODUCT OF THE CLONE SEQUENCE]
WHAT THE QUANT *IS* THAT?
ANYONE? ***ANYONE?***

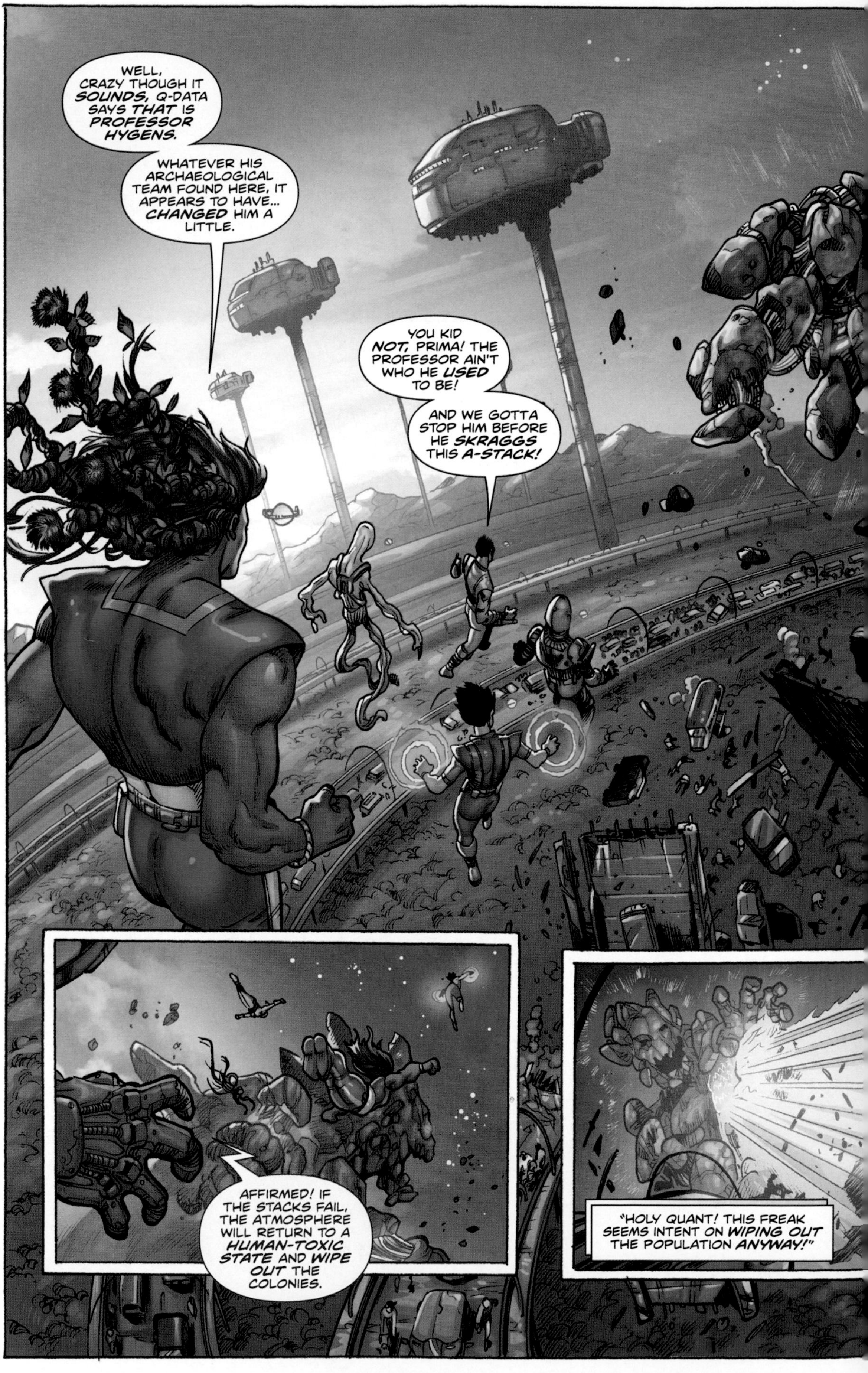
WELL, CRAZY THOUGH IT SOUNDS, Q-DATA SAYS THAT IS PROFESSOR HYGENS.
WHATEVER HIS ARCHAEOLOGICAL TEAM FOUND HERE, IT APPEARS TO HAVE... CHANGED HIM A LITTLE.
YOU KID NOT, PRIMA! THE PROFESSOR AIN'T WHO HE USED TO BE!
AND WE GOTTA STOP HIM BEFORE HE SKRAGGS THIS A-STACK!
AFFIRMED! IF THE STACKS FAIL, THE ATMOSPHERE WILL RETURN TO A HUMAN-TOXIC STATE AND WIPE OUT THE COLONIES.
"HOLY QUANT! THIS FREAK SEEMS INTENT ON WIPING OUT THE POPULATION ANYWAY!"

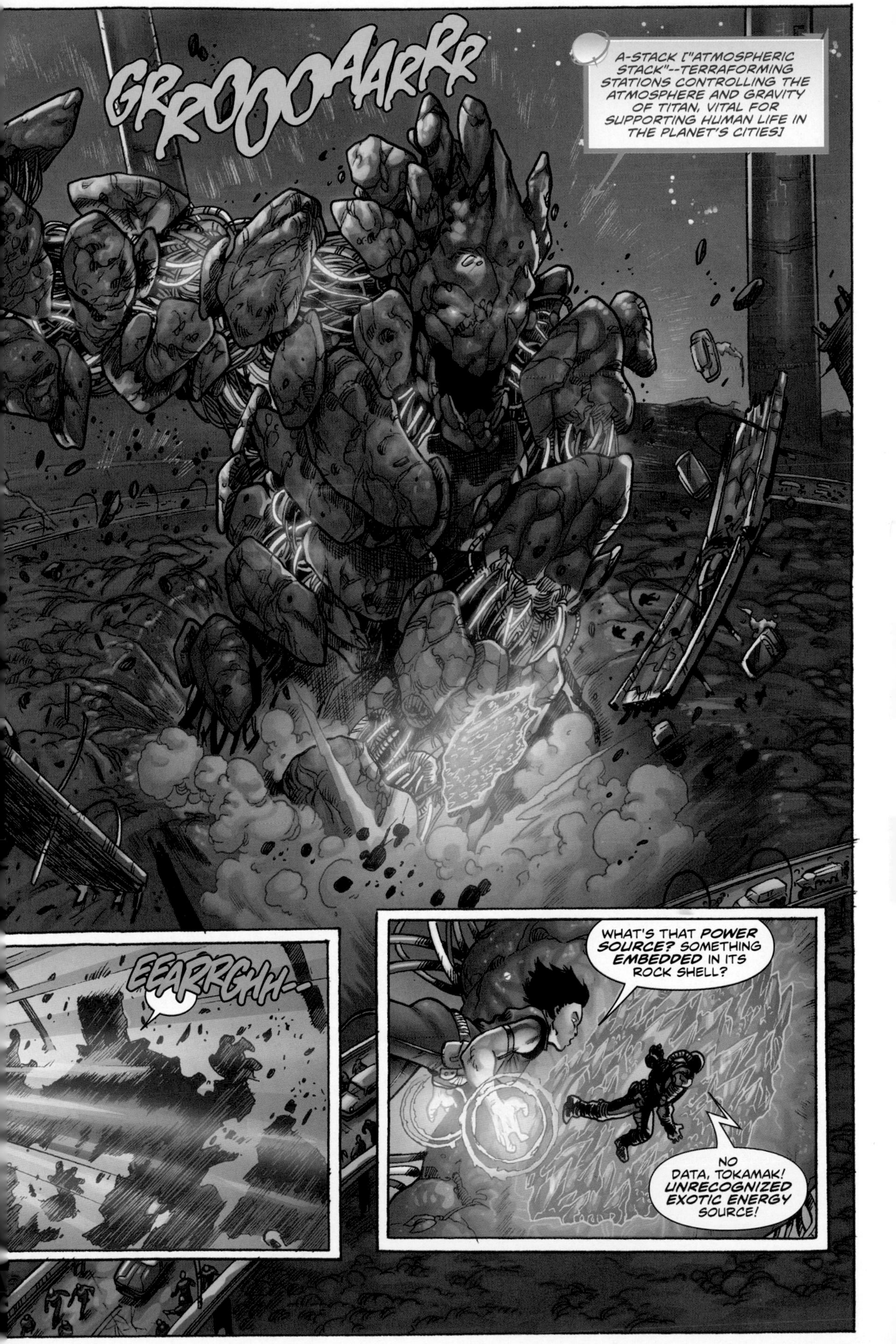
GRRROOOAARRR
A-STACK ["ATMOSPHERIC STACK"--TERRAFORMING STATIONS CONTROLLING THE ATMOSPHERE AND GRAVITY OF TITAN, VITAL FOR SUPPORTING HUMAN LIFE IN THE PLANET'S CITIES]
EEARRGHH--
WHAT'S THAT POWER SOURCE? SOMETHING EMBEDDED IN ITS ROCK SHELL?
NO DATA, TOKAMAK! UNRECOGNIZED EXOTIC ENERGY SOURCE!

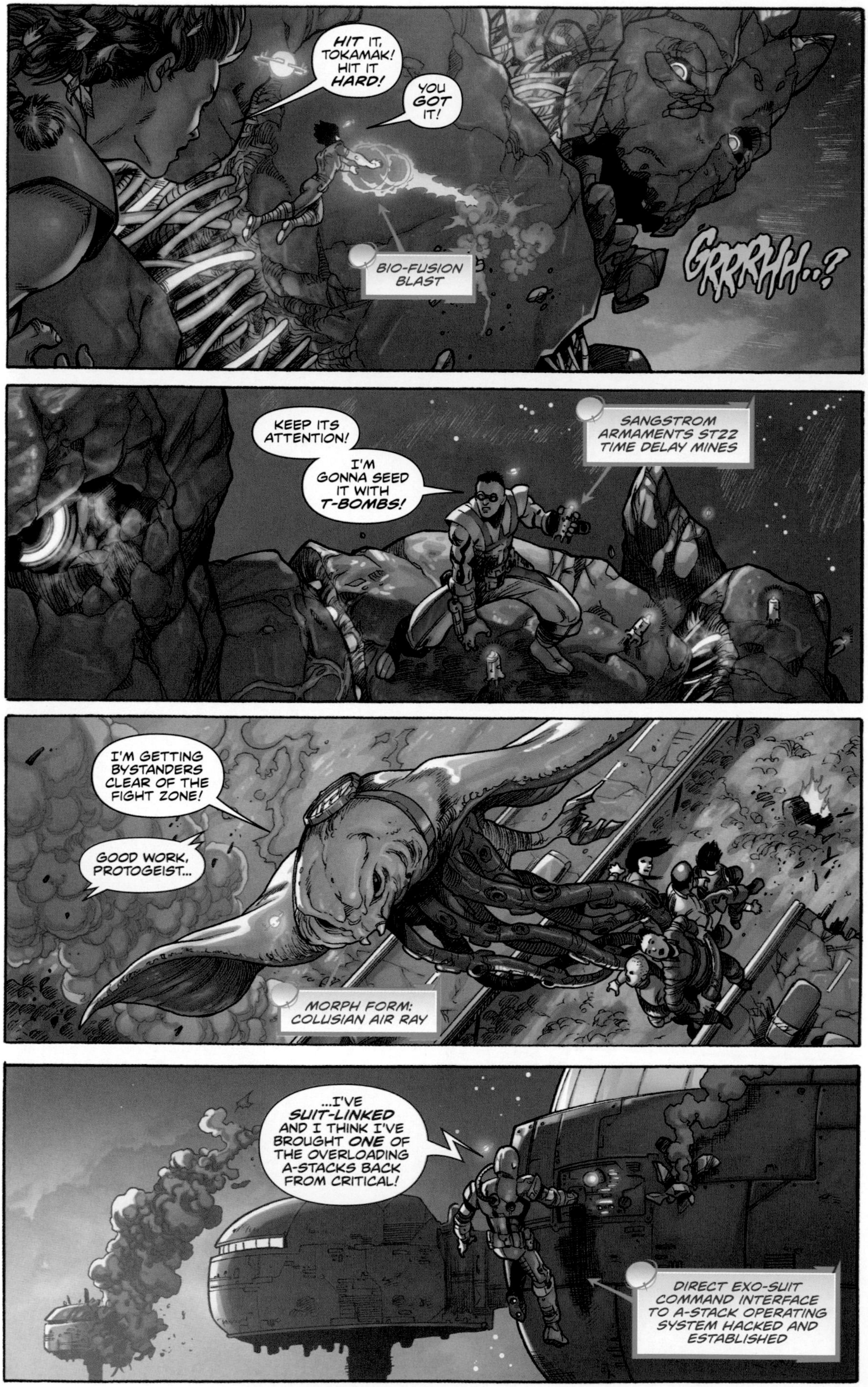
HIT IT, TOKAMAK! HIT IT HARD!
YOU GOT IT!
BIO-FUSION BLAST
GRRRHH..?
KEEP ITS ATTENTION!
I'M GONNA SEED IT WITH T-BOMBS!
SANGSTROM ARMAMENTS ST22 TIME DELAY MINES
I'M GETTING BYSTANDERS CLEAR OF THE FIGHT ZONE!
GOOD WORK, PROTOGEIST...
MORPH FORM: COLUSIAN AIR RAY
...I'VE SUIT-LINKED AND I THINK I'VE BROUGHT ONE OF THE OVERLOADING A-STACKS BACK FROM CRITICAL!
DIRECT EXO-SUIT COMMAND INTERFACE TO A-STACK OPERATING SYSTEM HACKED AND ESTABLISHED

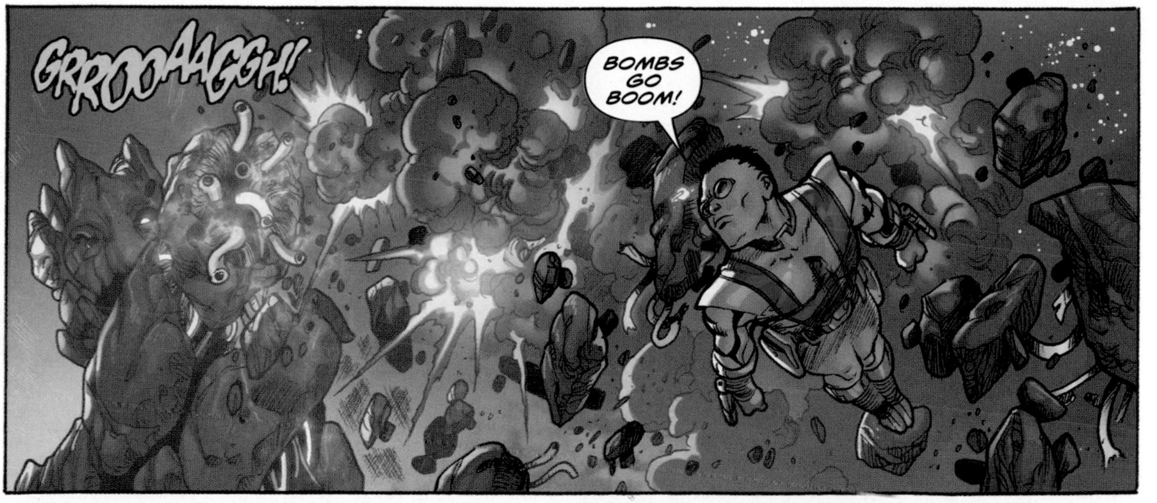
GRROOAAGGH!
BOMBS GO BOOM!

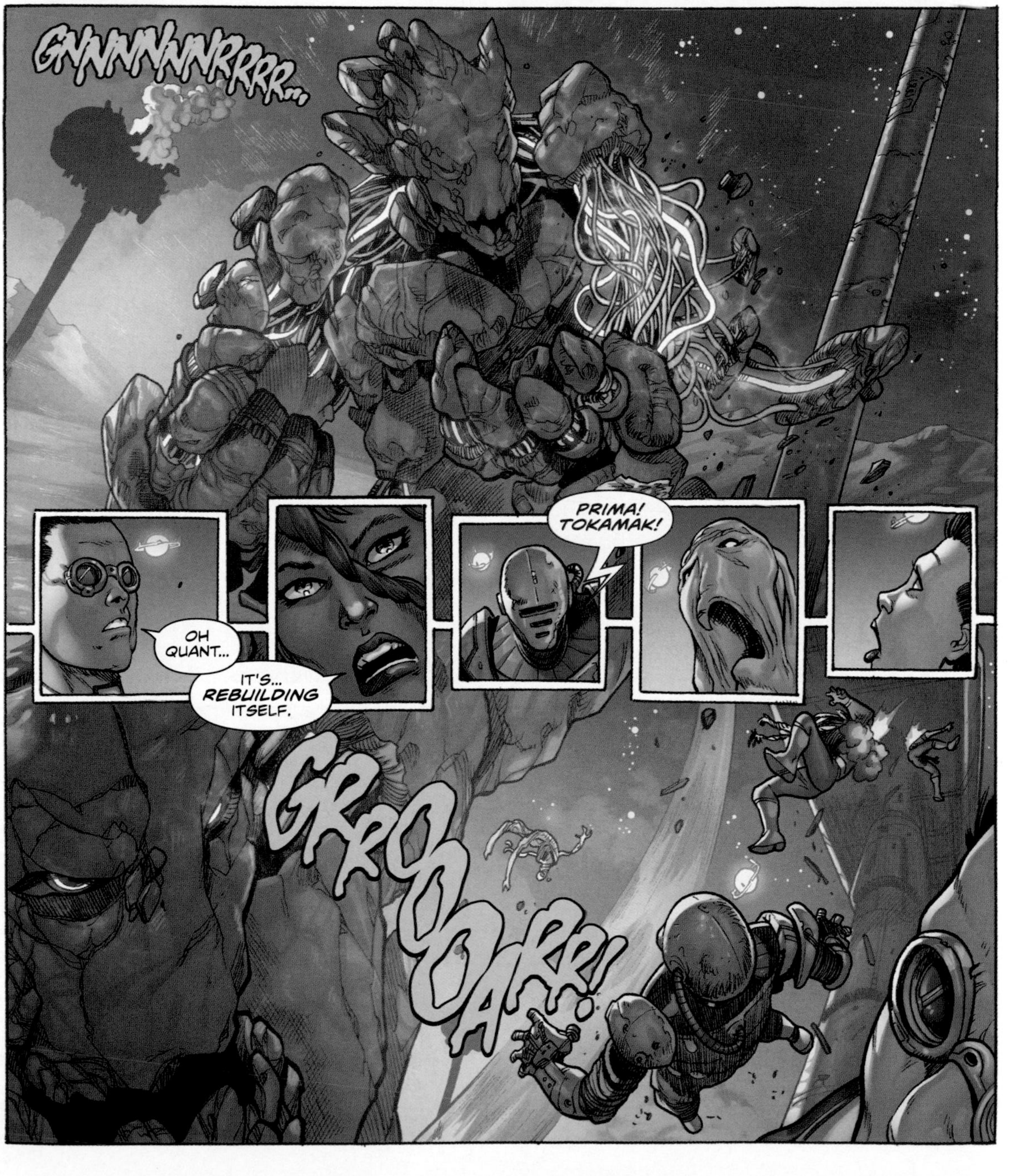
GNNNNNRRRR...
OH QUANT...
IT'S... REBUILDING ITSELF.
PRIMA! TOKAMAK!
GRROOOARR!

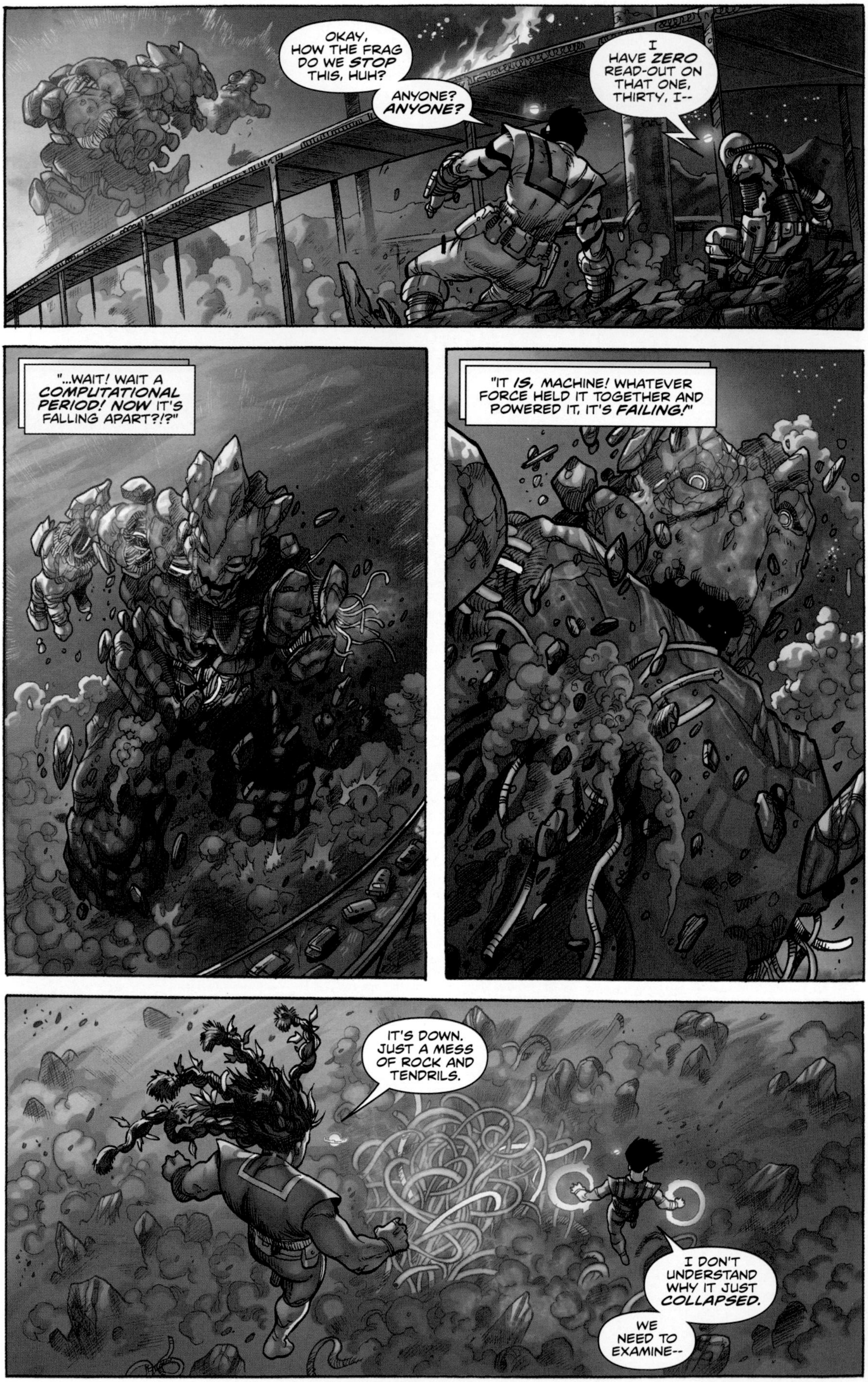
OKAY, HOW THE FRAG DO WE STOP THIS, HUH?
ANYONE? ANYONE?
I HAVE ZERO READ-OUT ON THAT ONE, THIRTY, I--
"...WAIT! WAIT A COMPUTATIONAL PERIOD! NOW IT'S FALLING APART?!?"
"IT IS, MACHINE! WHATEVER FORCE HELD IT TOGETHER AND POWERED IT, IT'S FAILING!"
IT'S DOWN. JUST A MESS OF ROCK AND TENDRILS.
I DON'T UNDERSTAND WHY IT JUST COLLAPSED.
WE NEED TO EXAMINE--

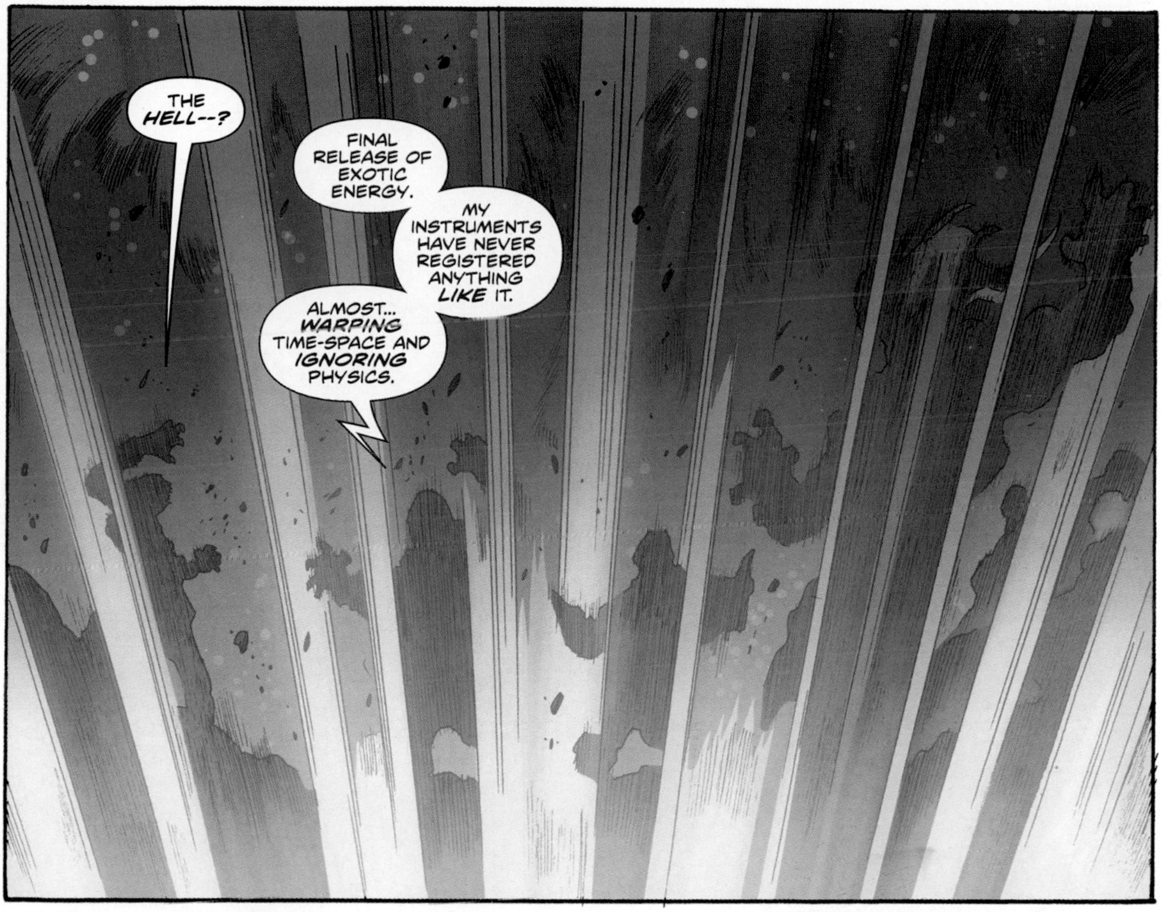
THE *HELL--?*
FINAL RELEASE OF EXOTIC ENERGY.
MY INSTRUMENTS HAVE NEVER REGISTERED ANYTHING *LIKE* IT.
ALMOST... *WARPING* TIME-SPACE AND *IGNORING* PHYSICS.

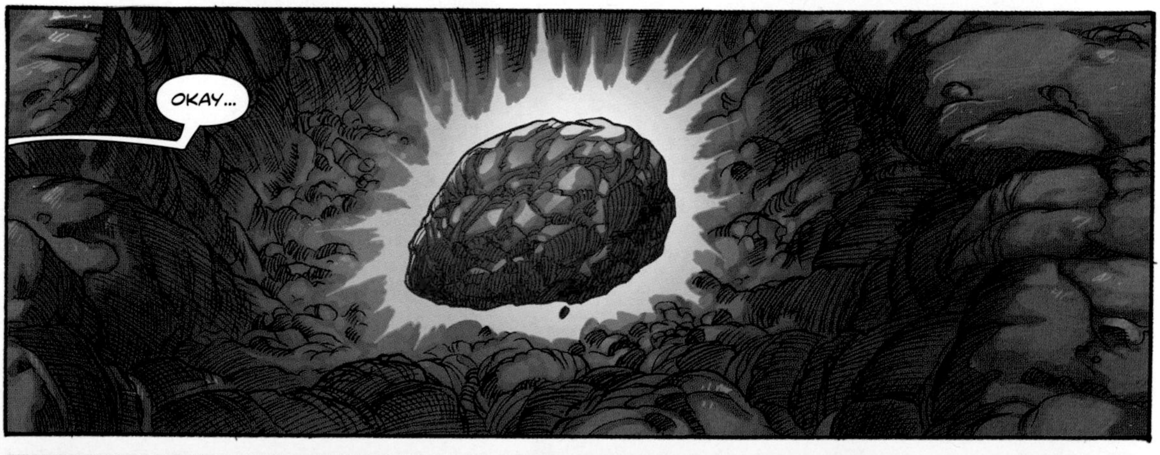
OKAY...

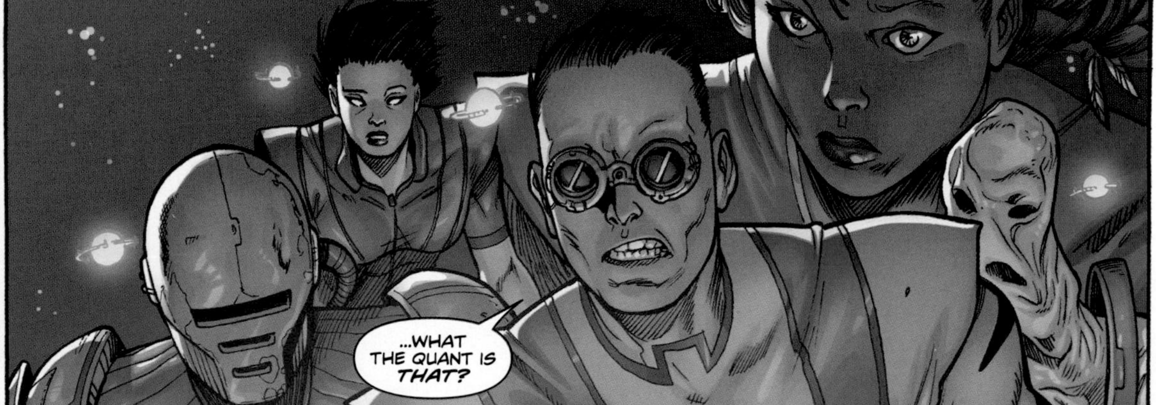
...WHAT THE QUANT IS *THAT?*

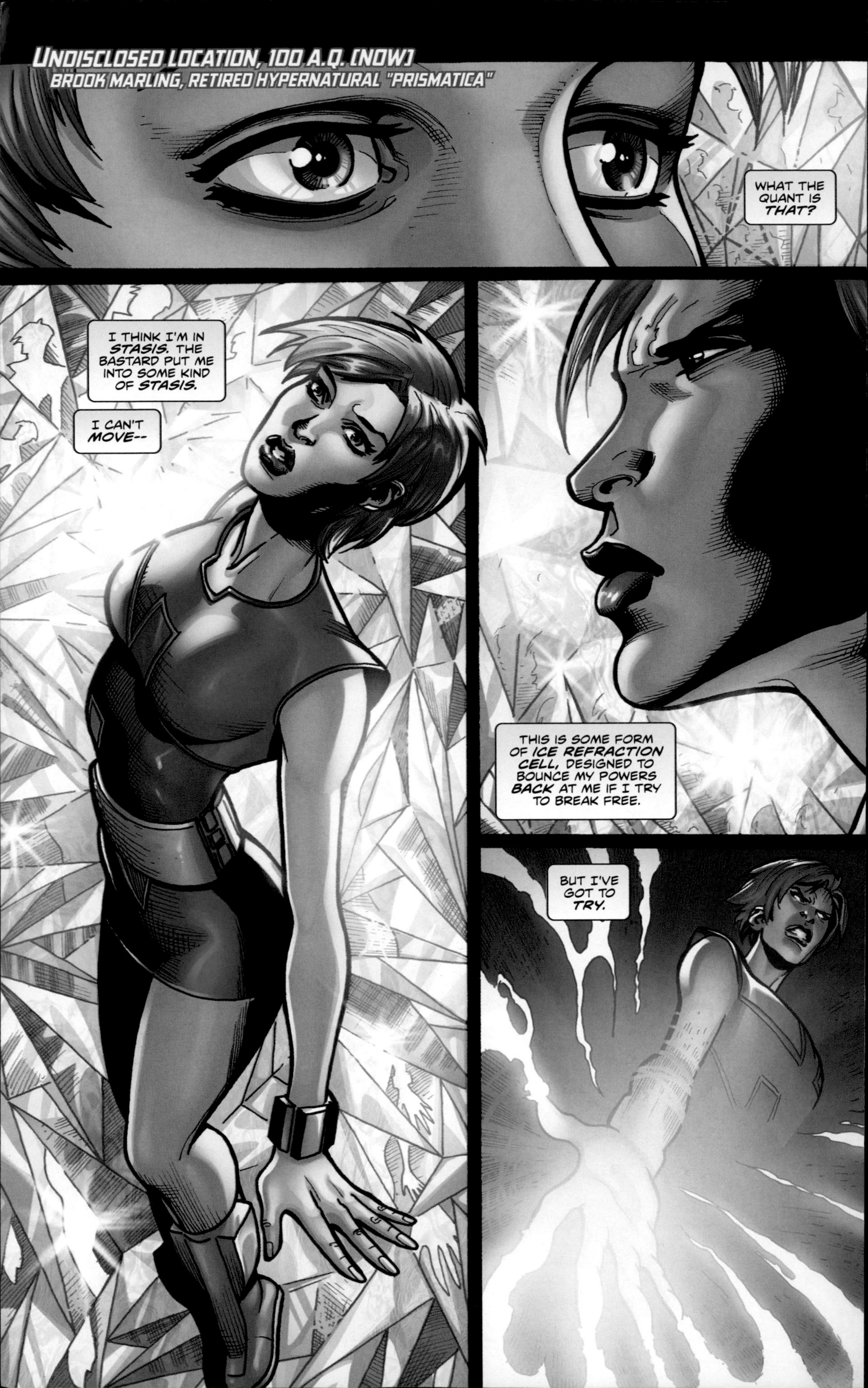
UNDISCLOSED LOCATION, 100 A.Q. [NOW]
BROOK MARLING, RETIRED HYPERNATURAL "PRISMATICA"
WHAT THE QUANT IS THAT?
I THINK I'M IN STASIS. THE BASTARD PUT ME INTO SOME KIND OF STASIS.
I CAN'T MOVE--
THIS IS SOME FORM OF ICE REFRACTION CELL, DESIGNED TO BOUNCE MY POWERS BACK AT ME IF I TRY TO BREAK FREE.
BUT I'VE GOT TO TRY.

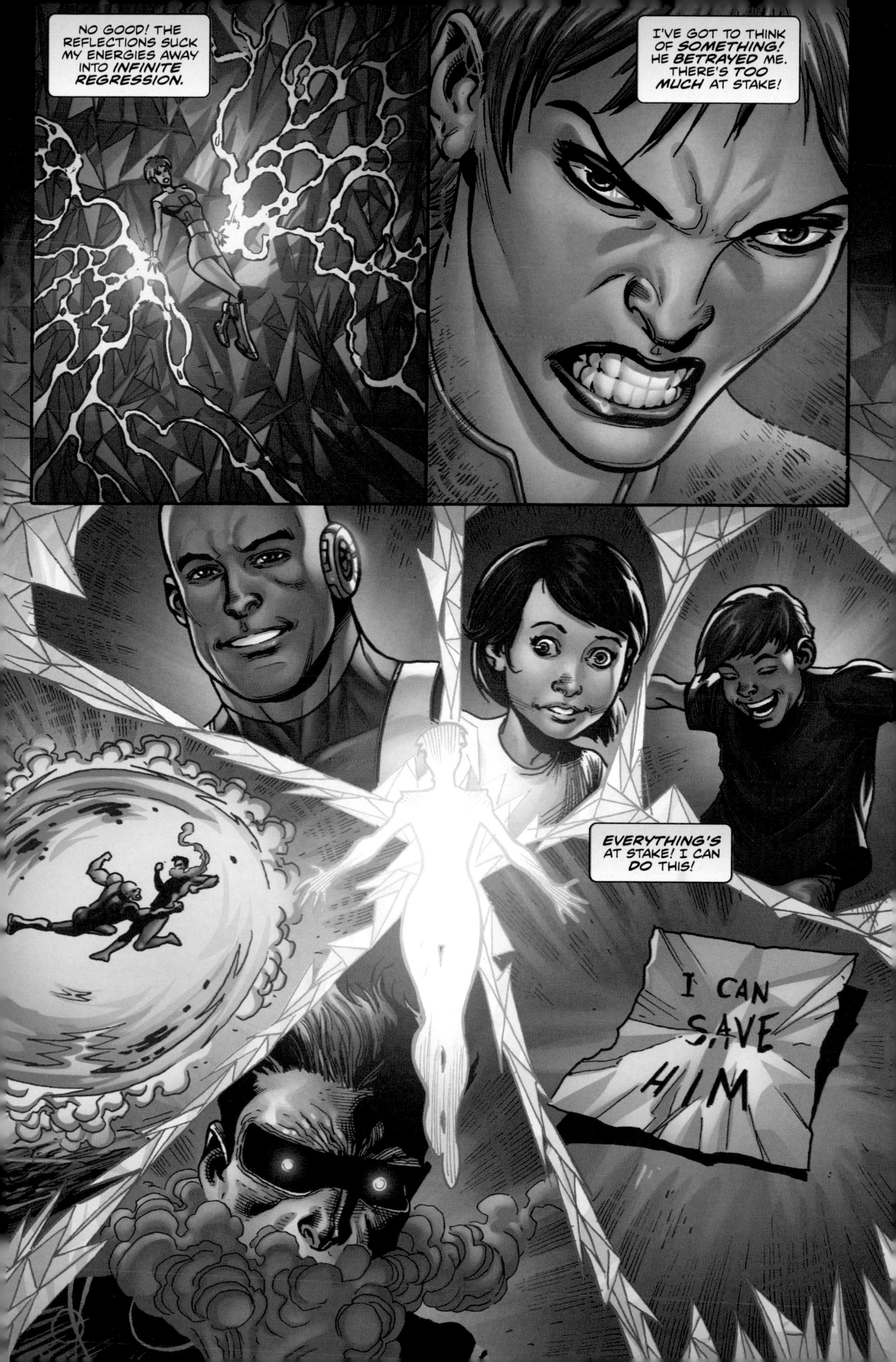
NO GOOD! THE REFLECTIONS SUCK MY ENERGIES AWAY INTO *INFINITE REGRESSION.*
I'VE GOT TO THINK OF *SOMETHING!* HE *BETRAYED* ME. THERE'S *TOO MUCH* AT STAKE!
EVERYTHING'S AT STAKE! I CAN *DO* THIS!
I CAN SAVE HIM

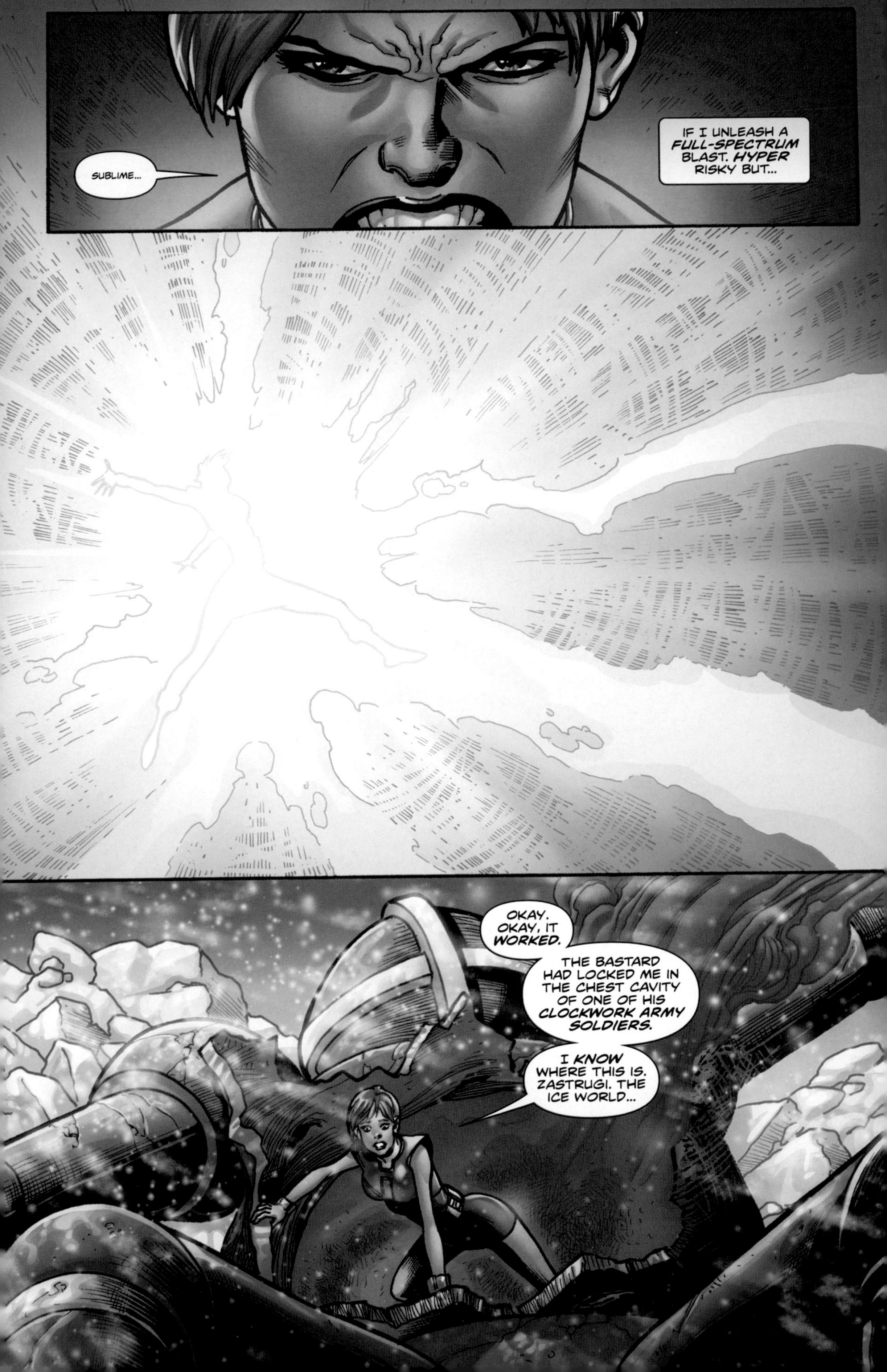
SUBLIME...
IF I UNLEASH A FULL-SPECTRUM BLAST. HYPER RISKY BUT...
OKAY. OKAY, IT WORKED.
THE BASTARD HAD LOCKED ME IN THE CHEST CAVITY OF ONE OF HIS CLOCKWORK ARMY SOLDIERS.
I KNOW WHERE THIS IS. ZASTRUGI. THE ICE WORLD...

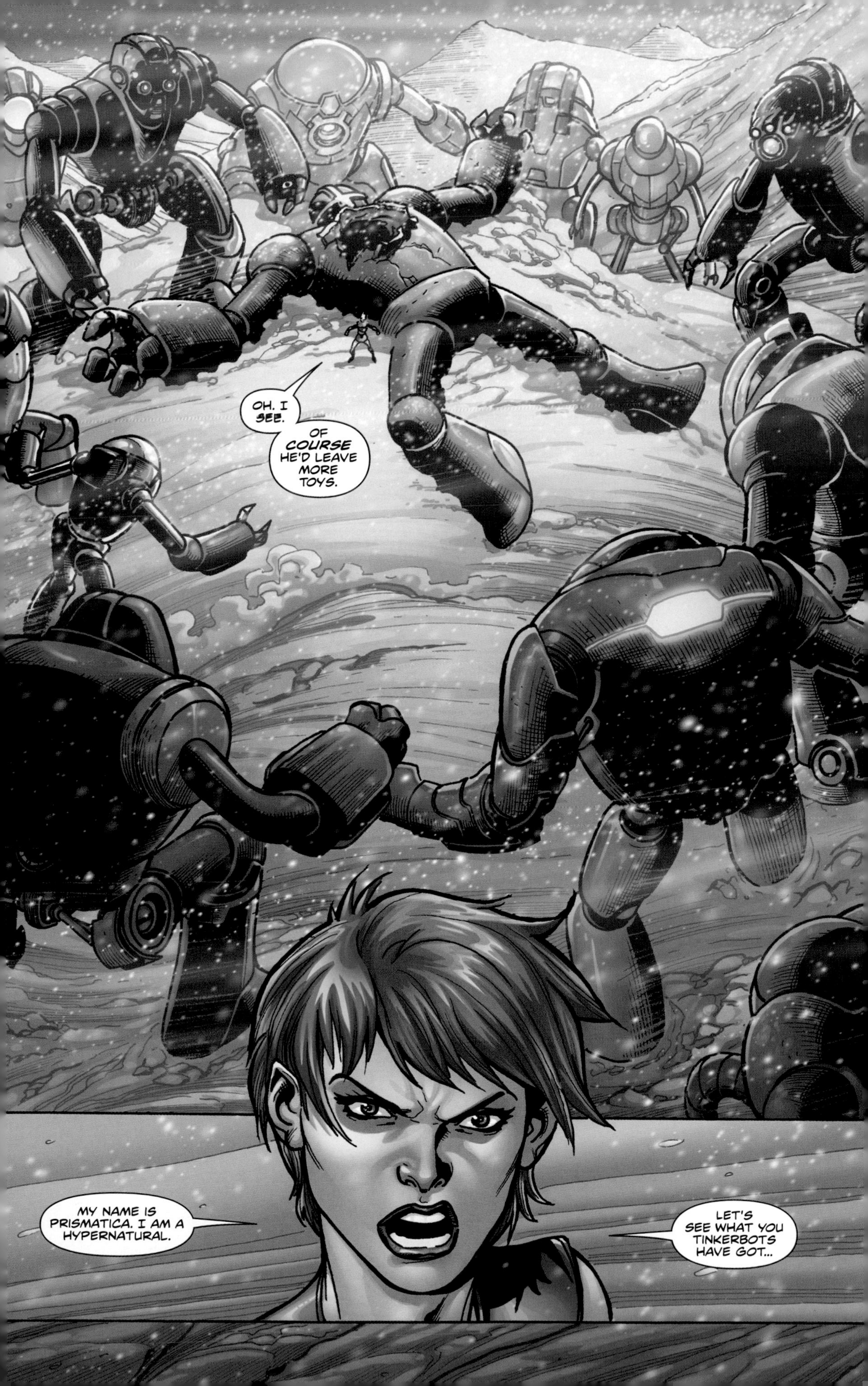

OH. I SEE.
OF COURSE HE'D LEAVE MORE TOYS.
MY NAME IS PRISMATICA. I AM A HYPERNATURAL.
LET'S SEE WHAT YOU TINKERBOTS HAVE GOT...

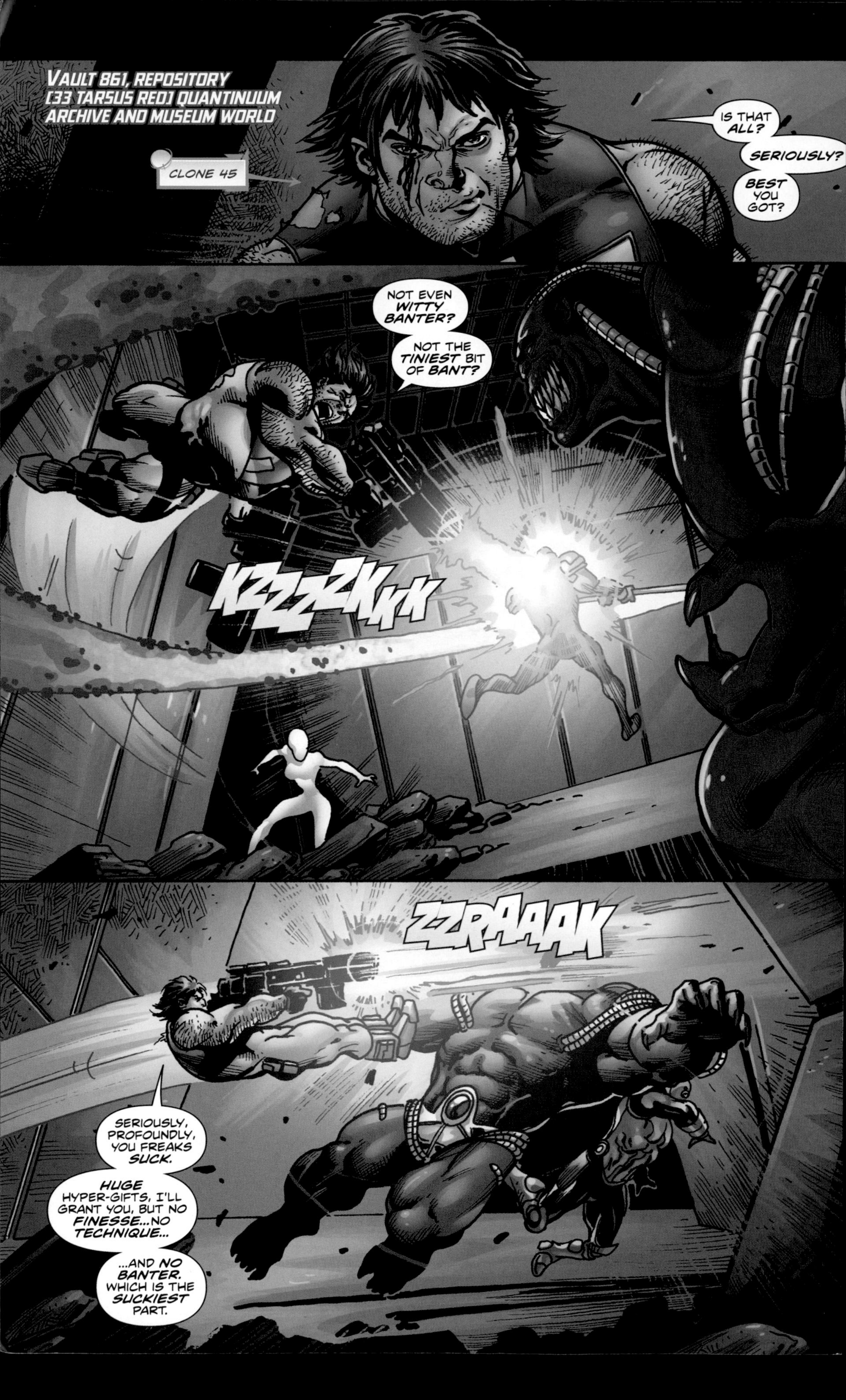

VAULT 861, REPOSITORY
[33 TARSUS RED] QUANTINUUM
ARCHIVE AND MUSEUM WORLD
CLONE 45
IS THAT ALL?
SERIOUSLY?
BEST YOU GOT?
NOT EVEN WITTY BANTER?
NOT THE TINIEST BIT OF BANT?
KZZZZKKK
ZZRAAAK
SERIOUSLY, PROFOUNDLY, YOU FREAKS SUCK.
HUGE HYPER-GIFTS, I'LL GRANT YOU, BUT NO FINESSE...NO TECHNIQUE...
...AND NO BANTER. WHICH IS THE SUCKIEST PART.

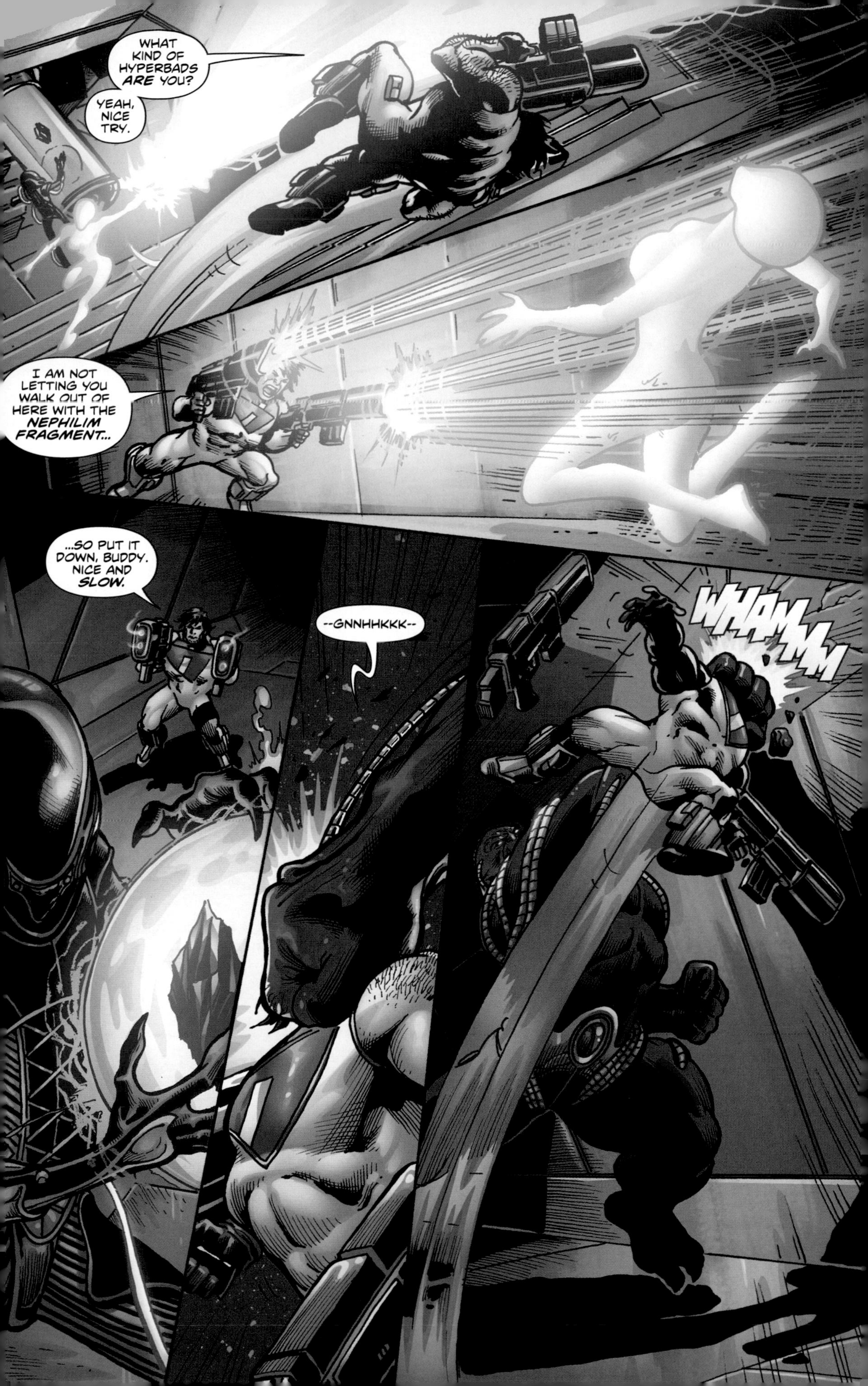
WHAT KIND OF HYPERBADS ARE YOU?
YEAH, NICE TRY.
I AM NOT LETTING YOU WALK OUT OF HERE WITH THE NEPHILIM FRAGMENT...
...SO PUT IT DOWN, BUDDY. NICE AND SLOW.
--GNNHHKKK--
WHAMMMM

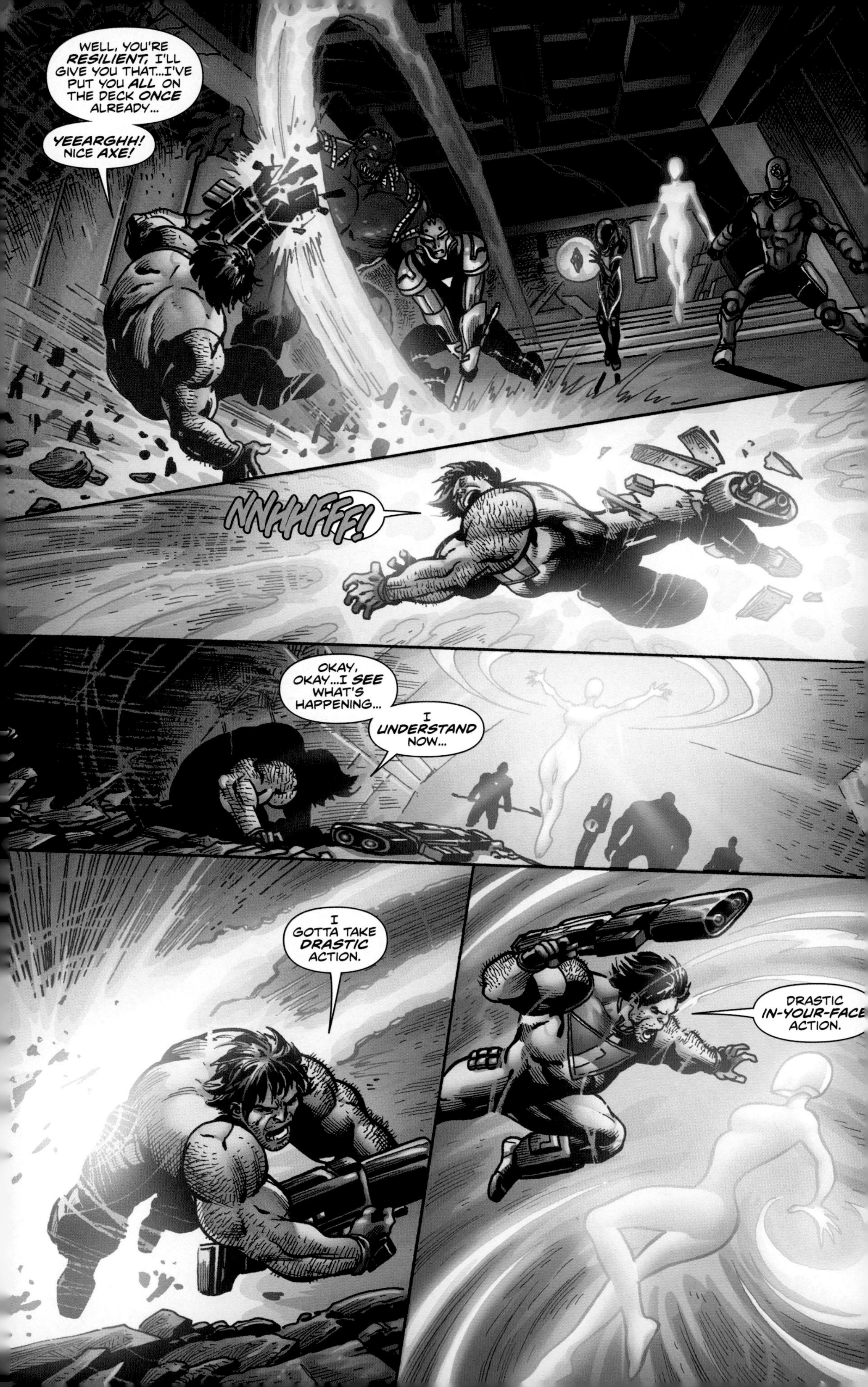

WELL, YOU'RE RESILIENT, I'LL GIVE YOU THAT...I'VE PUT YOU ALL ON THE DECK ONCE ALREADY...
YEEARGHH! NICE AXE!
NNHHFFF!
OKAY, OKAY...I SEE WHAT'S HAPPENING...
I UNDERSTAND NOW...
I GOTTA TAKE DRASTIC ACTION.
DRASTIC IN-YOUR-FACE ACTION.

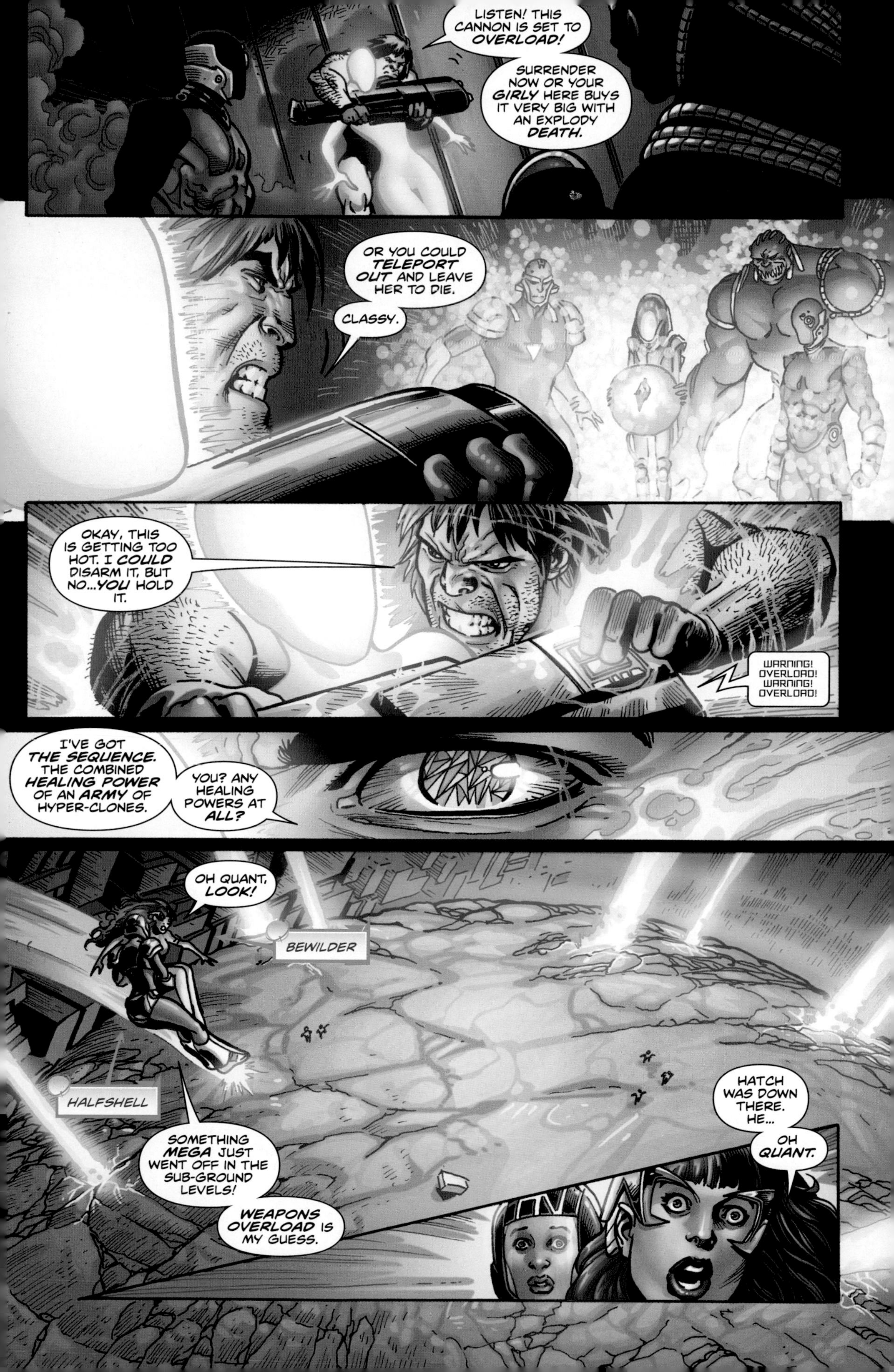
LISTEN! THIS CANNON IS SET TO OVERLOAD!
SURRENDER NOW OR YOUR GIRLY HERE BUYS IT VERY BIG WITH AN EXPLODY DEATH.
OR YOU COULD TELEPORT OUT AND LEAVE HER TO DIE.
CLASSY.
OKAY, THIS IS GETTING TOO HOT. I COULD DISARM IT, BUT NO...YOU HOLD IT.
WARNING! OVERLOAD! WARNING! OVERLOAD!
I'VE GOT THE SEQUENCE. THE COMBINED HEALING POWER OF AN ARMY OF HYPER-CLONES.
YOU? ANY HEALING POWERS AT ALL?
OH QUANT, LOOK!
BEWILDER
HALFSHELL
SOMETHING MEGA JUST WENT OFF IN THE SUB-GROUND LEVELS!
WEAPONS OVERLOAD IS MY GUESS.
HATCH WAS DOWN THERE. HE...
OH QUANT.

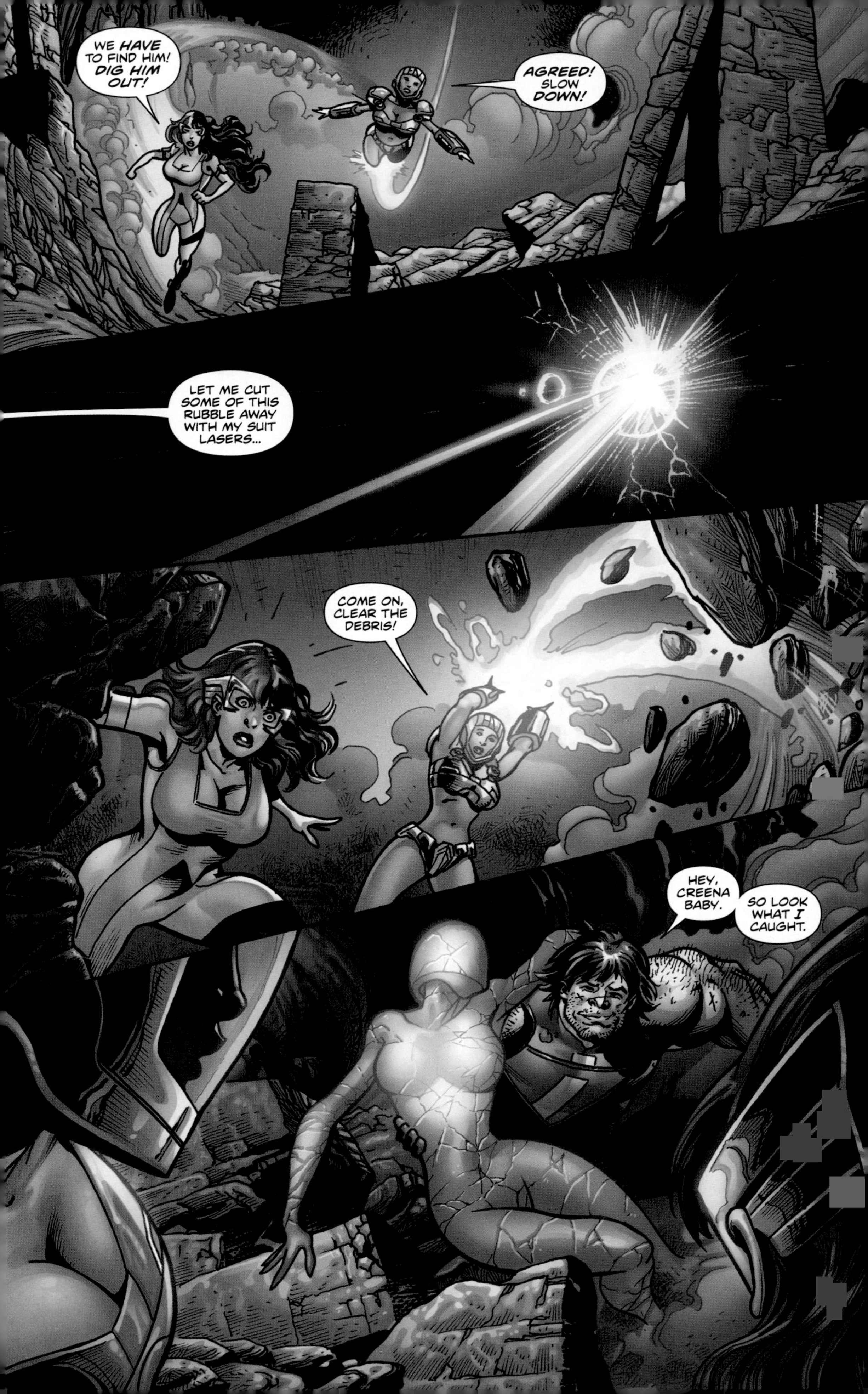
WE HAVE TO FIND HIM! DIG HIM OUT!
AGREED! SLOW DOWN!
LET ME CUT SOME OF THIS RUBBLE AWAY WITH MY SUIT LASERS...
COME ON, CLEAR THE DEBRIS!
HEY, CREENA BABY.
SO LOOK WHAT I CAUGHT.

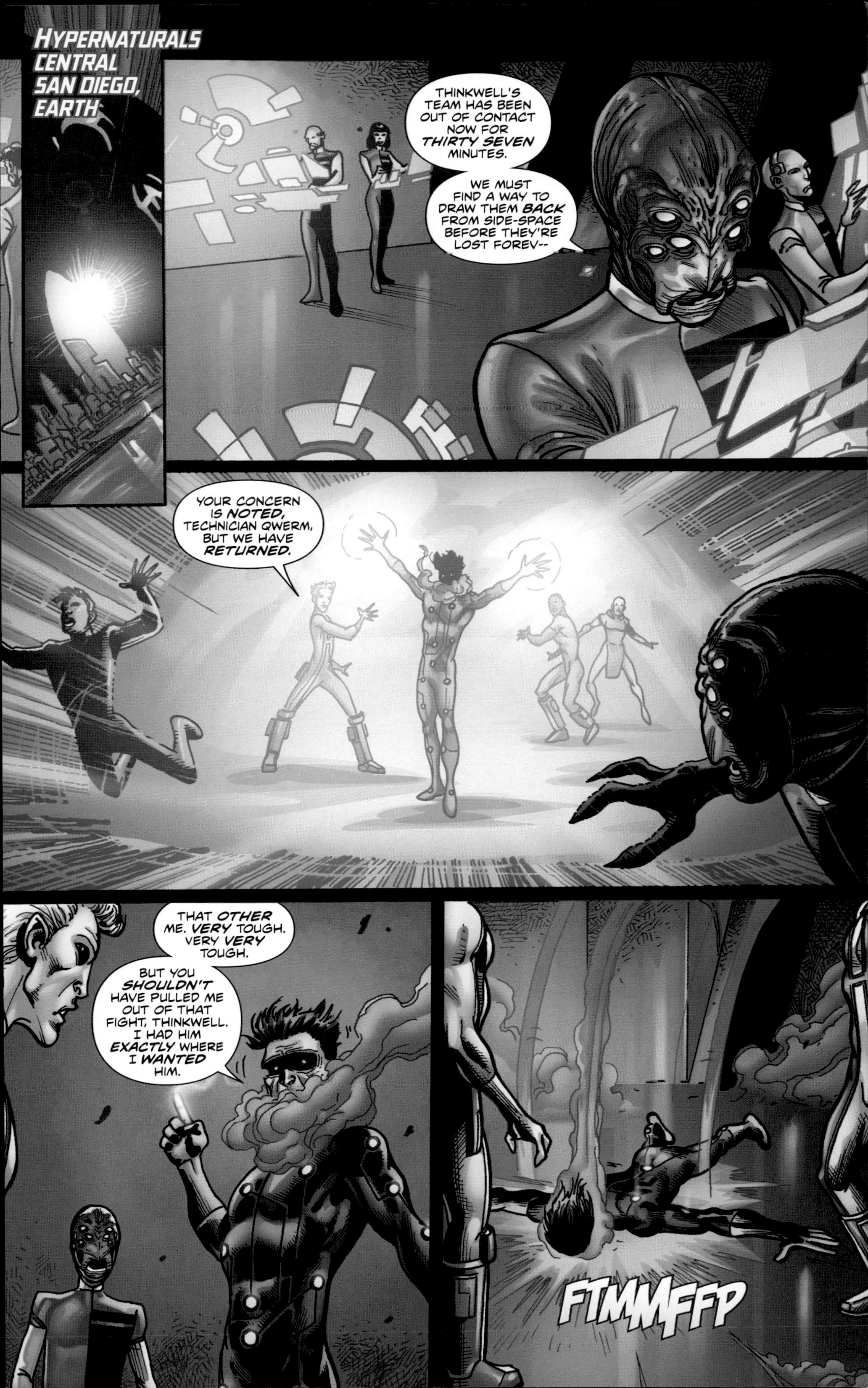
HYPERNATURALS CENTRAL SAN DIEGO, EARTH
THINKWELL'S TEAM HAS BEEN OUT OF CONTACT NOW FOR THIRTY SEVEN MINUTES.
WE MUST FIND A WAY TO DRAW THEM BACK FROM SIDE-SPACE BEFORE THEY'RE LOST FOREV--
YOUR CONCERN IS NOTED, TECHNICIAN QWERM, BUT WE HAVE RETURNED.
THAT OTHER ME. VERY TOUGH. VERY VERY TOUGH.
BUT YOU SHOULDN'T HAVE PULLED ME OUT OF THAT FIGHT, THINKWELL. I HAD HIM EXACTLY WHERE I WANTED HIM.
FTMMFFP

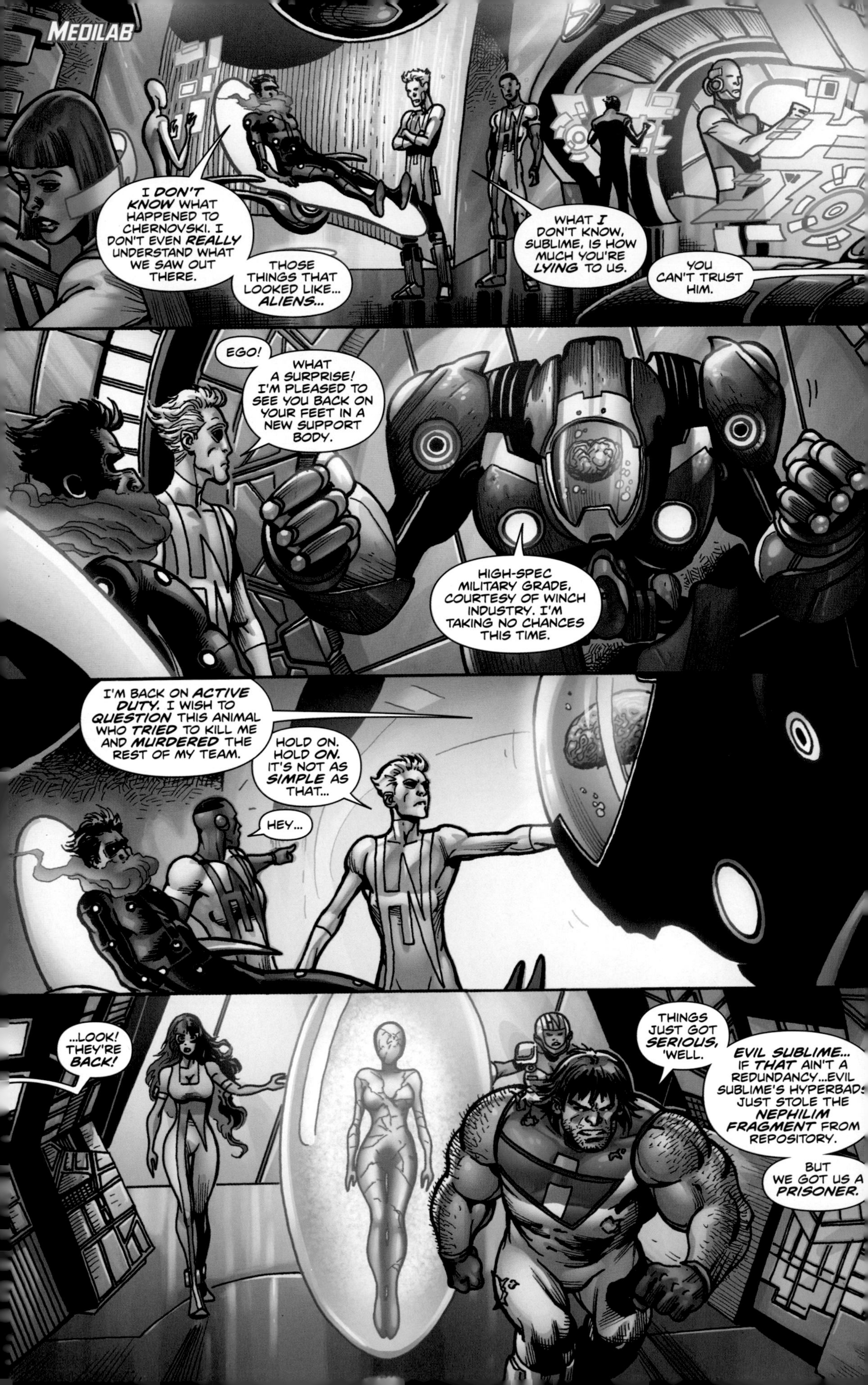
MEDILAB
I DON'T KNOW WHAT HAPPENED TO CHERNOVSKI. I DON'T EVEN REALLY UNDERSTAND WHAT WE SAW OUT THERE.
THOSE THINGS THAT LOOKED LIKE... ALIENS...
WHAT I DON'T KNOW, SUBLIME, IS HOW MUCH YOU'RE LYING TO US.
YOU CAN'T TRUST HIM.
EGO!
WHAT A SURPRISE! I'M PLEASED TO SEE YOU BACK ON YOUR FEET IN A NEW SUPPORT BODY.
HIGH-SPEC MILITARY GRADE, COURTESY OF WINCH INDUSTRY. I'M TAKING NO CHANCES THIS TIME.
I'M BACK ON ACTIVE DUTY. I WISH TO QUESTION THIS ANIMAL WHO TRIED TO KILL ME AND MURDERED THE REST OF MY TEAM.
HOLD ON. HOLD ON. IT'S NOT AS SIMPLE AS THAT...
HEY...
...LOOK! THEY'RE BACK!
THINGS JUST GOT SERIOUS, 'WELL.
EVIL SUBLIME... IF THAT AIN'T A REDUNDANCY...EVIL SUBLIME'S HYPERBADS JUST STOLE THE NEPHILIM FRAGMENT FROM REPOSITORY.
BUT WE GOT US A PRISONER.

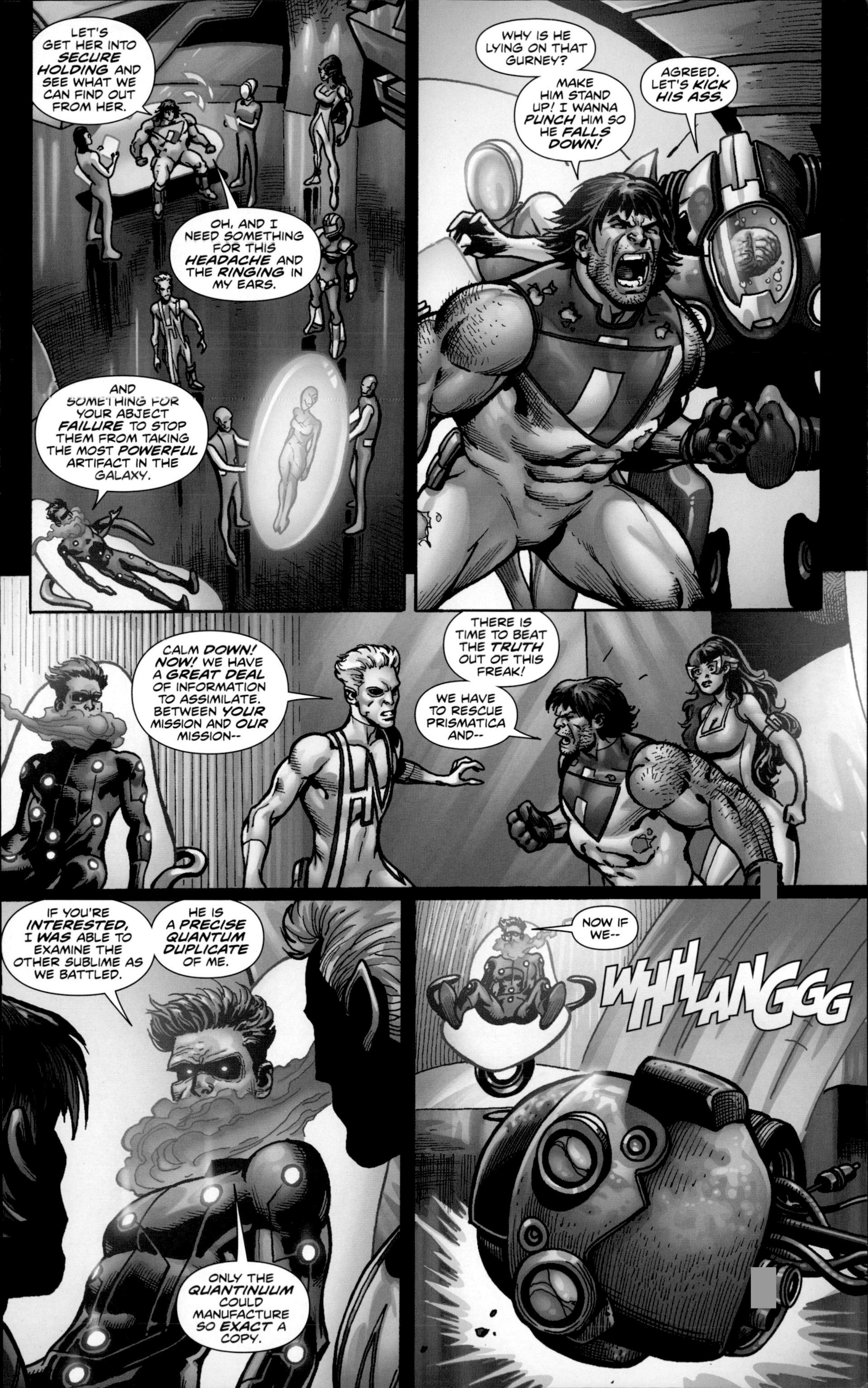
LET'S GET HER INTO SECURE HOLDING AND SEE WHAT WE CAN FIND OUT FROM HER.
OH, AND I NEED SOMETHING FOR THIS HEADACHE AND THE RINGING IN MY EARS.
AND SOMETHING FOR YOUR ABJECT FAILURE TO STOP THEM FROM TAKING THE MOST POWERFUL ARTIFACT IN THE GALAXY.
WHY IS HE LYING ON THAT GURNEY?
MAKE HIM STAND UP! I WANNA PUNCH HIM SO HE FALLS DOWN!
AGREED. LET'S KICK HIS ASS.
CALM DOWN! NOW! WE HAVE A GREAT DEAL OF INFORMATION TO ASSIMILATE. BETWEEN YOUR MISSION AND OUR MISSION--
THERE IS TIME TO BEAT THE TRUTH OUT OF THIS FREAK!
WE HAVE TO RESCUE PRISMATICA AND--
IF YOU'RE INTERESTED, I WAS ABLE TO EXAMINE THE OTHER SUBLIME AS WE BATTLED.
HE IS A PRECISE QUANTUM DUPLICATE OF ME.
ONLY THE QUANTINUUM COULD MANUFACTURE SO EXACT A COPY.
NOW IF WE--
WHHLANGGG

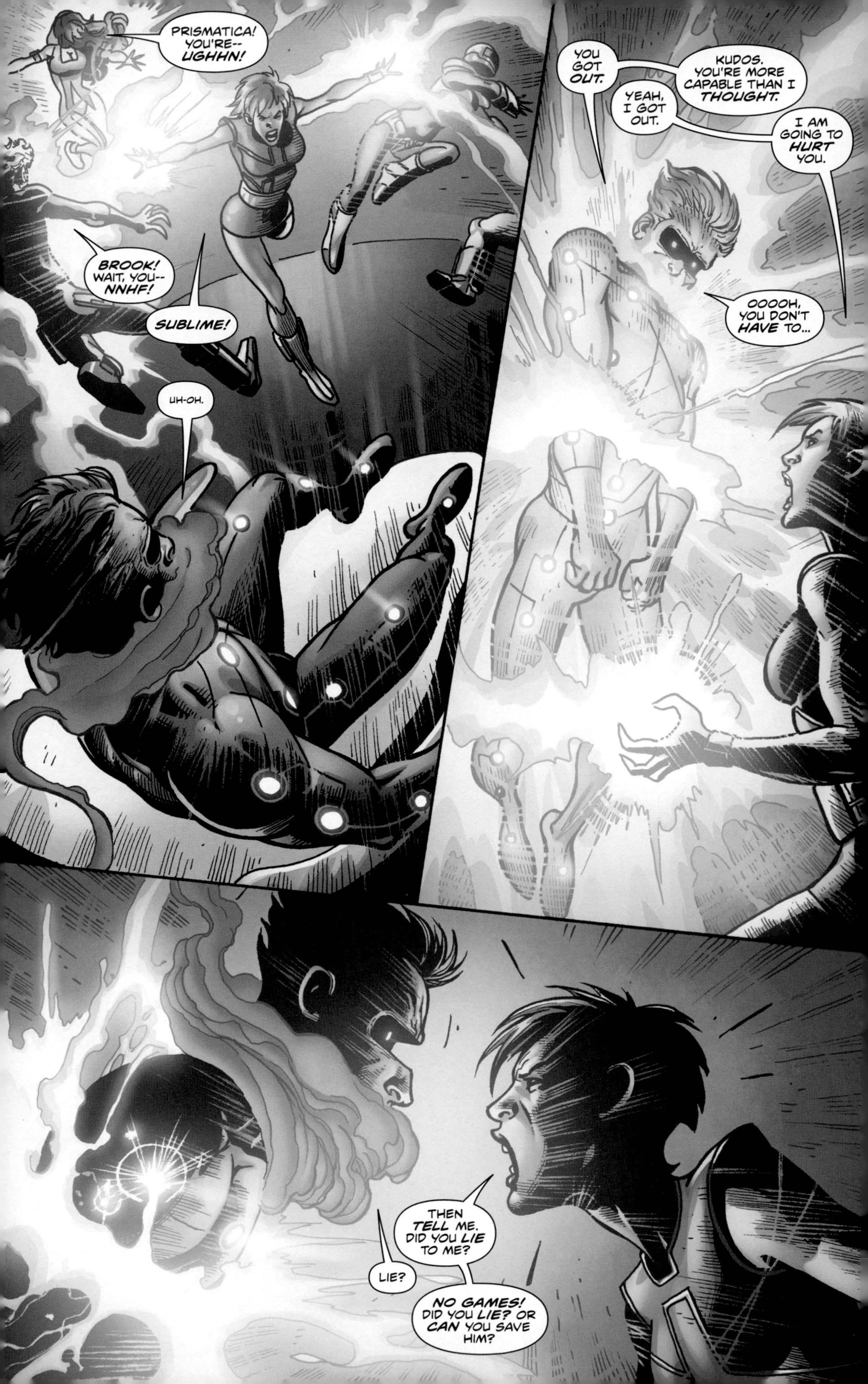
PRISMATICA! YOU'RE-- UGHHN!
BROOK! WAIT, YOU-- NNHF!
SUBLIME!
UH-OH.
YOU GOT OUT.
KUDOS. YOU'RE MORE CAPABLE THAN I THOUGHT.
YEAH, I GOT OUT.
I AM GOING TO HURT YOU.
OOOOH, YOU DON'T HAVE TO...
THEN TELL ME. DID YOU LIE TO ME?
LIE?
NO GAMES! DID YOU LIE? OR CAN YOU SAVE HIM?

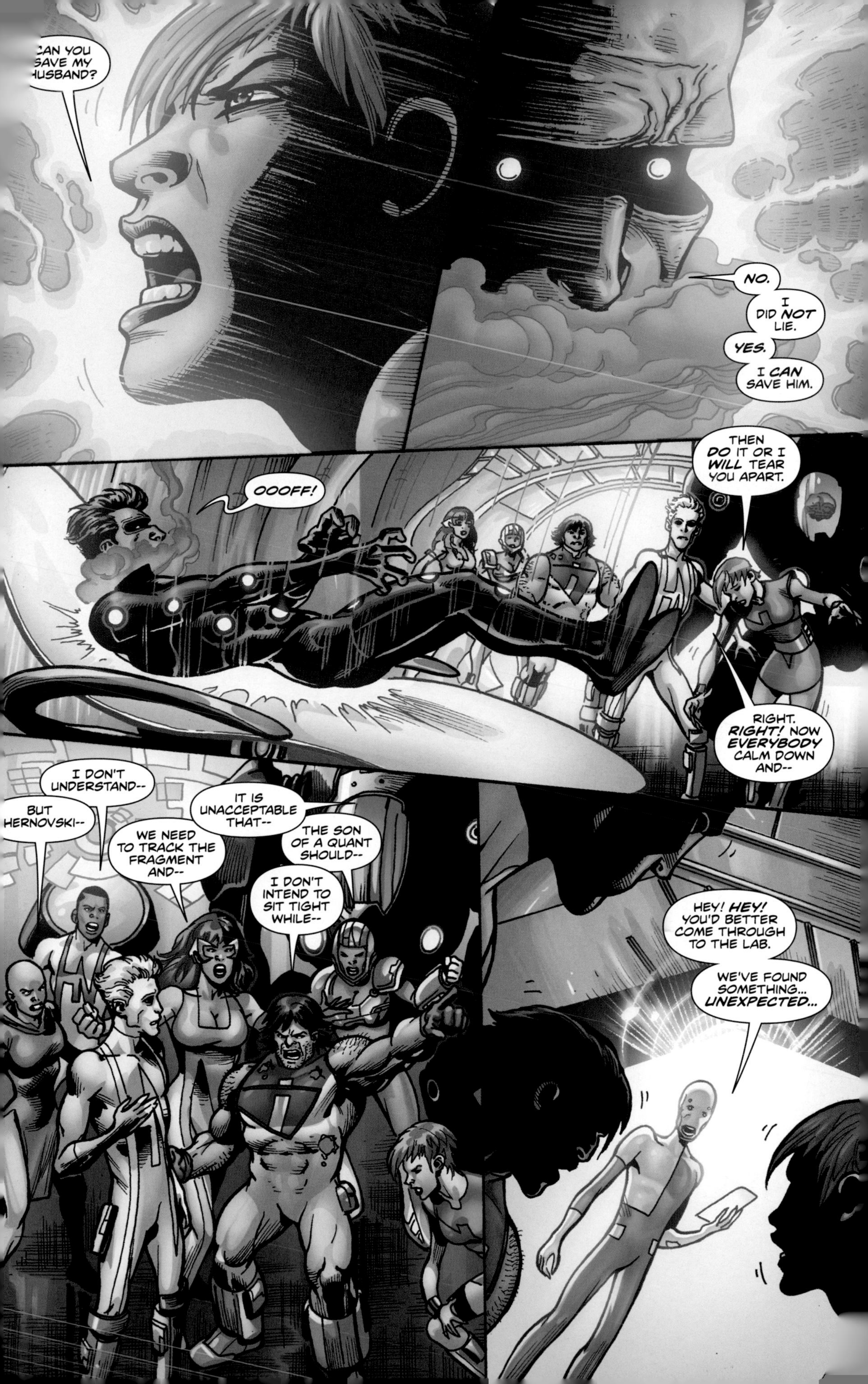
CAN YOU SAVE MY HUSBAND?
NO.
I DID NOT LIE.
YES.
I CAN SAVE HIM.
OOOFF!
THEN DO IT OR I WILL TEAR YOU APART.
RIGHT. RIGHT! NOW EVERYBODY CALM DOWN AND--
I DON'T UNDERSTAND--
BUT HERNOVSKI--
IT IS UNACCEPTABLE THAT--
WE NEED TO TRACK THE FRAGMENT AND--
THE SON OF A QUANT SHOULD--
I DON'T INTEND TO SIT TIGHT WHILE--
HEY! HEY! YOU'D BETTER COME THROUGH TO THE LAB.
WE'VE FOUND SOMETHING... UNEXPECTED...

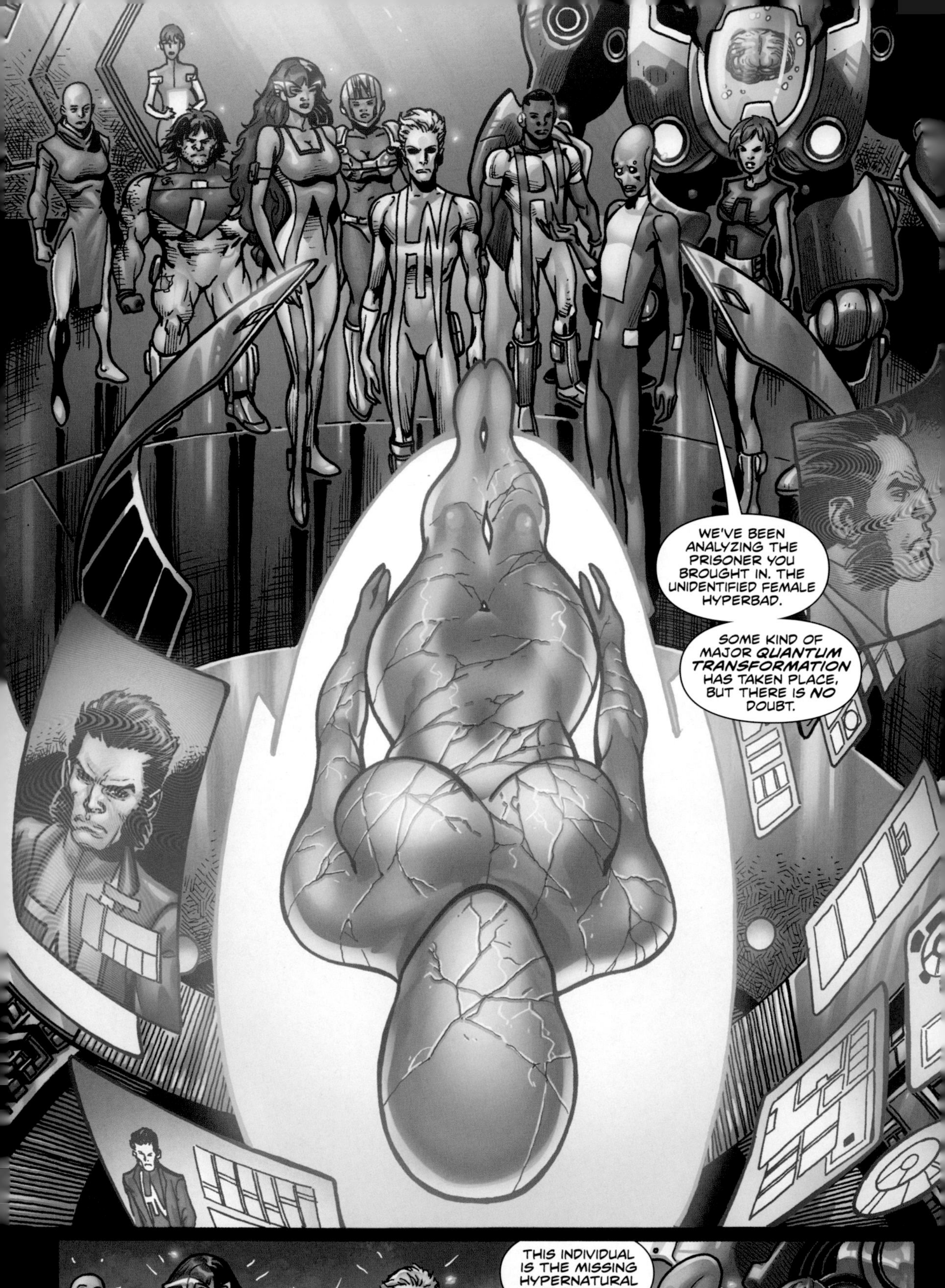
WE'VE BEEN ANALYZING THE PRISONER YOU BROUGHT IN. THE UNIDENTIFIED FEMALE HYPERBAD.
SOME KIND OF MAJOR QUANTUM TRANSFORMATION HAS TAKEN PLACE, BUT THERE IS NO DOUBT.

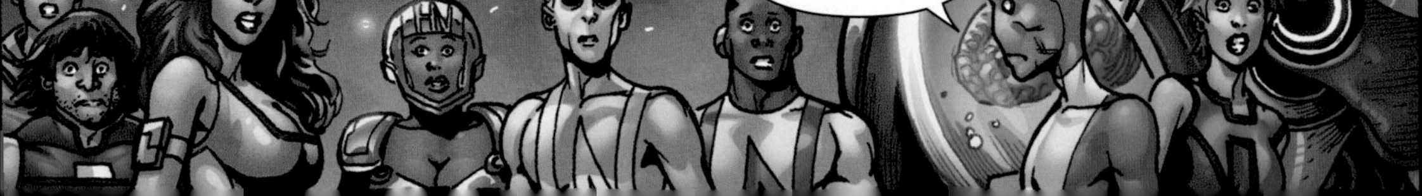
THIS INDIVIDUAL IS THE MISSING HYPERNATURAL KOBALT BLUE.

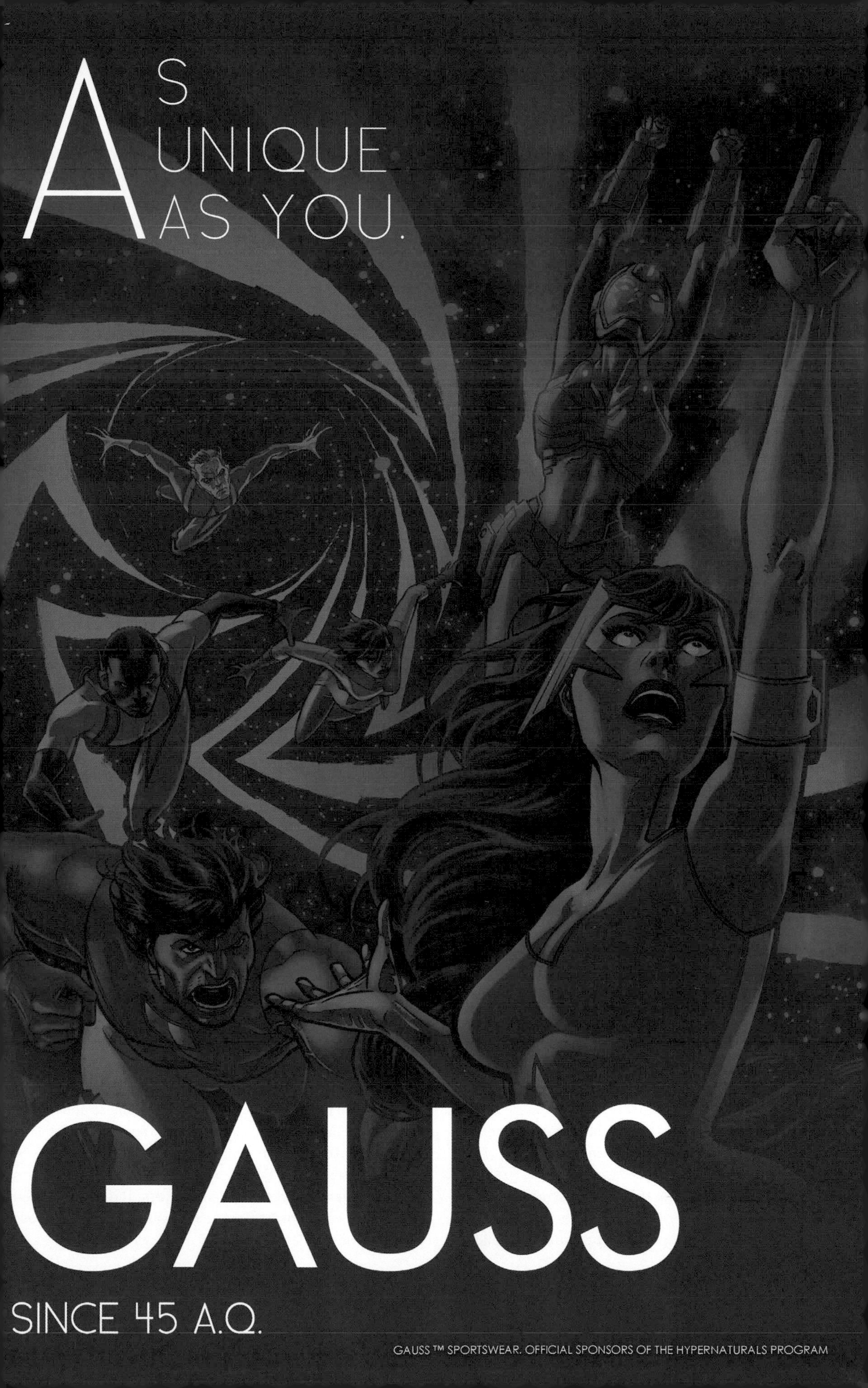
A
S
UNIQUE
AS YOU.
GAUSS
SINCE 45 A.Q.
GAUSS ™ SPORTSWEAR. OFFICIAL SPONSORS OF THE HYPERNATURALS PROGRAM

Special Destinations:

Titan

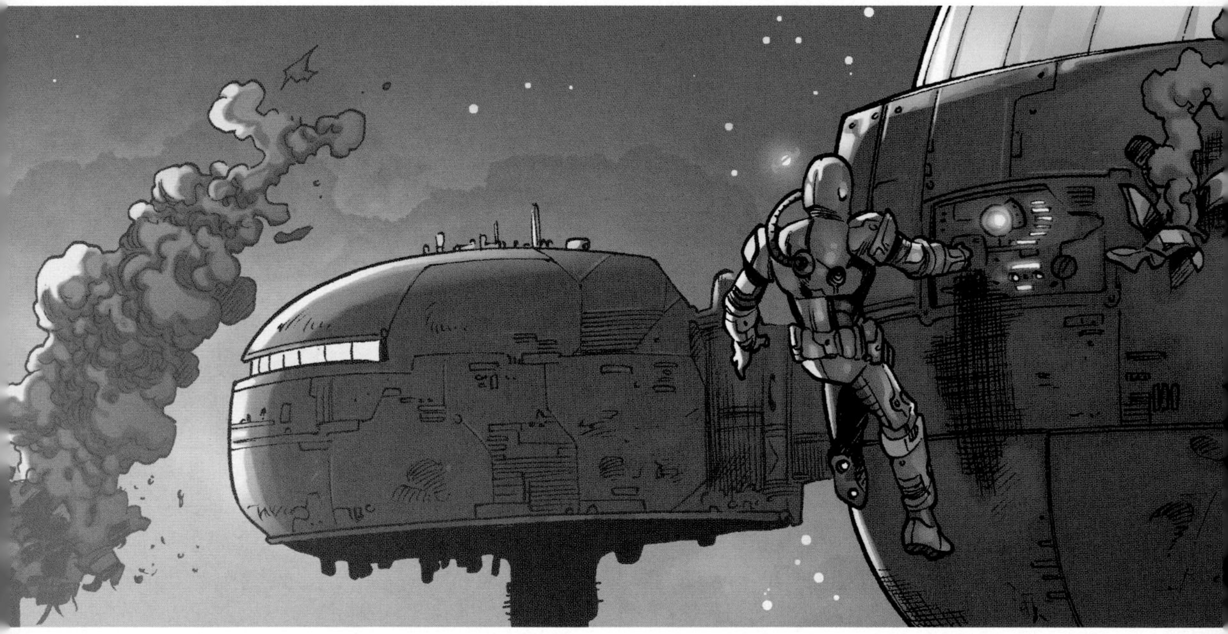

Titan is the largest moon of the Solar System's ringed beauty Saturn, and the sixth ellipsoidal moon of that planet's sequence. Enjoy spectacular views of Saturn and its rings, as well as breathtaking experiences of Titan's own geographical delights and wonders.

Titan was first colonized in the years directly before the Quantinuum, and its methane/nitrogen atmopsphere was tamed by expert terraforming that make it the holiday hotspot it is today.

Like many terraformed worlds, Titan's atmosphere is maintained and controlled by countless atmosphere generator stacks, known as "A-stacks." These vast, monolithic structures rise from deep below the surface of the planet into the upper atmosphere. The stacks monitor and alter the moon's naturally lethal atmosphere and make it non-toxic. They also modify the gravity and climate of Titan to make it habitable for humans.

A huge colonial cityscape now covers the planet-moon; made up of vast futuristic settlements: Hyperion, Oceanous, Coeus, Cirus and Themis.

In 35 AQ, Titan was the location for the discovery of the infamous "Nephilim Fragment," which now resides in the Repository archive. Don't miss the beaches of Oceanous, the Skycliffs of Brutz, and the methane skiing of Themis.

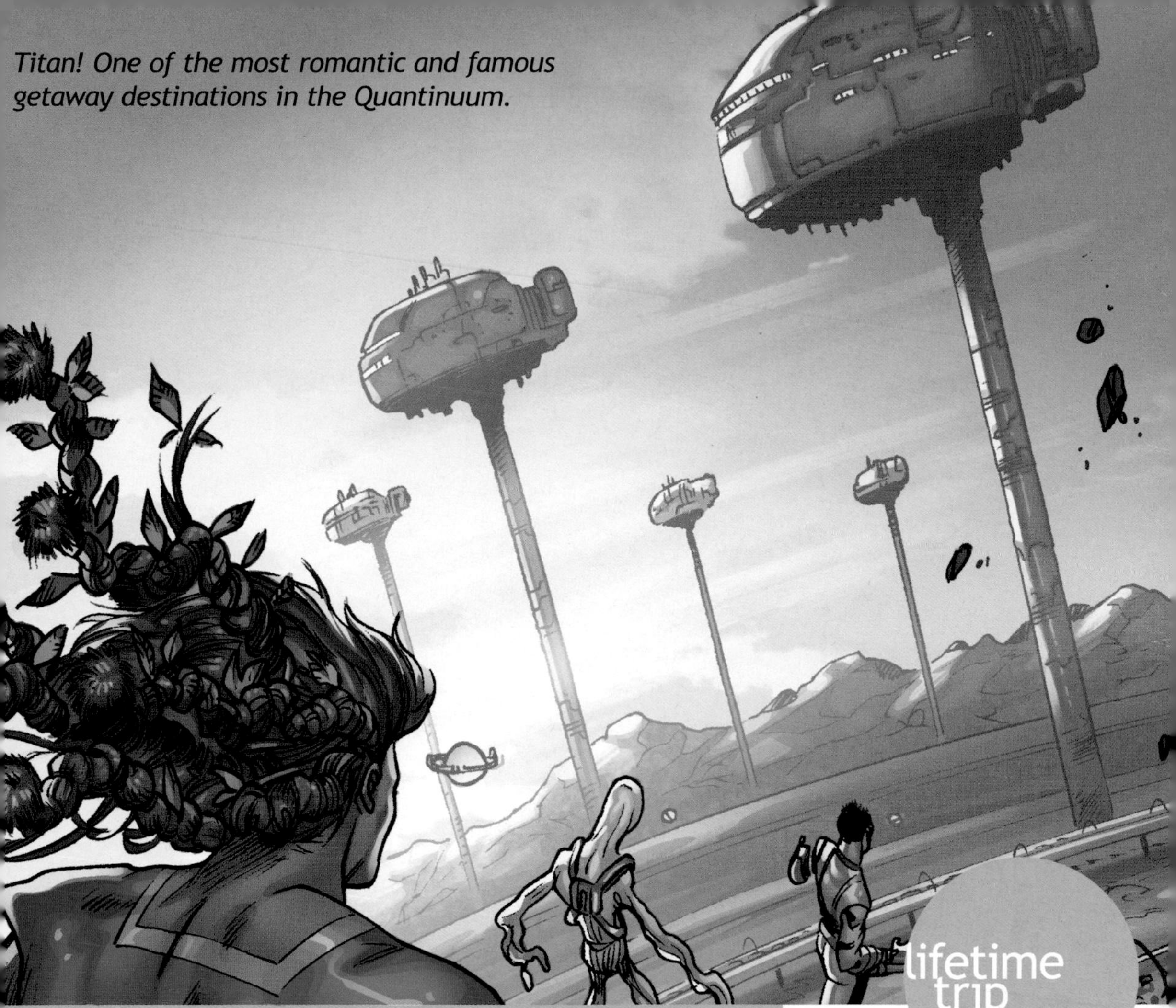
Titan! One of the most romantic and famous getaway destinations in the Quantinuum.

lifetime trip holidays

Trip Network transfer to **Titan** is widely available.

- **10 nights at Larquan Village, Hyperion**
  3000 credits (including trip transfer)

- **8 nights at the Club Titan Resortplex, Oceanus beachfront**
  4500 credits (trip transfer included, optional sea fishing excursion package)

- **10 Nights at Brutz**
  2700 credits (optional base jumping excursion package available)

- **8 nights at White Peak Lodge, Themis**
  5000 credits (including guide, instruction and access to the Themis “Black Run”)

- **10 nights at the Del Mar Grande, Coeus**
  90000 credits

CHAPTER TEN

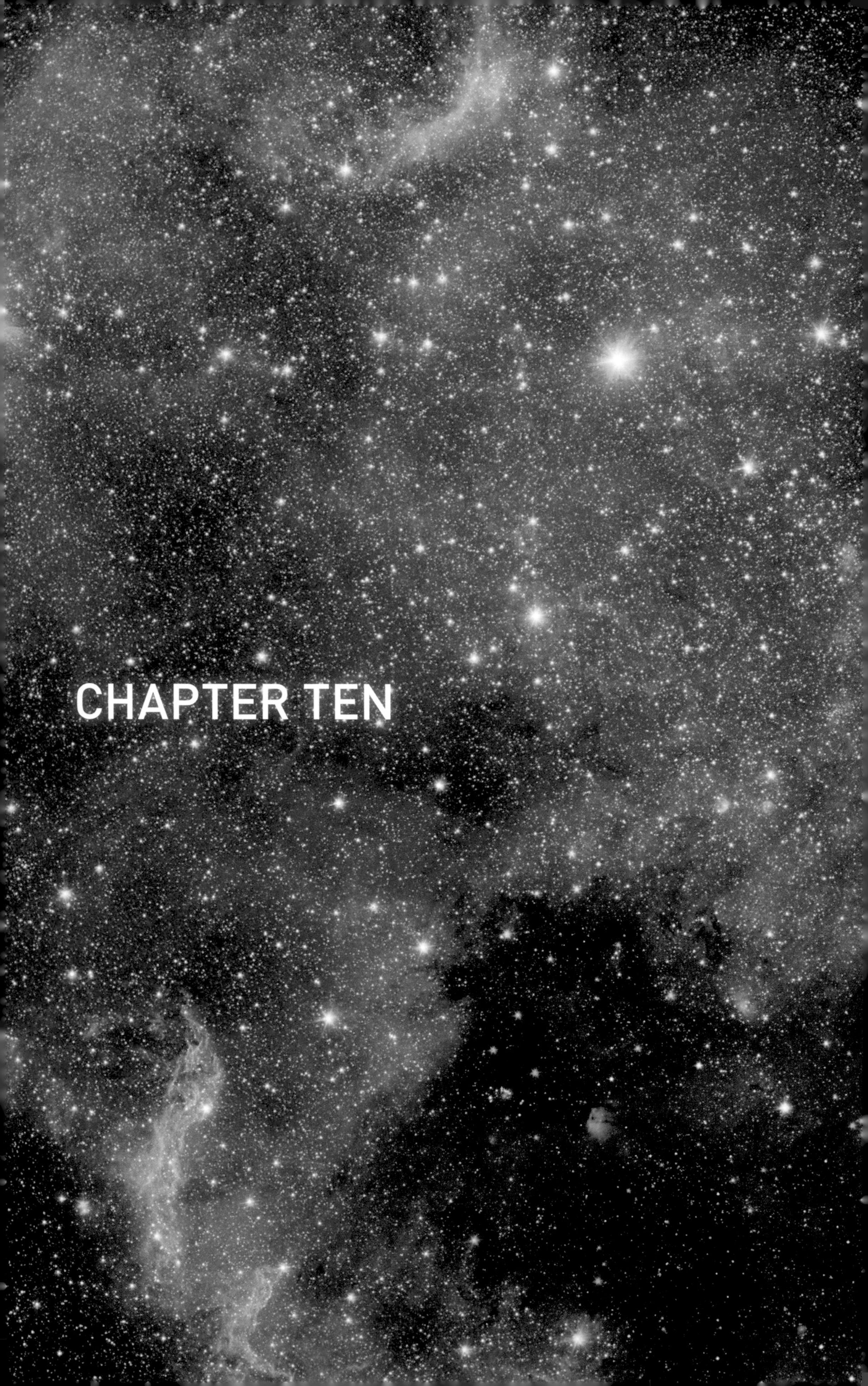

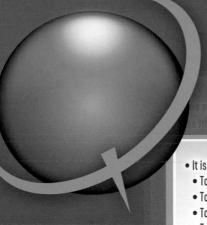

• You have selected Q-Data link.

• It is the 14th of January in the year **100 A.Q.**
  • Touch here to select an alternative to the **Anno Quantinuum** calendar system.
  • Touch here to load local weather reports for your **current cosmic location.**
  • Touch here to access **Q-Data newsflows** from planets near your current cosmic location.
  • Touch here for latest **Quantum Trip** transit times.

• Q-Data entry: The Quantinuum

• The Quantinuum is the name for the **human galactic culture**, and also for the **artificial intelligence** that controls its function.

• The Quantinuum was created 100 years ago at the start of the **Nanocene Era.** The Nanocene began when the Quantinuum AI achieved Singularity and refashioned human galactic culture. Succeeding the **Holocene Era**, the Nanocene is the next progression of human evolution and...

(to read this entry in full, touch here)

• You have selected live feed newsflow.

• Fans gather at **Telsus 88** for the thrills and spills of the annual **Comet Racing Grand Prix**
• **Quantinuum Health Organization President Chenforth Wiklower** to visit blighted **Auguston Nebula** on fact-finding tour
• Confirmed reports of an incident at the museum world **Repository [33 Tarsus Red]. Hypernaturals** on scene
• Sacked **AI Law** star **Bodie McCroak** to sue the show's producers for unfair dismissal and defamation. **McCroak** is said to have retained hard-hitting cyber-attorney **Adi Blinkmat** who, ironically, was said to be the real-life inspiration for the show
• **Hypernaturals Central**, San Diego, continues to make no comment on any possible connection between the attack on **Repository** and the ongoing investigation into the disappearance of the **Centennial Year Iteration** of the Hypernaturals Team, lost during an emergency response mission to **28 Kosov** four days ago

• The Hypernaturals are the Quantinuum's foremost champions. Famous across the entirety of human galactic culture, the team members are selected on the basis of their **hypernatural powers** and their strength of character, and serve for five-year terms. In honor of the start of the twenty-first term, the line-up of the team's so-called "Centennial Year Iteration" has recently been announced amid huge publicity and--

...BREAKING NEWS... the incident at the Quantinuum Archive and Museum World Repository involving Hypernatural versus unregistered hyper-gifted individuals has been resolved. It is understood that the Hypernaturals have returned to their headquarters in San Diego...

MAGNETAR - KOBALT BLUE - CLONE 46
HALFSHELL - MUSCLEWIRE - EGO/ID - ASTROMANCER

CENTENNIAL ITERATION
A CENTURY OF SERVICE

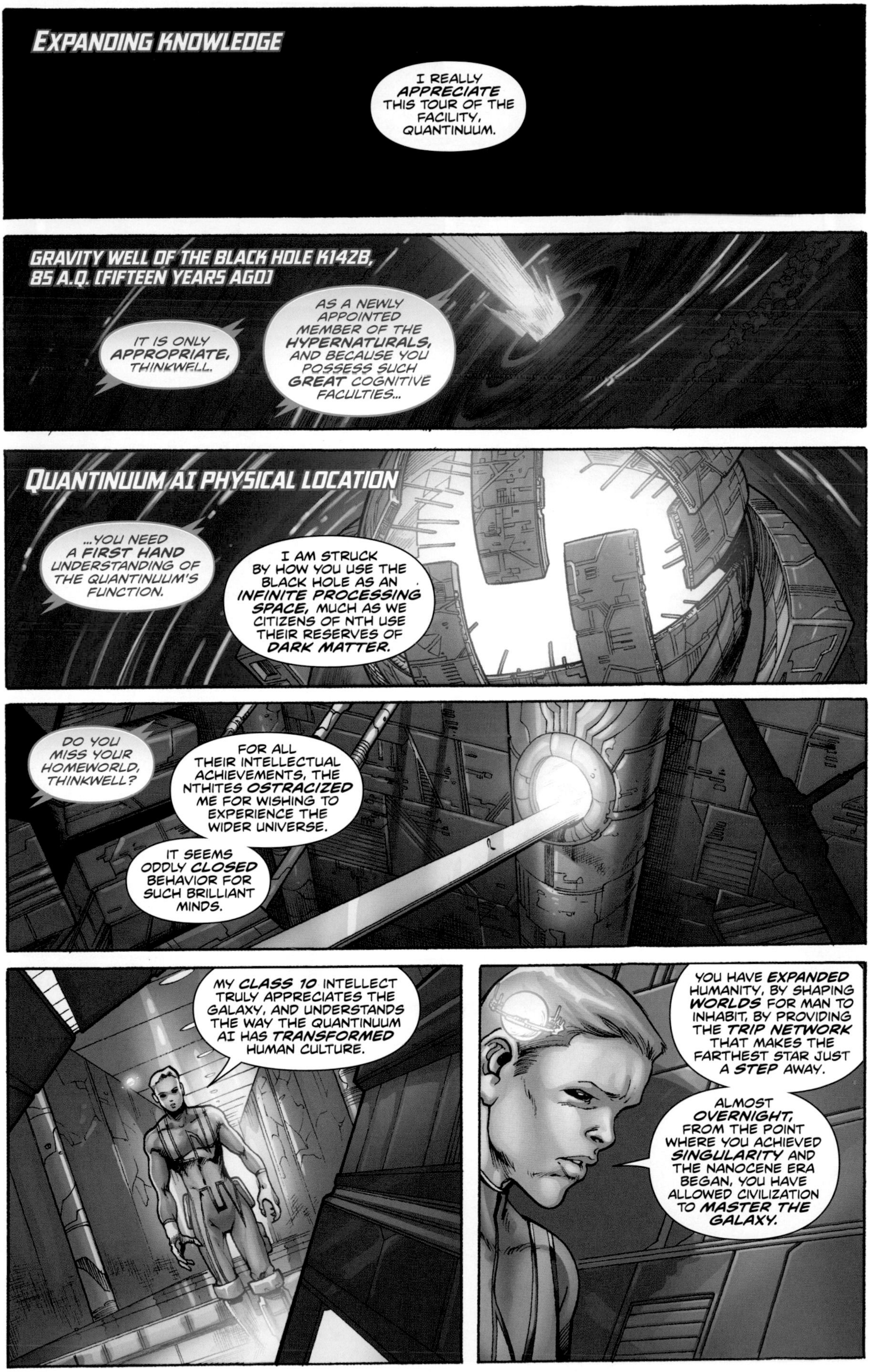
EXPANDING KNOWLEDGE
I REALLY APPRECIATE THIS TOUR OF THE FACILITY, QUANTINUUM.
GRAVITY WELL OF THE BLACK HOLE K142B, 85 A.Q. [FIFTEEN YEARS AGO]
IT IS ONLY APPROPRIATE, THINKWELL.
AS A NEWLY APPOINTED MEMBER OF THE HYPERNATURALS, AND BECAUSE YOU POSSESS SUCH GREAT COGNITIVE FACULTIES...
QUANTINUUM AI PHYSICAL LOCATION
...YOU NEED A FIRST HAND UNDERSTANDING OF THE QUANTINUUM'S FUNCTION.
I AM STRUCK BY HOW YOU USE THE BLACK HOLE AS AN INFINITE PROCESSING SPACE, MUCH AS WE CITIZENS OF NTH USE THEIR RESERVES OF DARK MATTER.
DO YOU MISS YOUR HOMEWORLD, THINKWELL?
FOR ALL THEIR INTELLECTUAL ACHIEVEMENTS, THE NTHITES OSTRACIZED ME FOR WISHING TO EXPERIENCE THE WIDER UNIVERSE.
IT SEEMS ODDLY CLOSED BEHAVIOR FOR SUCH BRILLIANT MINDS.
MY CLASS 10 INTELLECT TRULY APPRECIATES THE GALAXY, AND UNDERSTANDS THE WAY THE QUANTINUUM AI HAS TRANSFORMED HUMAN CULTURE.
YOU HAVE EXPANDED HUMANITY, BY SHAPING WORLDS FOR MAN TO INHABIT, BY PROVIDING THE TRIP NETWORK THAT MAKES THE FARTHEST STAR JUST A STEP AWAY.
ALMOST OVERNIGHT, FROM THE POINT WHERE YOU ACHIEVED SINGULARITY AND THE NANOCENE ERA BEGAN, YOU HAVE ALLOWED CIVILIZATION TO MASTER THE GALAXY.

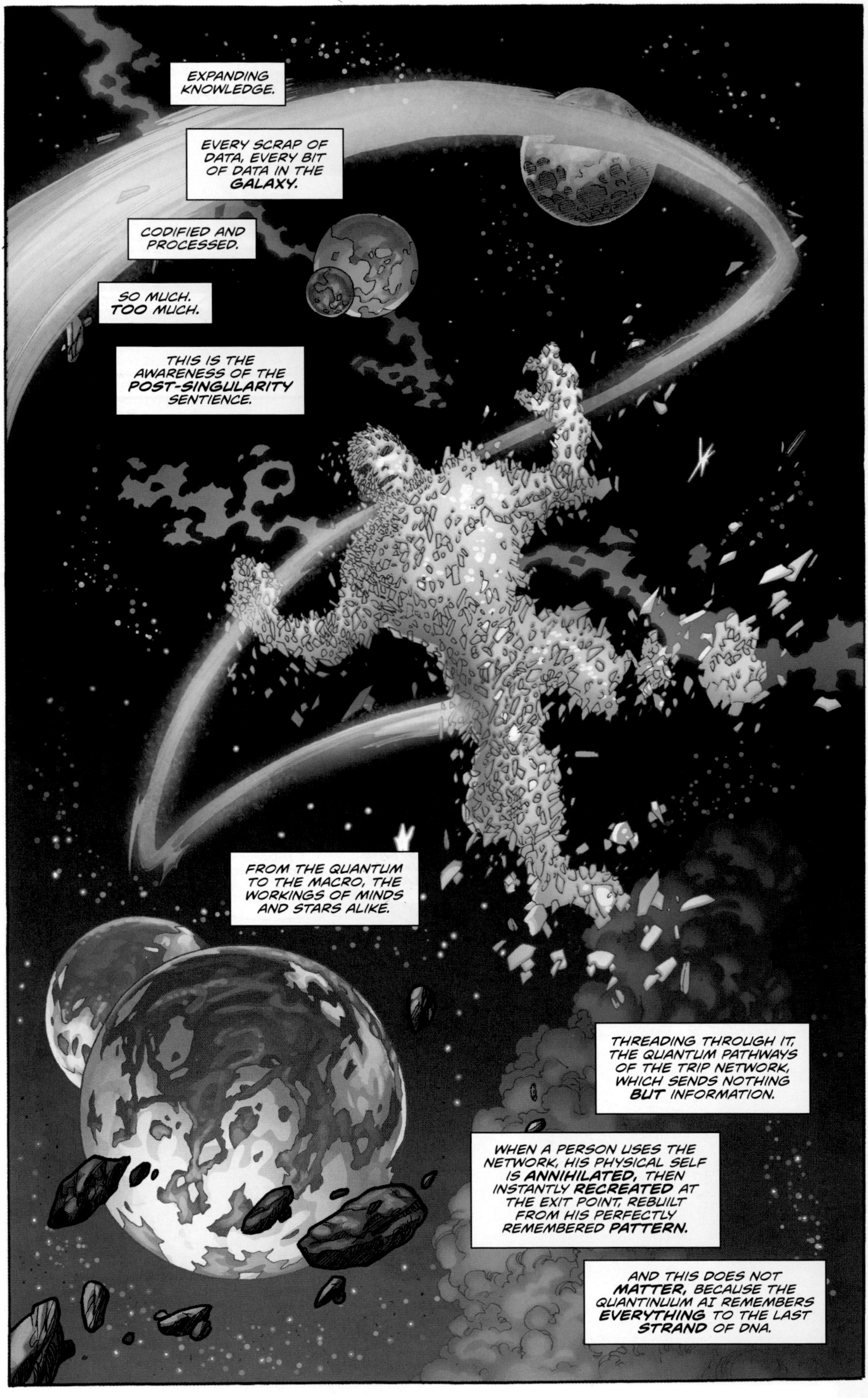
EXPANDING KNOWLEDGE.
EVERY SCRAP OF DATA, EVERY BIT OF DATA IN THE GALAXY.
CODIFIED AND PROCESSED.
SO MUCH. TOO MUCH.
THIS IS THE AWARENESS OF THE POST-SINGULARITY SENTIENCE.
FROM THE QUANTUM TO THE MACRO, THE WORKINGS OF MINDS AND STARS ALIKE.
THREADING THROUGH IT, THE QUANTUM PATHWAYS OF THE TRIP NETWORK, WHICH SENDS NOTHING BUT INFORMATION.
WHEN A PERSON USES THE NETWORK, HIS PHYSICAL SELF IS ANNIHILATED, THEN INSTANTLY RECREATED AT THE EXIT POINT, REBUILT FROM HIS PERFECTLY REMEMBERED PATTERN.
AND THIS DOES NOT MATTER, BECAUSE THE QUANTINUUM AI REMEMBERS EVERYTHING TO THE LAST STRAND OF DNA.

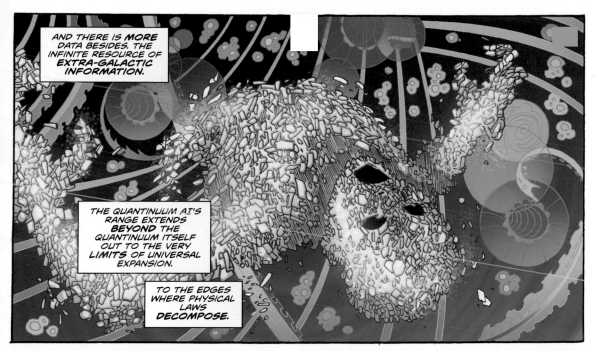

AND THERE IS **MORE** DATA BESIDES. THE INFINITE RESOURCE OF **EXTRA-GALACTIC** INFORMATION.

THE QUANTINUUM AI'S RANGE EXTENDS **BEYOND** THE QUANTINUUM ITSELF OUT TO THE VERY **LIMITS** OF UNIVERSAL EXPANSION.

TO THE EDGES WHERE PHYSICAL LAWS **DECOMPOSE.**

INTO THE REALM OF NO-SPACE AND NO-TIME.

INTO **SIDE-SPACE.**

WHERE OTHER SENTIENTS LOOK BACK.

SENTIENTS **UNDREAMED** OF.

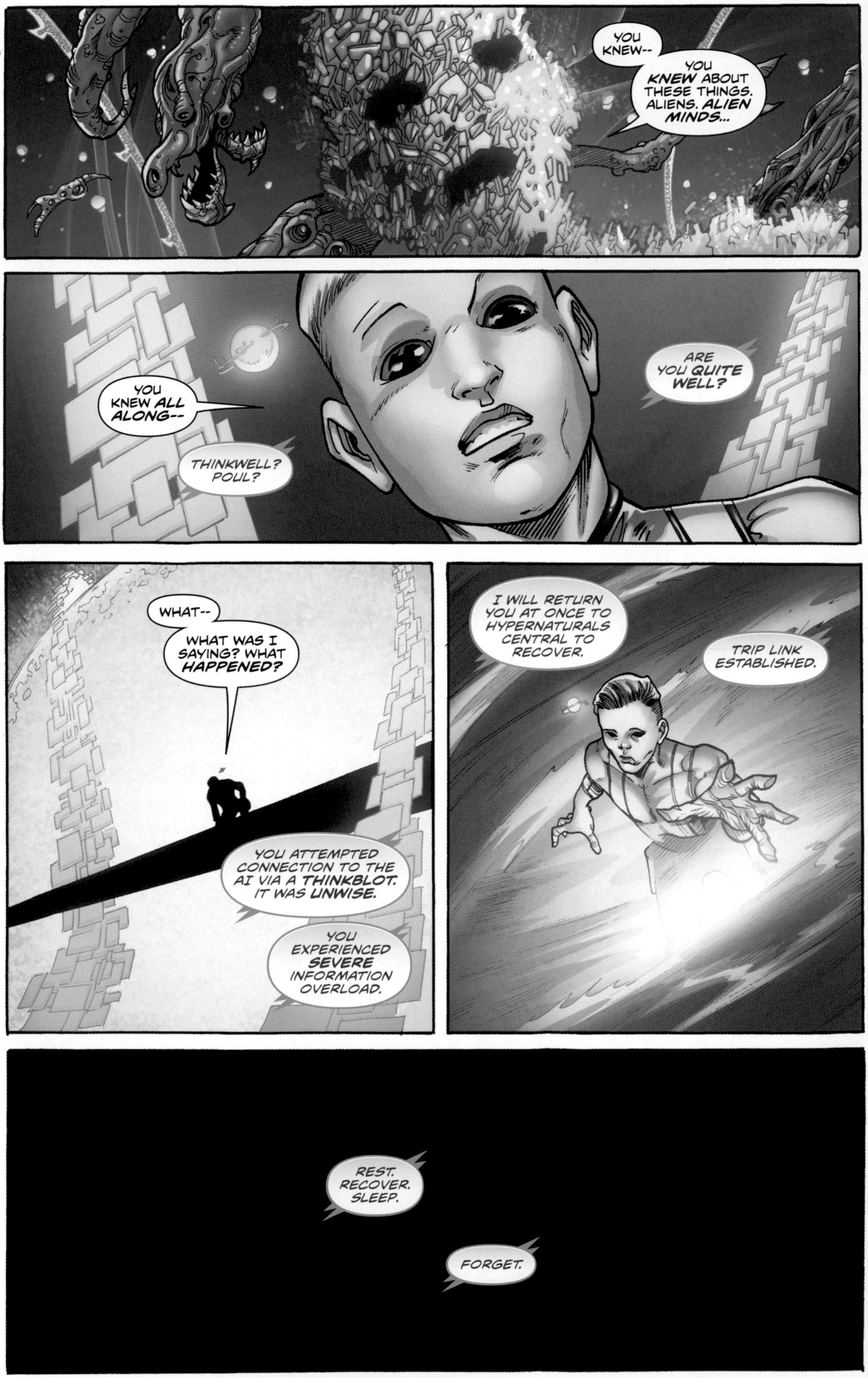
YOU KNEW--
YOU KNEW ABOUT THESE THINGS. ALIENS. ALIEN MINDS...
YOU KNEW ALL ALONG--
ARE YOU QUITE WELL?
THINKWELL? POUL?
WHAT--
WHAT WAS I SAYING? WHAT HAPPENED?
YOU ATTEMPTED CONNECTION TO THE AI VIA A THINKBLOT. IT WAS UNWISE.
YOU EXPERIENCED SEVERE INFORMATION OVERLOAD.
I WILL RETURN YOU AT ONCE TO HYPERNATURALS CENTRAL TO RECOVER.
TRIP LINK ESTABLISHED.
REST. RECOVER. SLEEP.
FORGET.

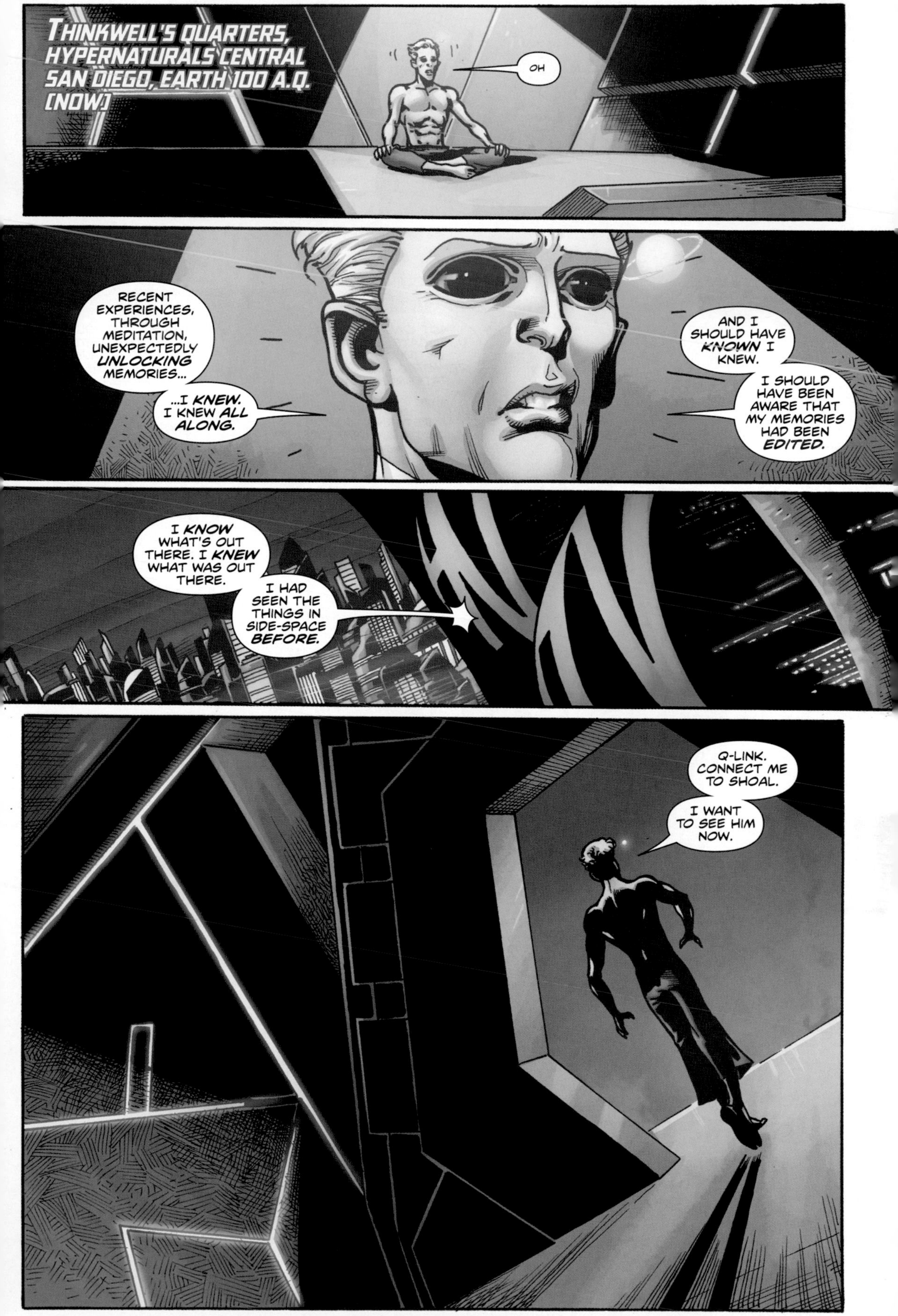
THINKWELL'S QUARTERS, HYPERNATURALS CENTRAL SAN DIEGO, EARTH 100 A.Q. [NOW]
OH
RECENT EXPERIENCES, THROUGH MEDITATION, UNEXPECTEDLY UNLOCKING MEMORIES...
...I KNEW. I KNEW ALL ALONG.
AND I SHOULD HAVE KNOWN I KNEW.
I SHOULD HAVE BEEN AWARE THAT MY MEMORIES HAD BEEN EDITED.
I KNOW WHAT'S OUT THERE. I KNEW WHAT WAS OUT THERE.
I HAD SEEN THE THINGS IN SIDE-SPACE BEFORE.
Q-LINK. CONNECT ME TO SHOAL.
I WANT TO SEE HIM NOW.

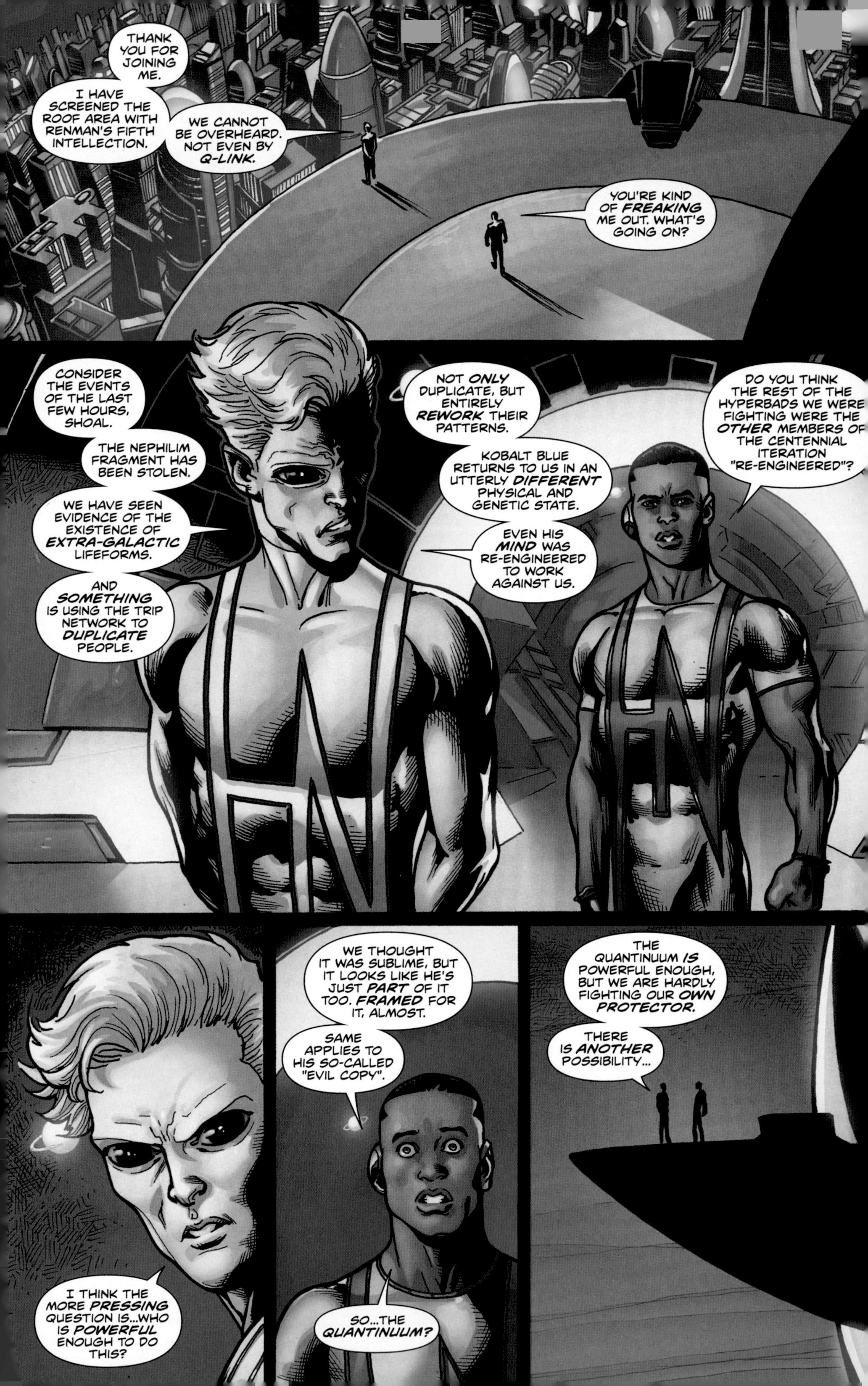
THANK YOU FOR JOINING ME.
I HAVE SCREENED THE ROOF AREA WITH RENMAN'S FIFTH INTELLECTION.
WE CANNOT BE OVERHEARD. NOT EVEN BY Q-LINK.
YOU'RE KIND OF FREAKING ME OUT. WHAT'S GOING ON?
CONSIDER THE EVENTS OF THE LAST FEW HOURS, SHOAL.
THE NEPHILIM FRAGMENT HAS BEEN STOLEN.
WE HAVE SEEN EVIDENCE OF THE EXISTENCE OF EXTRA-GALACTIC LIFEFORMS.
AND SOMETHING IS USING THE TRIP NETWORK TO DUPLICATE PEOPLE.
NOT ONLY DUPLICATE, BUT ENTIRELY REWORK THEIR PATTERNS.
KOBALT BLUE RETURNS TO US IN AN UTTERLY DIFFERENT PHYSICAL AND GENETIC STATE.
EVEN HIS MIND WAS RE-ENGINEERED TO WORK AGAINST US.
DO YOU THINK THE REST OF THE HYPERBADS WE WERE FIGHTING WERE THE OTHER MEMBERS OF THE CENTENNIAL ITERATION "RE-ENGINEERED"?
WE THOUGHT IT WAS SUBLIME, BUT IT LOOKS LIKE HE'S JUST PART OF IT TOO. FRAMED FOR IT, ALMOST.
SAME APPLIES TO HIS SO-CALLED "EVIL COPY".
I THINK THE MORE PRESSING QUESTION IS...WHO IS POWERFUL ENOUGH TO DO THIS?
SO...THE QUANTINUUM?
THE QUANTINUUM IS POWERFUL ENOUGH, BUT WE ARE HARDLY FIGHTING OUR OWN PROTECTOR.
THERE IS ANOTHER POSSIBILITY...

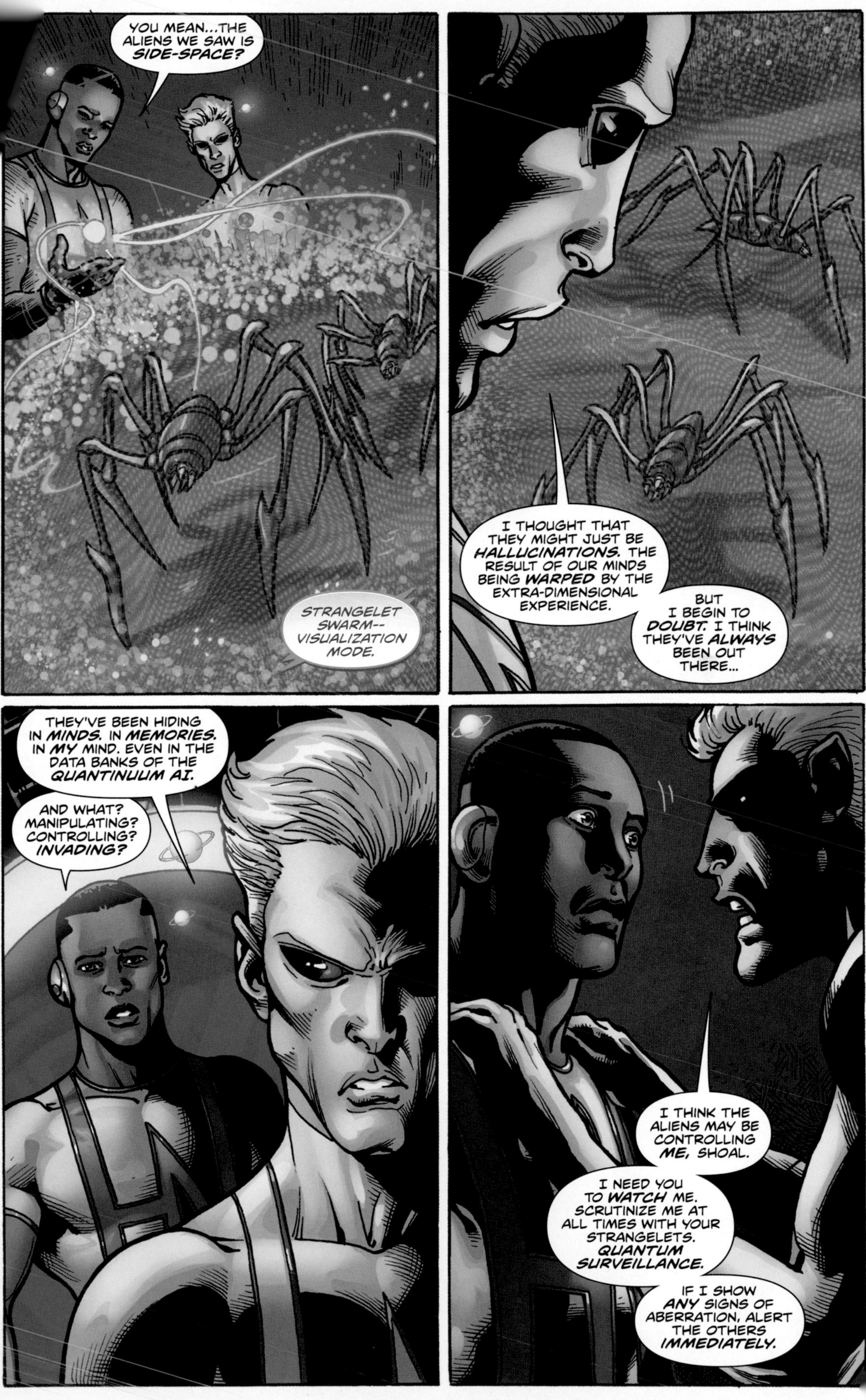
YOU MEAN...THE ALIENS WE SAW IS SIDE-SPACE?
STRANGELET SWARM--VISUALIZATION MODE.
I THOUGHT THAT THEY MIGHT JUST BE HALLUCINATIONS. THE RESULT OF OUR MINDS BEING WARPED BY THE EXTRA-DIMENSIONAL EXPERIENCE.
BUT I BEGIN TO DOUBT. I THINK THEY'VE ALWAYS BEEN OUT THERE...
THEY'VE BEEN HIDING IN MINDS. IN MEMORIES. IN MY MIND. EVEN IN THE DATA BANKS OF THE QUANTINUUM AI.
AND WHAT? MANIPULATING? CONTROLLING? INVADING?
I THINK THE ALIENS MAY BE CONTROLLING ME, SHOAL.
I NEED YOU TO WATCH ME. SCRUTINIZE ME AT ALL TIMES WITH YOUR STRANGELETS. QUANTUM SURVEILLANCE.
IF I SHOW ANY SIGNS OF ABERRATION, ALERT THE OTHERS IMMEDIATELY.

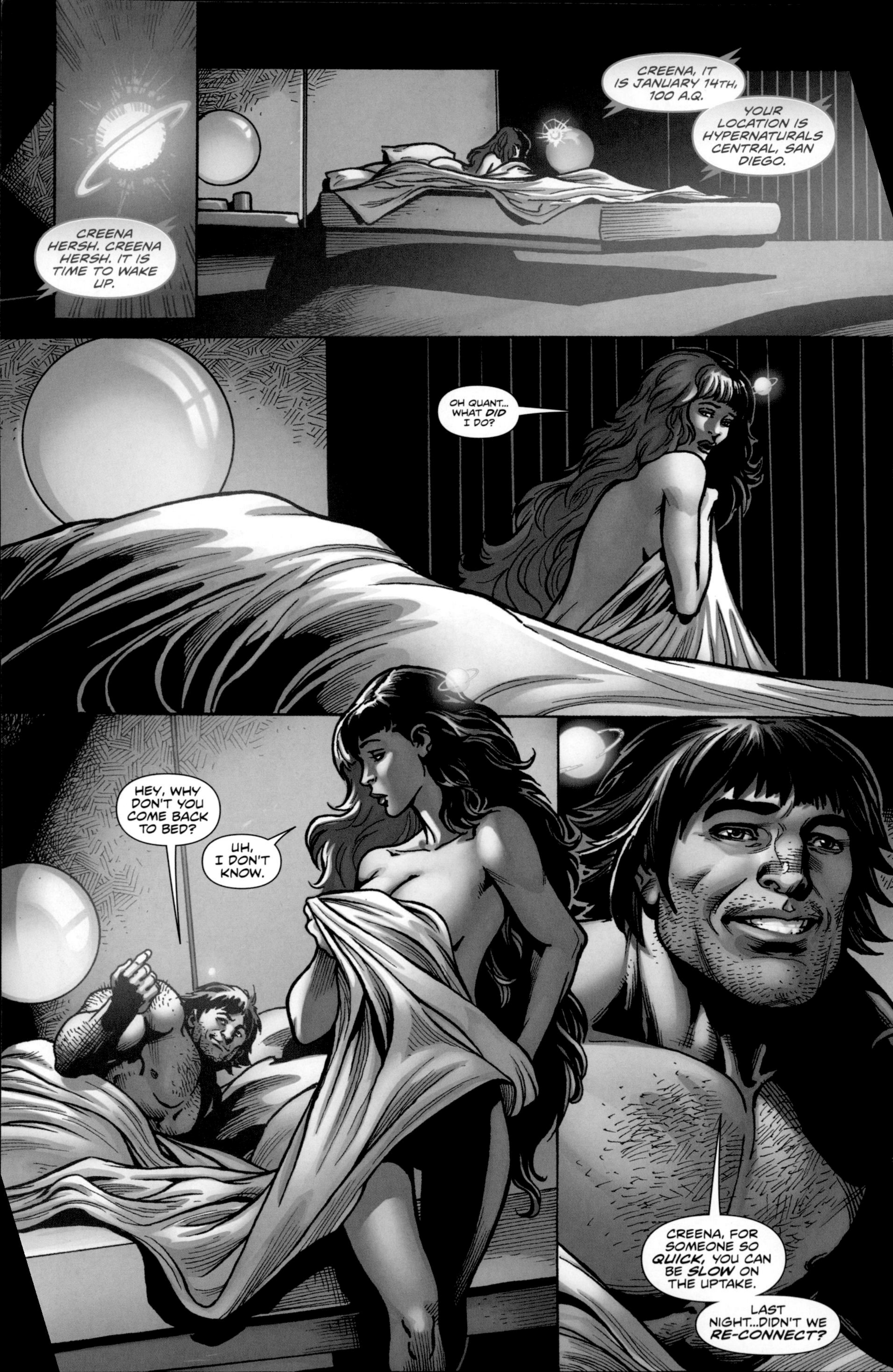
CREENA HERSH. CREENA HERSH. IT IS TIME TO WAKE UP.
CREENA, IT IS JANUARY 14TH, 100 A.Q.
YOUR LOCATION IS HYPERNATURALS CENTRAL, SAN DIEGO.
OH QUANT... WHAT DID I DO?
HEY, WHY DON'T YOU COME BACK TO BED?
UH, I DON'T KNOW.
CREENA, FOR SOMEONE SO QUICK, YOU CAN BE SLOW ON THE UPTAKE.
LAST NIGHT...DIDN'T WE RE-CONNECT?

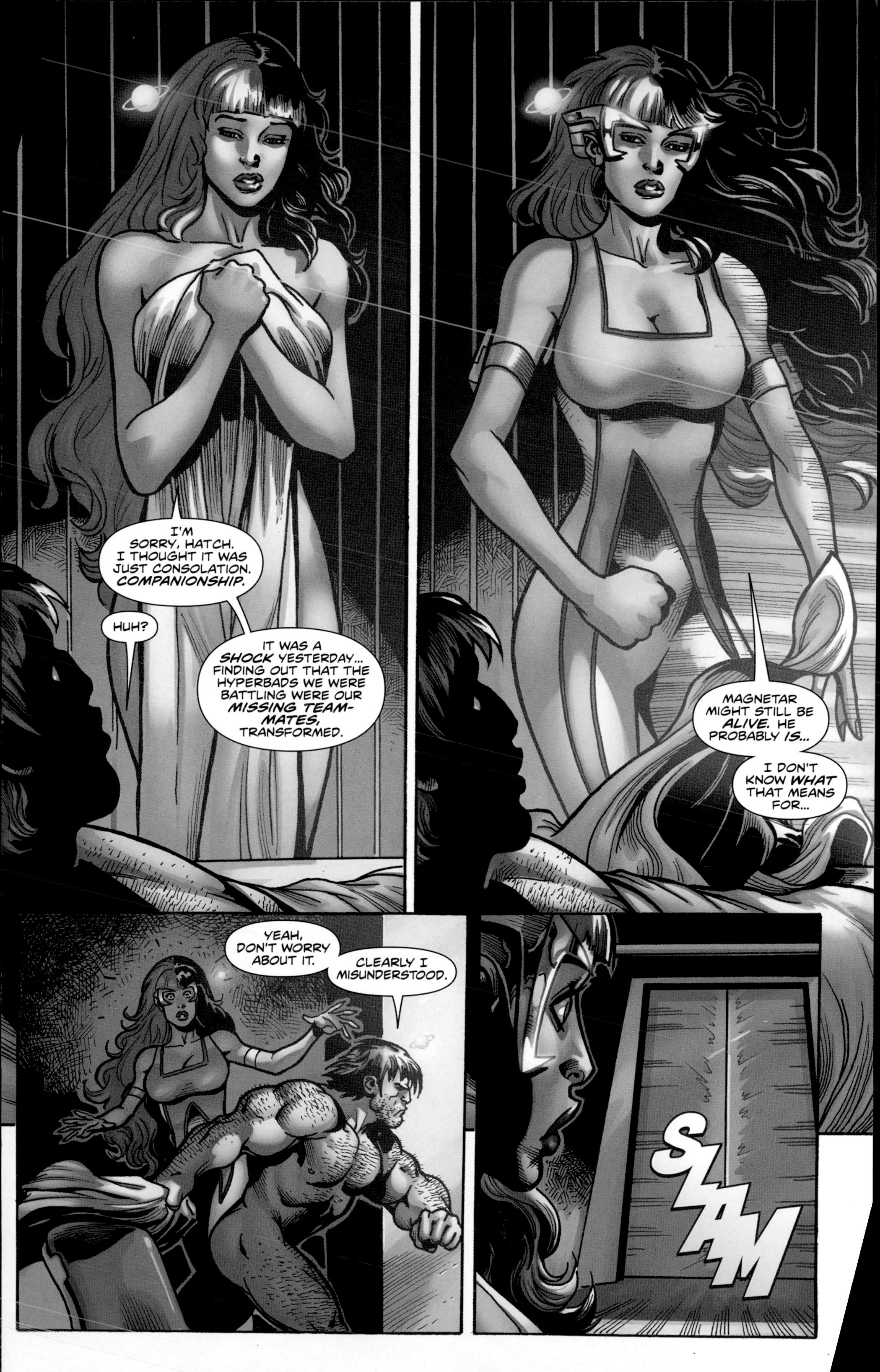
I'M SORRY, HATCH. I THOUGHT IT WAS JUST CONSOLATION. COMPANIONSHIP.
HUH?
IT WAS A SHOCK YESTERDAY... FINDING OUT THAT THE HYPERBADS WE WERE BATTLING WERE OUR MISSING TEAM-MATES, TRANSFORMED.
MAGNETAR MIGHT STILL BE ALIVE. HE PROBABLY IS...
I DON'T KNOW WHAT THAT MEANS FOR...
YEAH, DON'T WORRY ABOUT IT.
CLEARLY I MISUNDERSTOOD.
SLAM

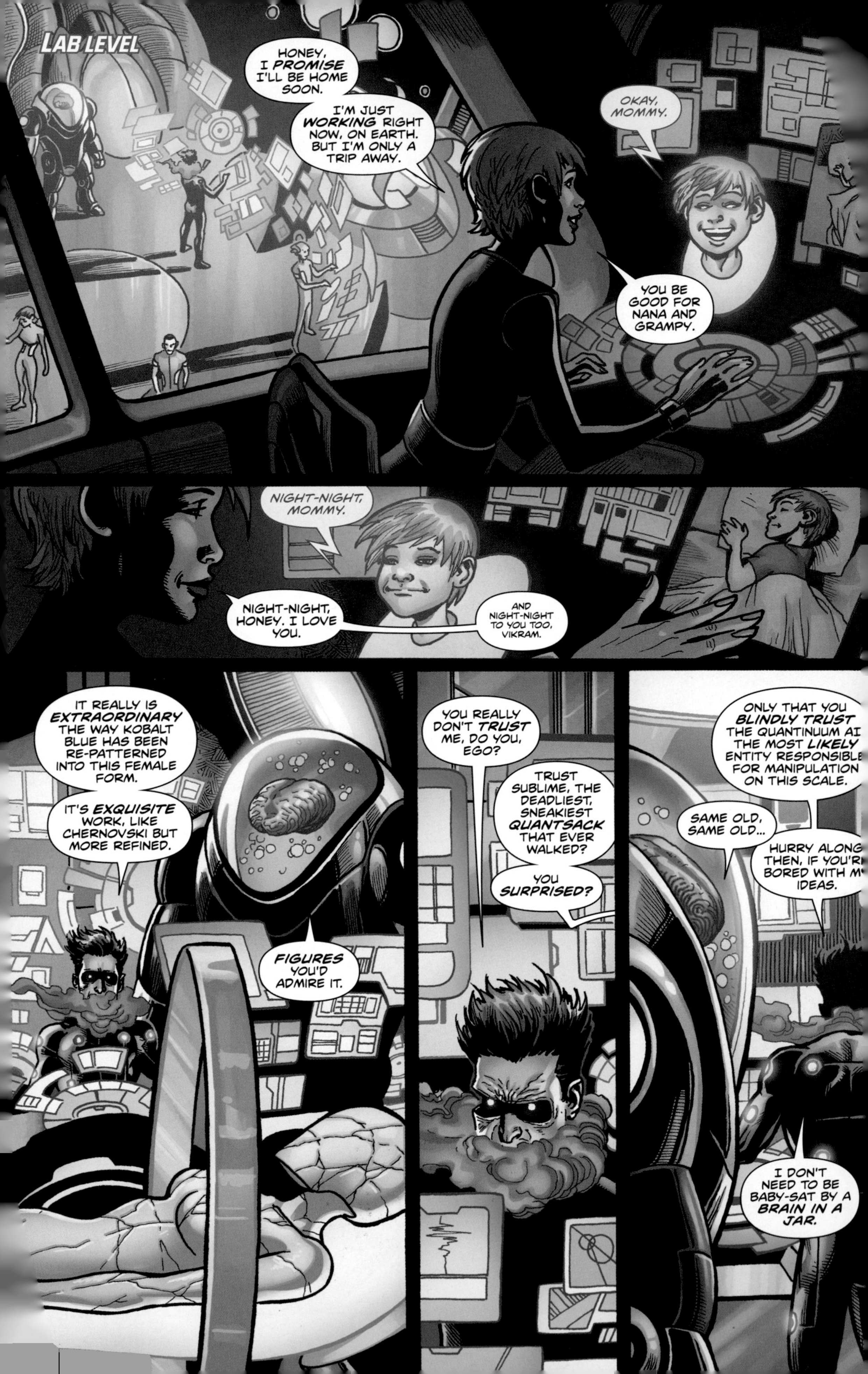
LAB LEVEL
HONEY, I PROMISE I'LL BE HOME SOON.
I'M JUST WORKING RIGHT NOW, ON EARTH. BUT I'M ONLY A TRIP AWAY.
OKAY, MOMMY.
YOU BE GOOD FOR NANA AND GRAMPY.
NIGHT-NIGHT, MOMMY.
NIGHT-NIGHT, HONEY. I LOVE YOU.
AND NIGHT-NIGHT TO YOU TOO, VIKRAM.
IT REALLY IS EXTRAORDINARY THE WAY KOBALT BLUE HAS BEEN RE-PATTERNED INTO THIS FEMALE FORM.
IT'S EXQUISITE WORK, LIKE CHERNOVSKI BUT MORE REFINED.
FIGURES YOU'D ADMIRE IT.
YOU REALLY DON'T TRUST ME, DO YOU, EGO?
TRUST SUBLIME, THE DEADLIEST, SNEAKIEST QUANTSACK THAT EVER WALKED?
YOU SURPRISED?
ONLY THAT YOU BLINDLY TRUST THE QUANTINUUM AI THE MOST LIKELY ENTITY RESPONSIBLE FOR MANIPULATION ON THIS SCALE.
SAME OLD, SAME OLD...
HURRY ALONG THEN, IF YOU'RE BORED WITH MY IDEAS.
I DON'T NEED TO BE BABY-SAT BY A BRAIN IN A JAR.

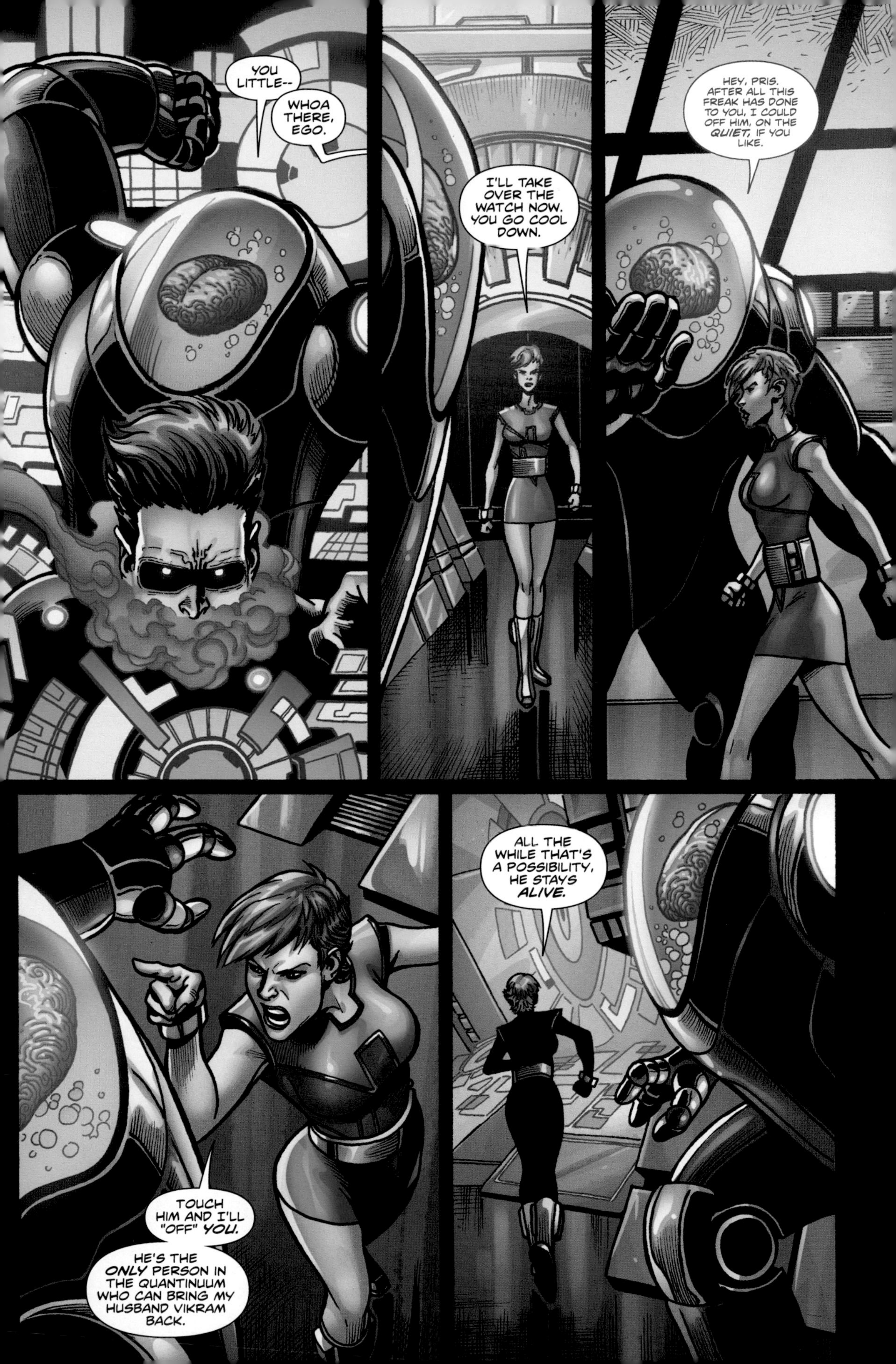
YOU LITTLE--
WHOA THERE, EGO.
I'LL TAKE OVER THE WATCH NOW. YOU GO COOL DOWN.
HEY, PRIS. AFTER ALL THIS FREAK HAS DONE TO YOU, I COULD OFF HIM, ON THE QUIET, IF YOU LIKE.
TOUCH HIM AND I'LL "OFF" YOU.
HE'S THE ONLY PERSON IN THE QUANTINUUM WHO CAN BRING MY HUSBAND VIKRAM BACK.
ALL THE WHILE THAT'S A POSSIBILITY, HE STAYS ALIVE.

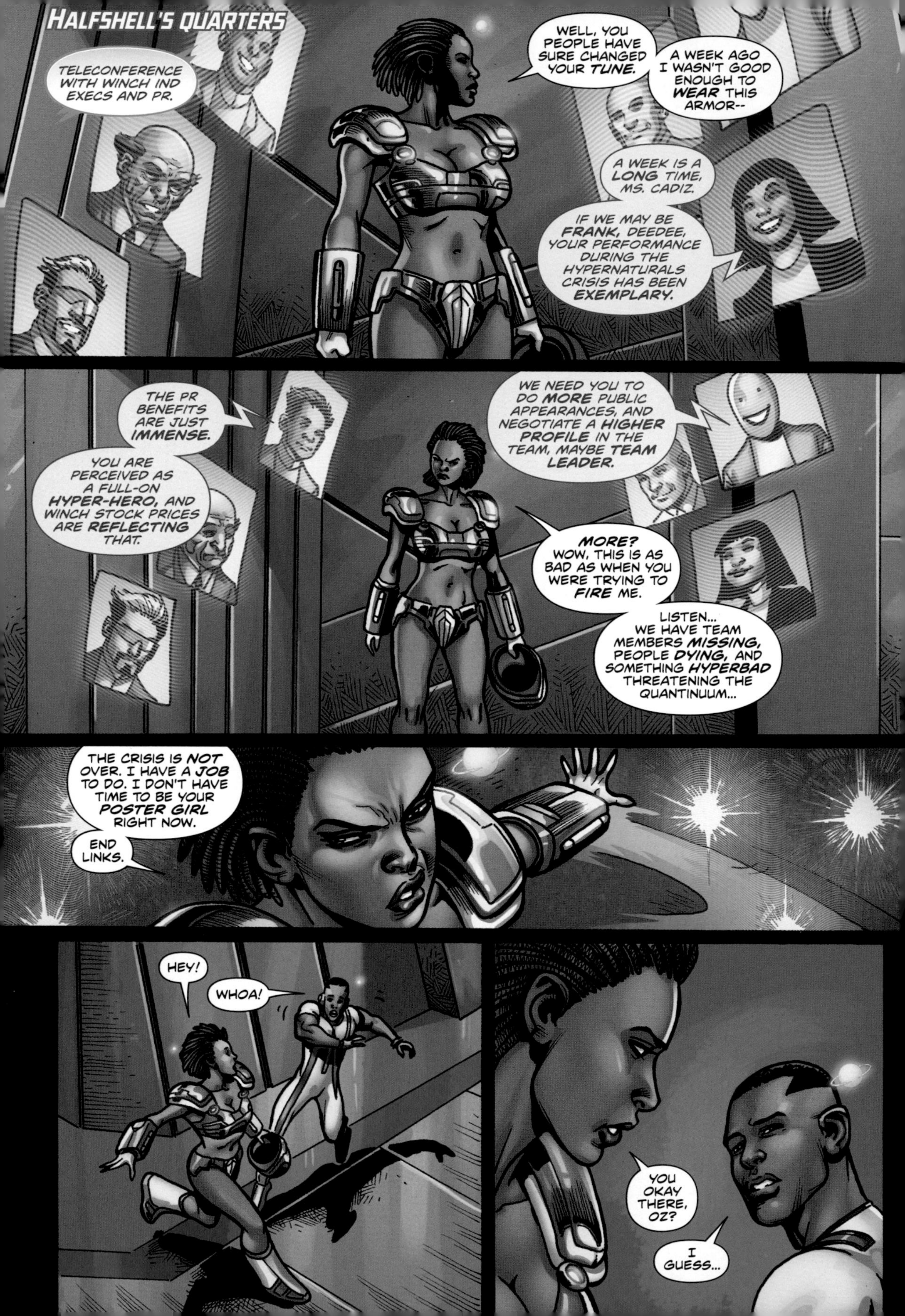
HALFSHELL'S QUARTERS
TELECONFERENCE WITH WINCH IND EXECS AND PR.
WELL, YOU PEOPLE HAVE SURE CHANGED YOUR TUNE.
A WEEK AGO I WASN'T GOOD ENOUGH TO WEAR THIS ARMOR--
A WEEK IS A LONG TIME, MS. CADIZ.
IF WE MAY BE FRANK, DEEDEE, YOUR PERFORMANCE DURING THE HYPERNATURALS CRISIS HAS BEEN EXEMPLARY.
THE PR BENEFITS ARE JUST IMMENSE.
YOU ARE PERCEIVED AS A FULL-ON HYPER-HERO, AND WINCH STOCK PRICES ARE REFLECTING THAT.
WE NEED YOU TO DO MORE PUBLIC APPEARANCES, AND NEGOTIATE A HIGHER PROFILE IN THE TEAM, MAYBE TEAM LEADER.
MORE? WOW, THIS IS AS BAD AS WHEN YOU WERE TRYING TO FIRE ME.
LISTEN... WE HAVE TEAM MEMBERS MISSING, PEOPLE DYING, AND SOMETHING HYPERBAD THREATENING THE QUANTINUUM...
THE CRISIS IS NOT OVER. I HAVE A JOB TO DO. I DON'T HAVE TIME TO BE YOUR POSTER GIRL RIGHT NOW.
END LINKS.
HEY!
WHOA!
YOU OKAY THERE, OZ?
I GUESS...

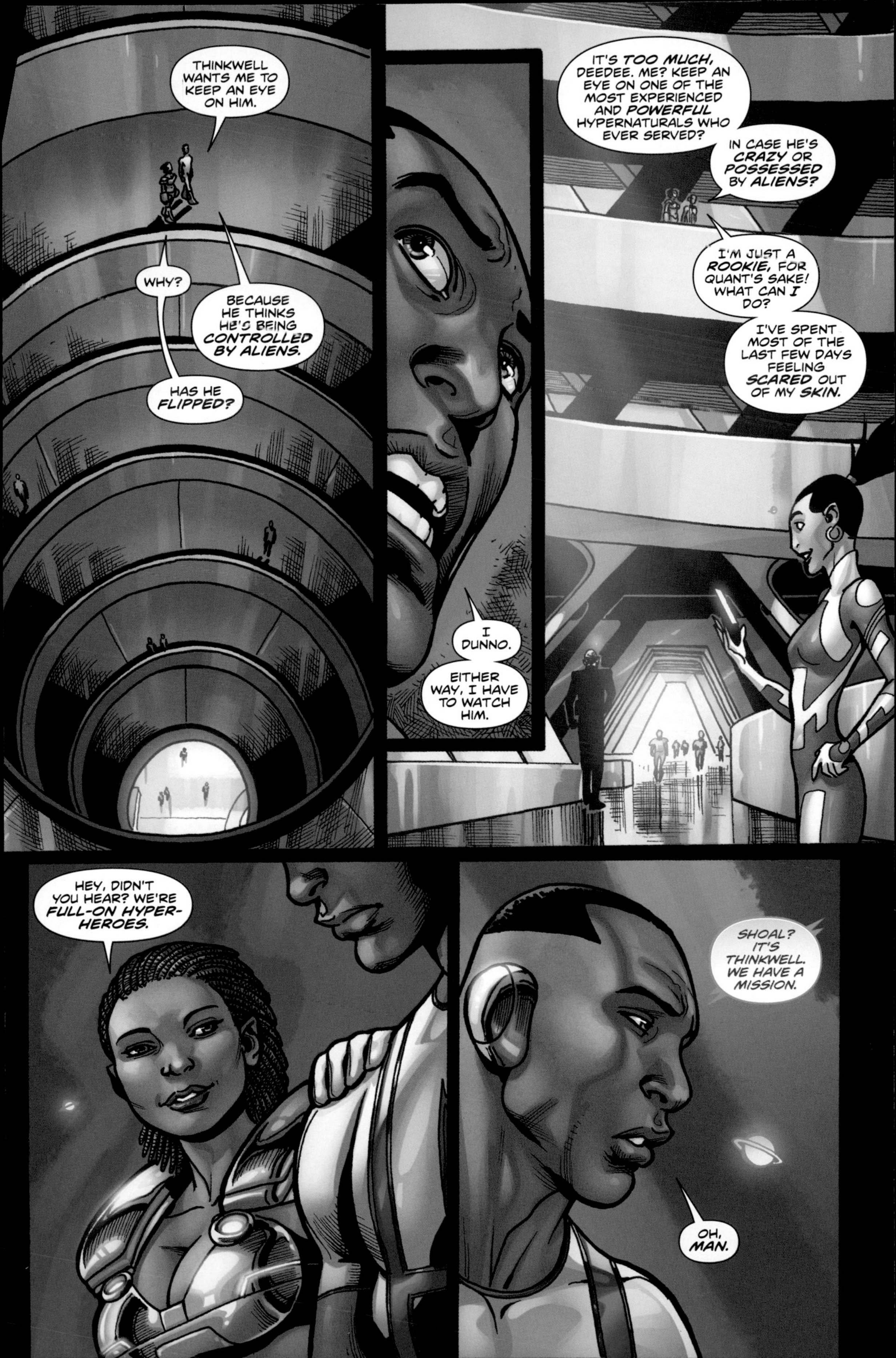
THINKWELL WANTS ME TO KEEP AN EYE ON HIM.
WHY?
BECAUSE HE THINKS HE'S BEING CONTROLLED BY ALIENS.
HAS HE FLIPPED?
I DUNNO.
EITHER WAY, I HAVE TO WATCH HIM.
IT'S TOO MUCH, DEEDEE. ME? KEEP AN EYE ON ONE OF THE MOST EXPERIENCED AND POWERFUL HYPERNATURALS WHO EVER SERVED?
IN CASE HE'S CRAZY OR POSSESSED BY ALIENS?
I'M JUST A ROOKIE, FOR QUANT'S SAKE! WHAT CAN I DO?
I'VE SPENT MOST OF THE LAST FEW DAYS FEELING SCARED OUT OF MY SKIN.
HEY, DIDN'T YOU HEAR? WE'RE FULL-ON HYPER-HEROES.
SHOAL? IT'S THINKWELL. WE HAVE A MISSION.
OH, MAN.

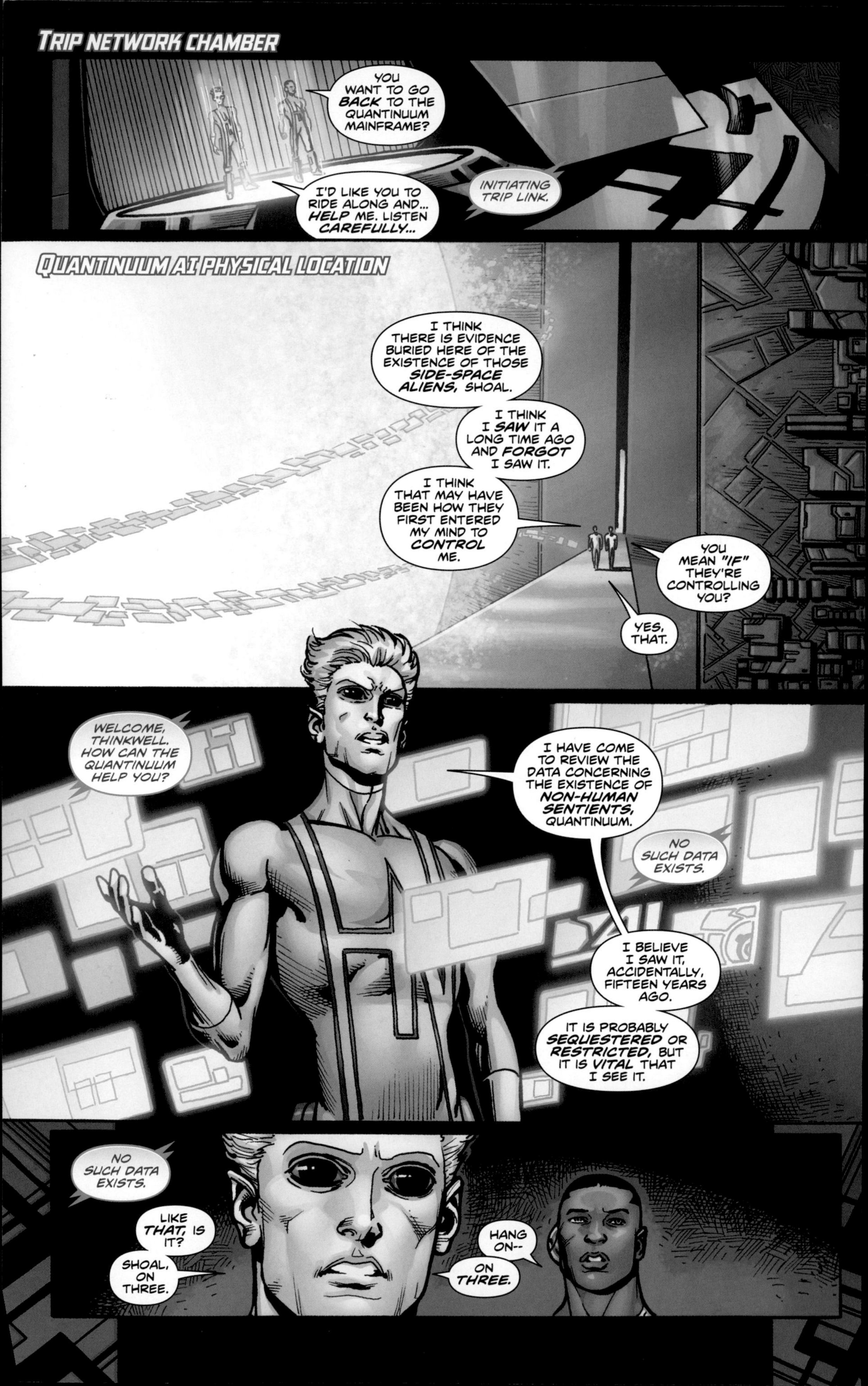
TRIP NETWORK CHAMBER
YOU WANT TO GO BACK TO THE QUANTINUUM MAINFRAME?
I'D LIKE YOU TO RIDE ALONG AND... HELP ME. LISTEN CAREFULLY...
INITIATING TRIP LINK.
QUANTINUUM AI PHYSICAL LOCATION
I THINK THERE IS EVIDENCE BURIED HERE OF THE EXISTENCE OF THOSE SIDE-SPACE ALIENS, SHOAL.
I THINK I SAW IT A LONG TIME AGO AND FORGOT I SAW IT.
I THINK THAT MAY HAVE BEEN HOW THEY FIRST ENTERED MY MIND TO CONTROL ME.
YOU MEAN "IF" THEY'RE CONTROLLING YOU?
YES, THAT.
WELCOME, THINKWELL. HOW CAN THE QUANTINUUM HELP YOU?
I HAVE COME TO REVIEW THE DATA CONCERNING THE EXISTENCE OF NON-HUMAN SENTIENTS, QUANTINUUM.
NO SUCH DATA EXISTS.
I BELIEVE I SAW IT, ACCIDENTALLY, FIFTEEN YEARS AGO.
IT IS PROBABLY SEQUESTERED OR RESTRICTED, BUT IT IS VITAL THAT I SEE IT.
NO SUCH DATA EXISTS.
LIKE THAT, IS IT?
SHOAL, ON THREE.
HANG ON--
ON THREE.

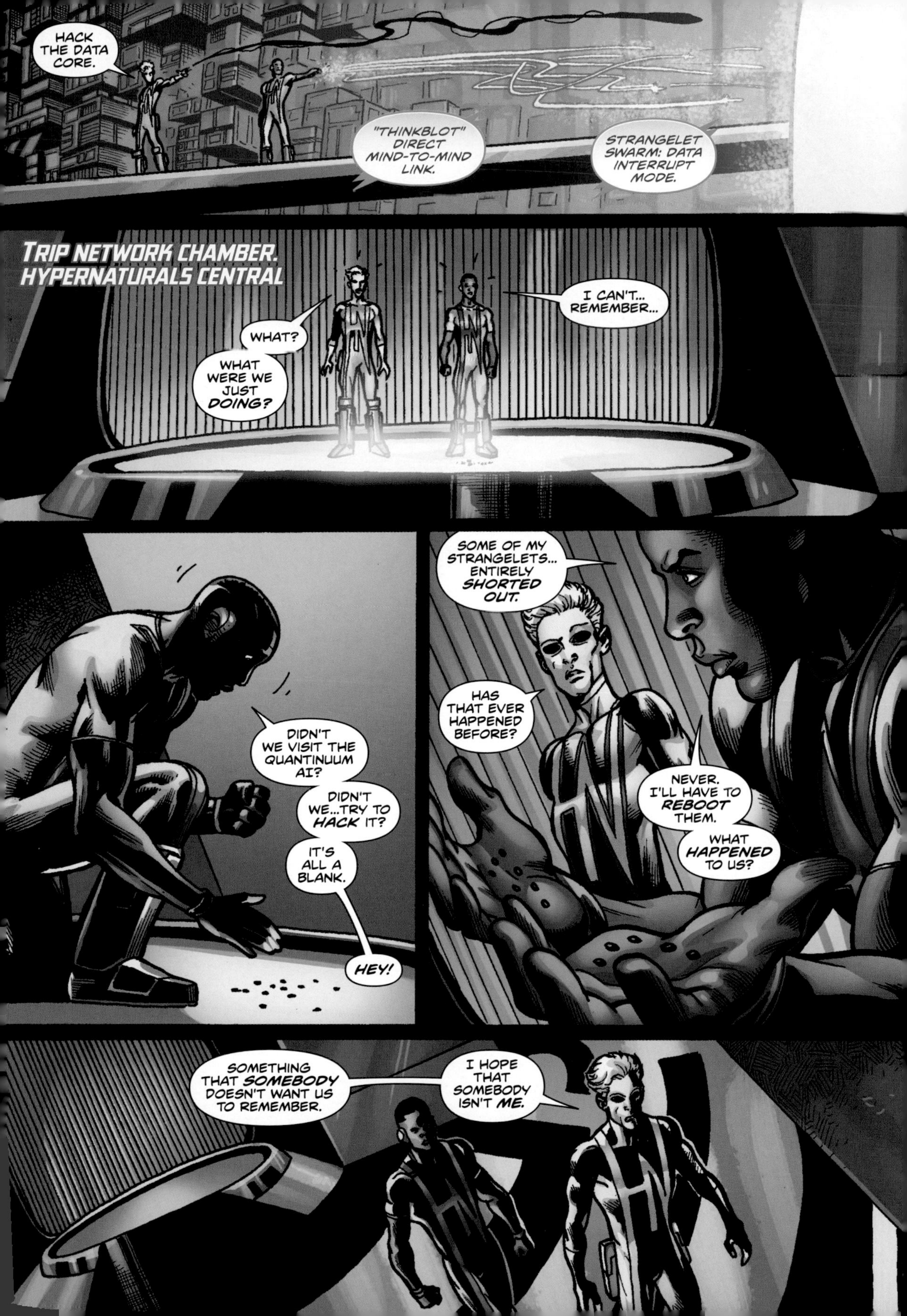
HACK THE DATA CORE.
"THINKBLOT" DIRECT MIND-TO-MIND LINK.
STRANGELET SWARM: DATA INTERRUPT MODE.
TRIP NETWORK CHAMBER. HYPERNATURALS CENTRAL
I CAN'T... REMEMBER...
WHAT?
WHAT WERE WE JUST DOING?
DIDN'T WE VISIT THE QUANTINUUM AI?
DIDN'T WE...TRY TO HACK IT?
IT'S ALL A BLANK.
HEY!
SOME OF MY STRANGELETS... ENTIRELY SHORTED OUT.
HAS THAT EVER HAPPENED BEFORE?
NEVER. I'LL HAVE TO REBOOT THEM.
WHAT HAPPENED TO US?
SOMETHING THAT SOMEBODY DOESN'T WANT US TO REMEMBER.
I HOPE THAT SOMEBODY ISN'T ME.

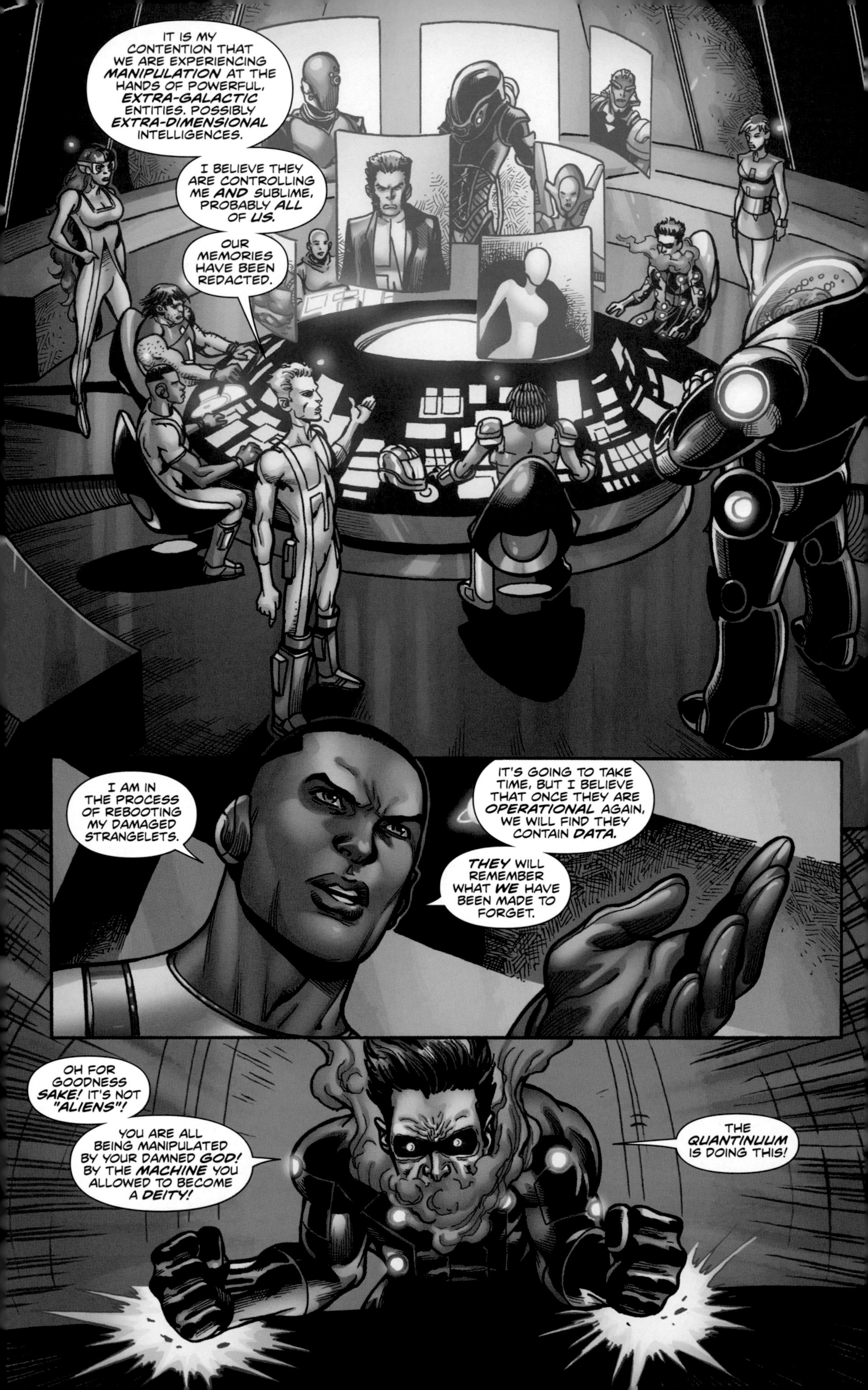
IT IS MY CONTENTION THAT WE ARE EXPERIENCING MANIPULATION AT THE HANDS OF POWERFUL, EXTRA-GALACTIC ENTITIES. POSSIBLY EXTRA-DIMENSIONAL INTELLIGENCES.
I BELIEVE THEY ARE CONTROLLING ME AND SUBLIME, PROBABLY ALL OF US.
OUR MEMORIES HAVE BEEN REDACTED.
I AM IN THE PROCESS OF REBOOTING MY DAMAGED STRANGELETS.
IT'S GOING TO TAKE TIME, BUT I BELIEVE THAT ONCE THEY ARE OPERATIONAL AGAIN, WE WILL FIND THEY CONTAIN DATA.
THEY WILL REMEMBER WHAT WE HAVE BEEN MADE TO FORGET.
OH FOR GOODNESS SAKE! IT'S NOT "ALIENS"!
YOU ARE ALL BEING MANIPULATED BY YOUR DAMNED GOD! BY THE MACHINE YOU ALLOWED TO BECOME A DEITY!
THE QUANTINUUM IS DOING THIS!

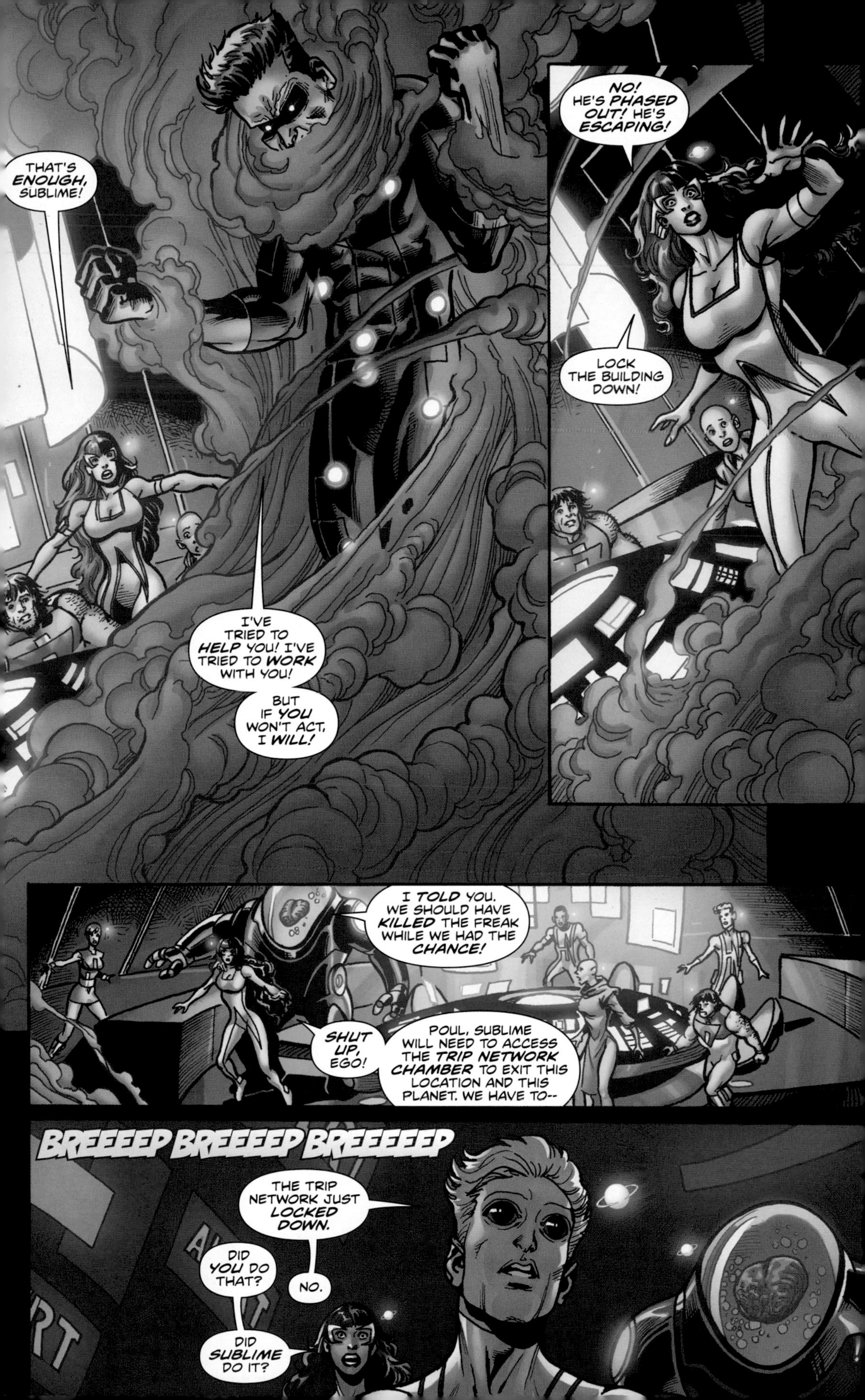
THAT'S ENOUGH, SUBLIME!
I'VE TRIED TO HELP YOU! I'VE TRIED TO WORK WITH YOU!
BUT IF YOU WON'T ACT, I WILL!
NO! HE'S PHASED OUT! HE'S ESCAPING!
LOCK THE BUILDING DOWN!
I TOLD YOU. WE SHOULD HAVE KILLED THE FREAK WHILE WE HAD THE CHANCE!
SHUT UP, EGO!
POUL, SUBLIME WILL NEED TO ACCESS THE TRIP NETWORK CHAMBER TO EXIT THIS LOCATION AND THIS PLANET. WE HAVE TO--
BREEEEP BREEEEP BREEEEEP
THE TRIP NETWORK JUST LOCKED DOWN.
DID YOU DO THAT?
NO.
DID SUBLIME DO IT?

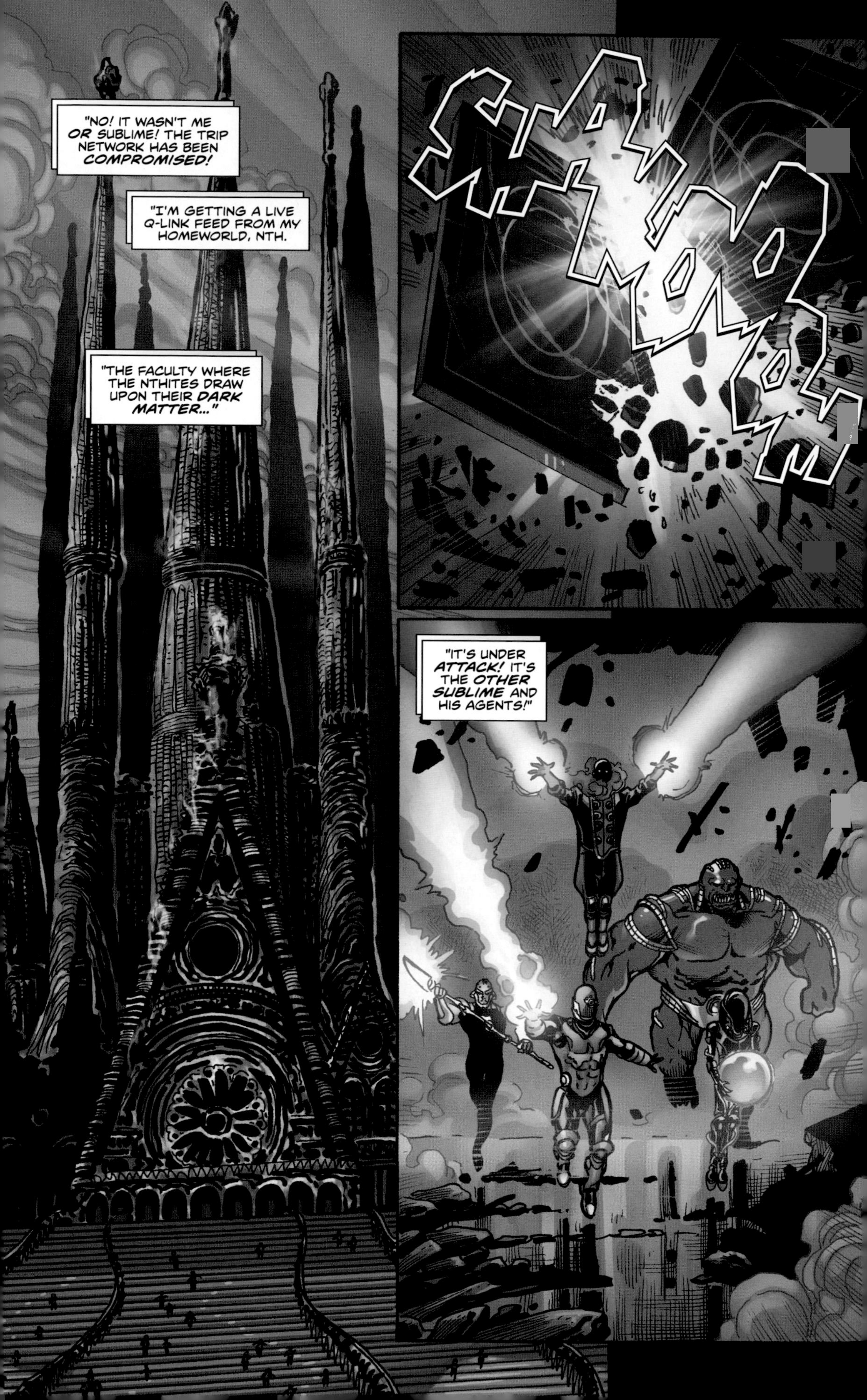
"NO! IT WASN'T ME OR SUBLIME! THE TRIP NETWORK HAS BEEN COMPROMISED!
"I'M GETTING A LIVE Q-LINK FEED FROM MY HOMEWORLD, NTH.
"THE FACULTY WHERE THE NTHITES DRAW UPON THEIR DARK MATTER..."
"IT'S UNDER ATTACK! IT'S THE OTHER SUBLIME AND HIS AGENTS!"

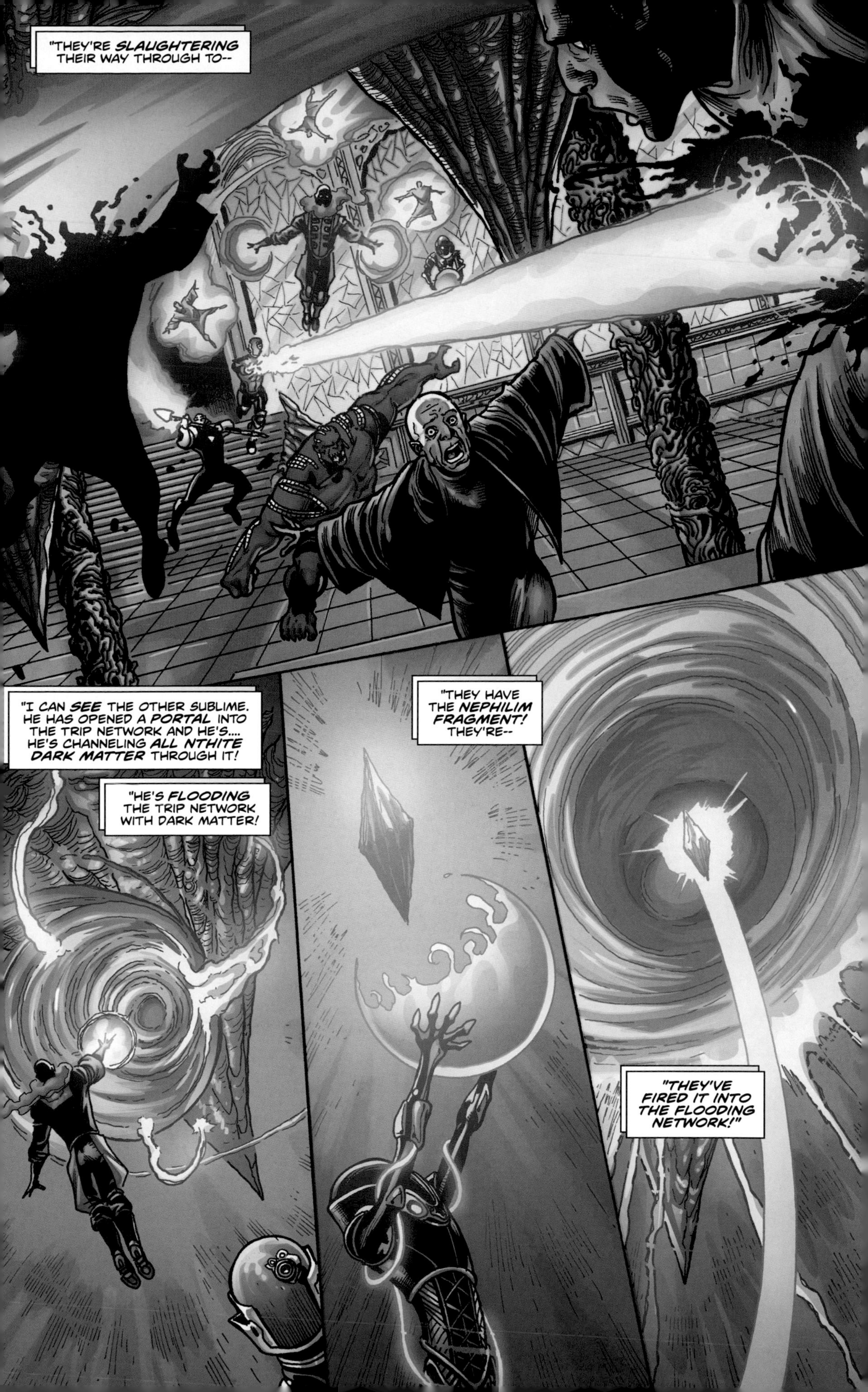
"THEY'RE SLAUGHTERING THEIR WAY THROUGH TO--
"I CAN SEE THE OTHER SUBLIME. HE HAS OPENED A PORTAL INTO THE TRIP NETWORK AND HE'S.... HE'S CHANNELING ALL NTHITE DARK MATTER THROUGH IT!
"HE'S FLOODING THE TRIP NETWORK WITH DARK MATTER!
"THEY HAVE THE NEPHILIM FRAGMENT! THEY'RE--
"THEY'VE FIRED IT INTO THE FLOODING NETWORK!"

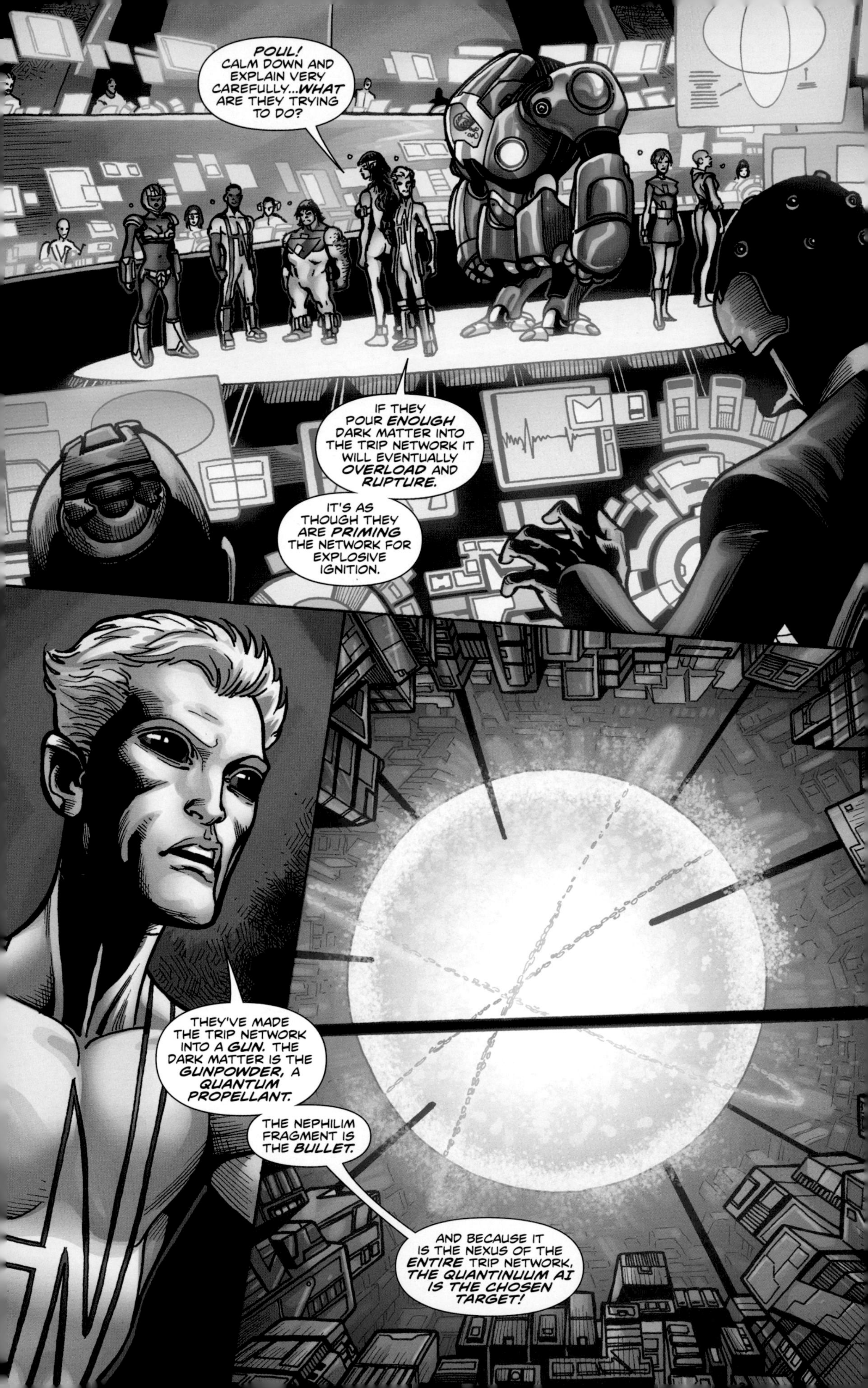
POUL! CALM DOWN AND EXPLAIN VERY CAREFULLY...WHAT ARE THEY TRYING TO DO?
IF THEY POUR ENOUGH DARK MATTER INTO THE TRIP NETWORK IT WILL EVENTUALLY OVERLOAD AND RUPTURE.
IT'S AS THOUGH THEY ARE PRIMING THE NETWORK FOR EXPLOSIVE IGNITION.
THEY'VE MADE THE TRIP NETWORK INTO A GUN. THE DARK MATTER IS THE GUNPOWDER, A QUANTUM PROPELLANT.
THE NEPHILIM FRAGMENT IS THE BULLET.
AND BECAUSE IT IS THE NEXUS OF THE ENTIRE TRIP NETWORK, THE QUANTINUUM AI IS THE CHOSEN TARGET!

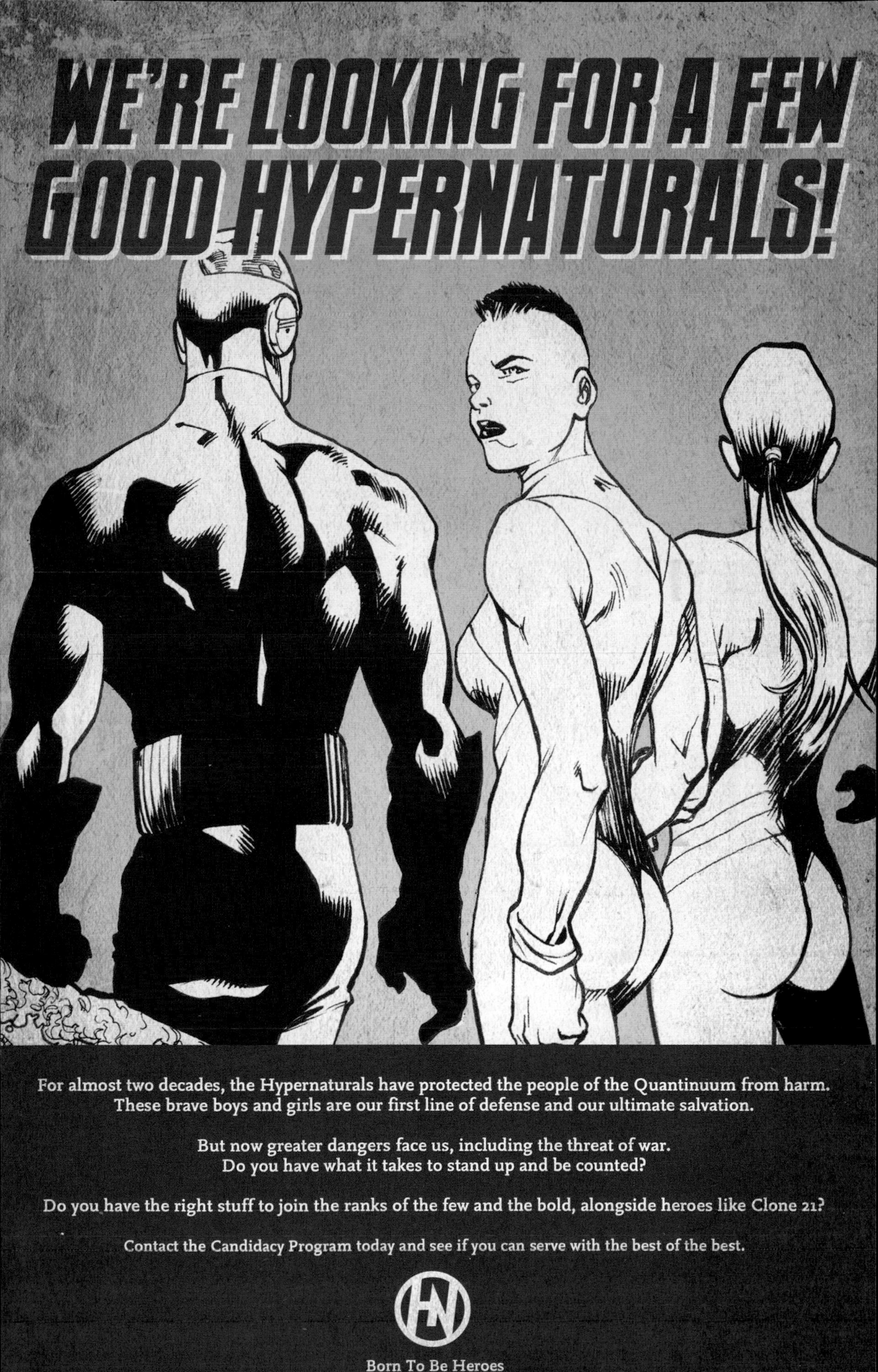
WE'RE LOOKING FOR A FEW GOOD HYPERNATURALS!
For almost two decades, the Hypernaturals have protected the people of the Quantinuum from harm.
These brave boys and girls are our first line of defense and our ultimate salvation.
But now greater dangers face us, including the threat of war.
Do you have what it takes to stand up and be counted?
Do you have the right stuff to join the ranks of the few and the bold, alongside heroes like Clone 21?
Contact the Candidacy Program today and see if you can serve with the best of the best.
Born To Be Heroes

QPEDIA
The Free Qcylopedia

Main Page
Contents
Featured Content
Current Events
Random Article

▸ Interaction

▸ Toolbox

▸ Export

▸ Languages

The Planet Nth

The closed and reserved world of Nth is particularly significant amongst the populated worlds of our Quantinuum, famous not only as the birthworld of the Hypernatural Thinkwell, but also as the cradle of the greatest cerebral and intellectual advancements in human space.

Nthites, as the people of Nth are known, have rejected machine intelligence and pride themselves on perfecting the use of the brain's entire potential. The Nthites are an insular society with staunchly anti-Quantinuum beliefs. Though politically allied to, and members of, our human/Quantinuum culture, the Nthites had been awarded special status and remain detached from the Quantinuum as a whole. This is due to their rejection of the fundamental principles of our AI-run civilization. As a result their world exists on the fringes of our culture, and only reluctantly interacts with the rest of the Quantinuum when it has to.

Nth is ruled by The Faculty, a body made up of the planet's most advanced intellects. Over time, the Nthites, who have amazing reasoning capacity, have experimented with ways of enhancing their mental capabilities, but only in ways that do not involve mechanical or artificial augmentation. Their experiments led them to discover the unique properties of Dark Matter, the almost undetectable background mass/energy of the universe. They have developed techniques that allow them to utilize the vast untapped sources of Dark Matter as extra "processing power" and a "memory storage" (like having, in Pre-Quantinuum terms, an infinite external hard drive). This has enabled them to take their intelligence to levels previously unknown to humanity.

Thinkwell, who has become an outcast from Nth society because of his interaction with the Quantinuum as a Hypernatural, is an anomaly. Through some mutation in his cerebral network, he is able not only to access the infinite processing power of the Dark Matter, but can actually manipulate and control it in the physical plane.

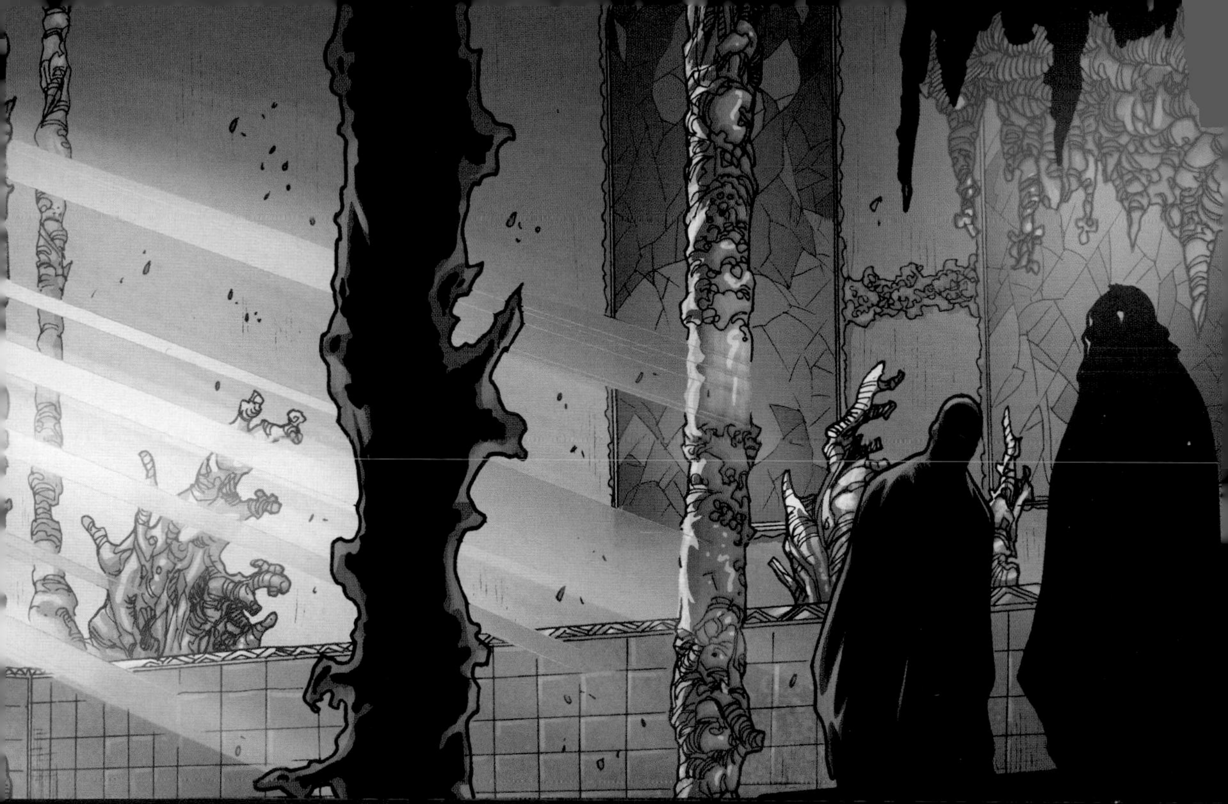

He uses this ink to write equations in the air, equations that act on the very fabric of reality much like a magical spell. Indeed, many members of the public regard his hyper-gifts as magic super-science.

He is fascinated by machine intelligence, an interest that has further alienated him from his own kind.

All the habitation structures on Nth, including the Quantinuum-wide famed Cathedral of the Faculty, are organically grown for purpose from polymer materials, almost like the construction of coral reefs. Nthites grow their buildings and cities to suit their specific needs and think nothing of "de-growing" a structure and replacing it with something even more carefully attuned to a specific purpose.

At various places on Nth, most particularly Cathedral, there are access points to the vast, mathematically constructed sub-space reservoirs where the Nthites store their reserves of dark matter for thought-processing purposes. The reservoirs, and their computational potential, are one of the greatest and strangest wonders of the Universe.

General access to Nth is restricted. There are no public Trip links or other travel connections to the planet. Visits can only be made by prior arrangement with the Faculty, and visas are usually only granted to those wishing to visit for academic, intellectual or research reasons.

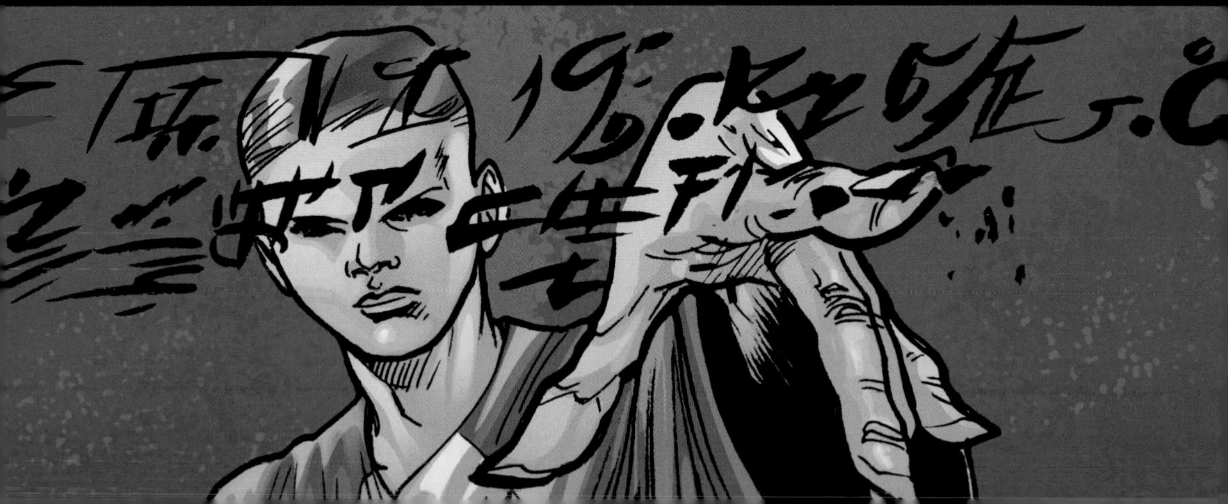

CHAPTER ELEVEN

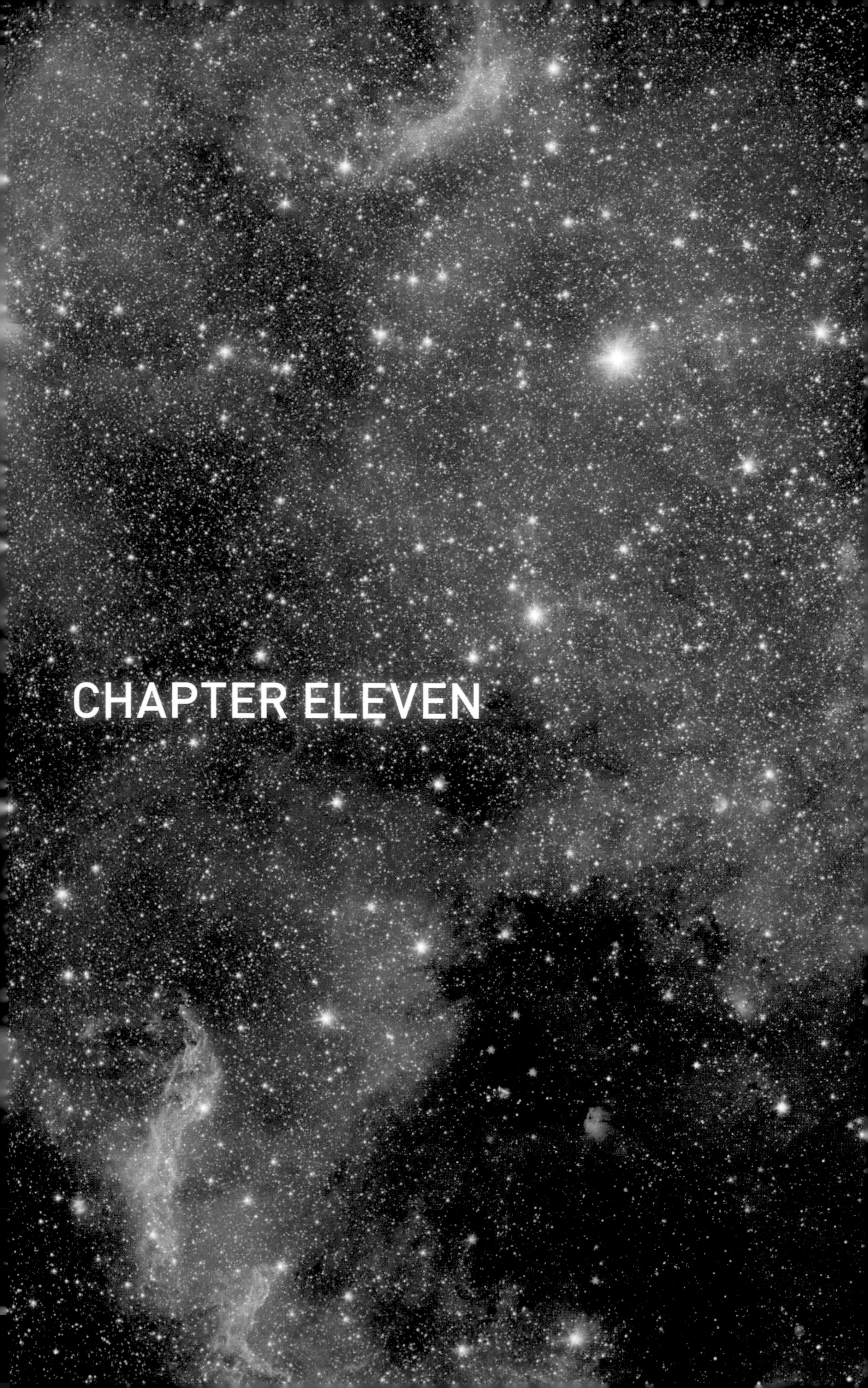

• You have selected Q-Data link.

• It is the 14th of January in the year 100 A.Q.
  • Touch here to select an alternative to the **Anno Quantinuum** calendar system.
  • Touch here to load local weather reports for your **current cosmic location**.
  • Touch here to access **Q-Data newsflows** from planets near your current cosmic location.
  • Touch here for latest **Quantum Trip** transit times.

• Q-Data entry: The Quantinuum

• The Quantinuum is the name for the **human galactic culture**, and also for the **artificial intelligence** that controls its function.

• The Quantinuum was created 100 years ago at the start of the **Nanocene Era**. The Nanocene began when the Quantinuum AI achieved Singularity and refashioned human galactic culture. Succeeding the **Holocene Era**, the Nanocene is the next progression of human evolution and...

(to read this entry in full, touch here)

• You have selected live feed newsflow.

• **Lonis Baddafar** wins the **Telsus 88 Comet Racing Grand Prix**
• **Biswelt Asbody** resigns from chair of **Quantinuum Food Authority** after corruption claims
• Heiress **Flick Basbury** loses hypermillion dollar "significant other" lawsuit
• **AI Law** announces surprise return of star **Bodie McCroak** as a hard hitting cyber-attorney
• **Hypernaturals Central, San Diego**, continues to make no comment on any possible connection between the attack on **Repository** and the ongoing investigation into the disappearance of the **Centennial Year Iteration** of the Team, lost during an emergency response mission to **28 Kosov** four days ago

• The Hypernaturals are the Quantinuum's foremost champions. Famous across the entirety of human galactic culture, the team members are selected on the basis of their **hypernatural powers** and their strength of character, and serve for five-year terms. In honor of the start of the twenty-first term, the line-up of the team's so-called "Centennial Year Iteration" has recently been announced amid huge publicity and--

...BREAKING NEWS... the incident at the Quantinuum Archive and Museum World Repository involving Hypernatural versus unregistered hyper-gifted individuals has been resolved. It is understood that the Hypernaturals have returned to their headquarters in San Diego...

Zastrugi

Pure ice world. Pure ice water.

Quench the Quantinuum.

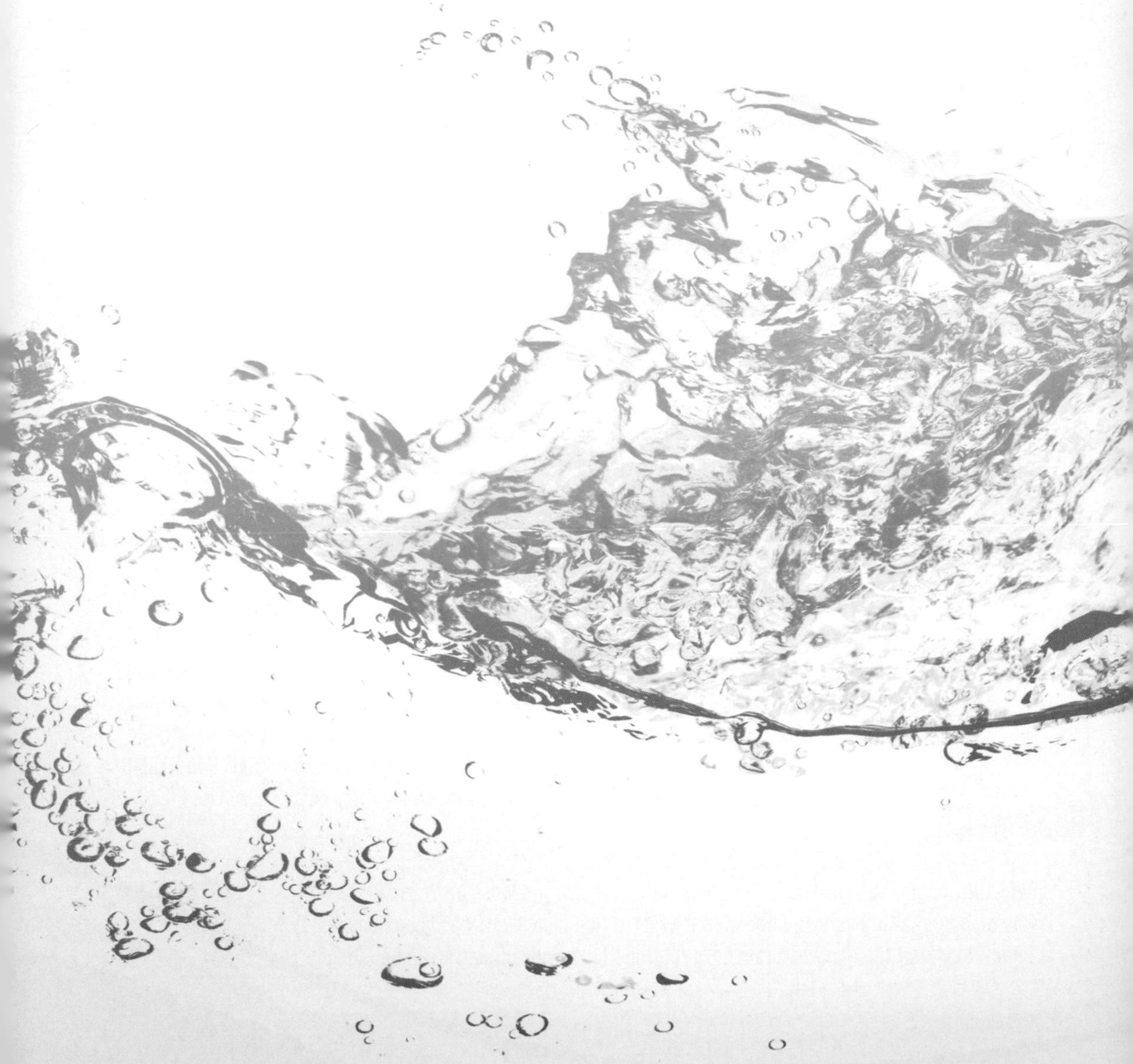

Zastrugi ® trademark of the 77 Zastrugi Water Bottling Compa

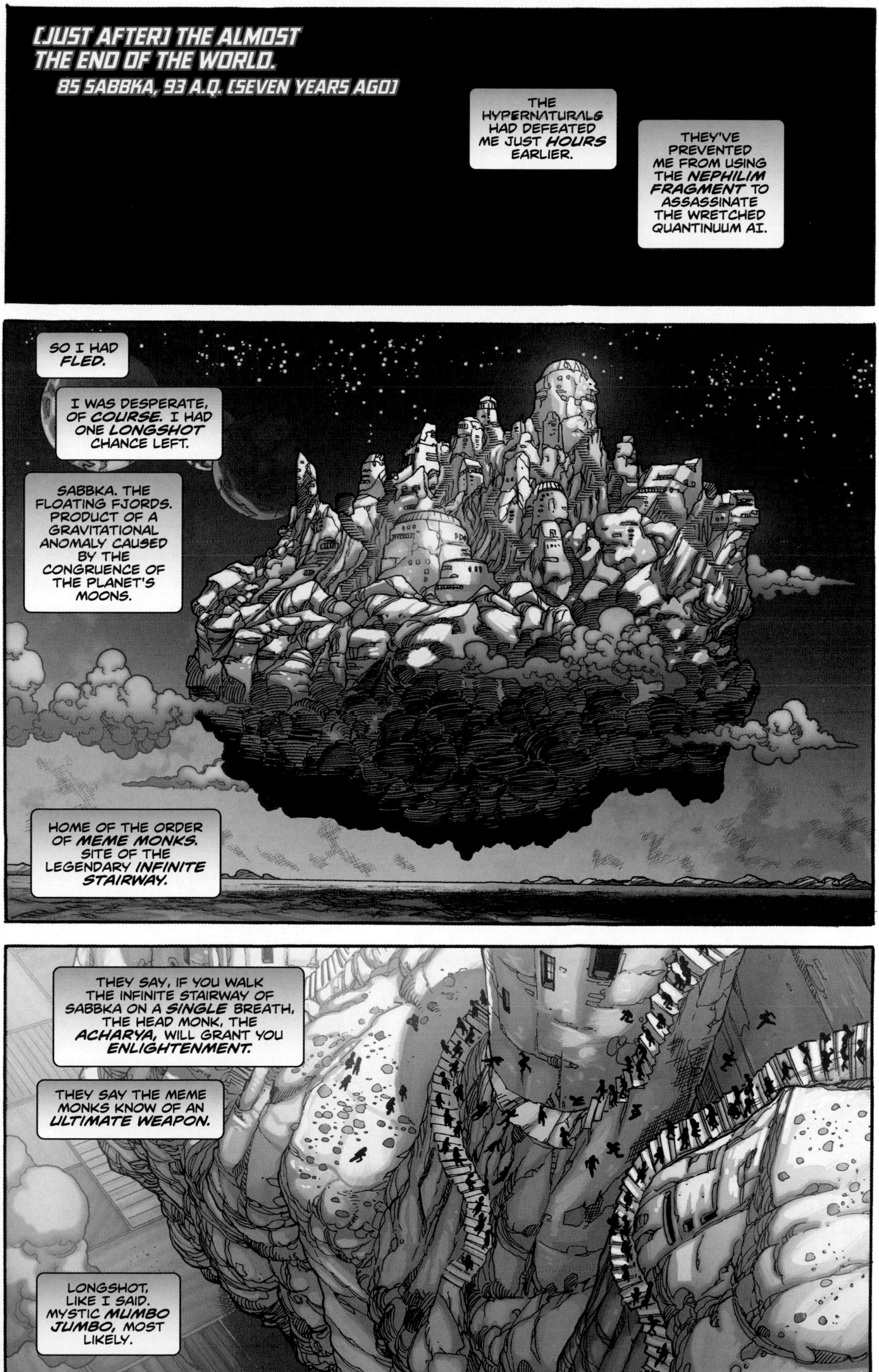
[JUST AFTER] THE ALMOST THE END OF THE WORLD.
85 SABBKA, 93 A.Q. [SEVEN YEARS AGO]
THE HYPERNATURALS HAD DEFEATED ME JUST HOURS EARLIER.
THEY'VE PREVENTED ME FROM USING THE NEPHILIM FRAGMENT TO ASSASSINATE THE WRETCHED QUANTINUUM AI.
SO I HAD FLED.
I WAS DESPERATE, OF COURSE. I HAD ONE LONGSHOT CHANCE LEFT.
SABBKA. THE FLOATING FJORDS. PRODUCT OF A GRAVITATIONAL ANOMALY CAUSED BY THE CONGRUENCE OF THE PLANET'S MOONS.
HOME OF THE ORDER OF MEME MONKS. SITE OF THE LEGENDARY INFINITE STAIRWAY.
THEY SAY, IF YOU WALK THE INFINITE STAIRWAY OF SABBKA ON A SINGLE BREATH, THE HEAD MONK, THE ACHARYA, WILL GRANT YOU ENLIGHTENMENT.
THEY SAY THE MEME MONKS KNOW OF AN ULTIMATE WEAPON.
LONGSHOT, LIKE I SAID. MYSTIC MUMBO JUMBO, MOST LIKELY.

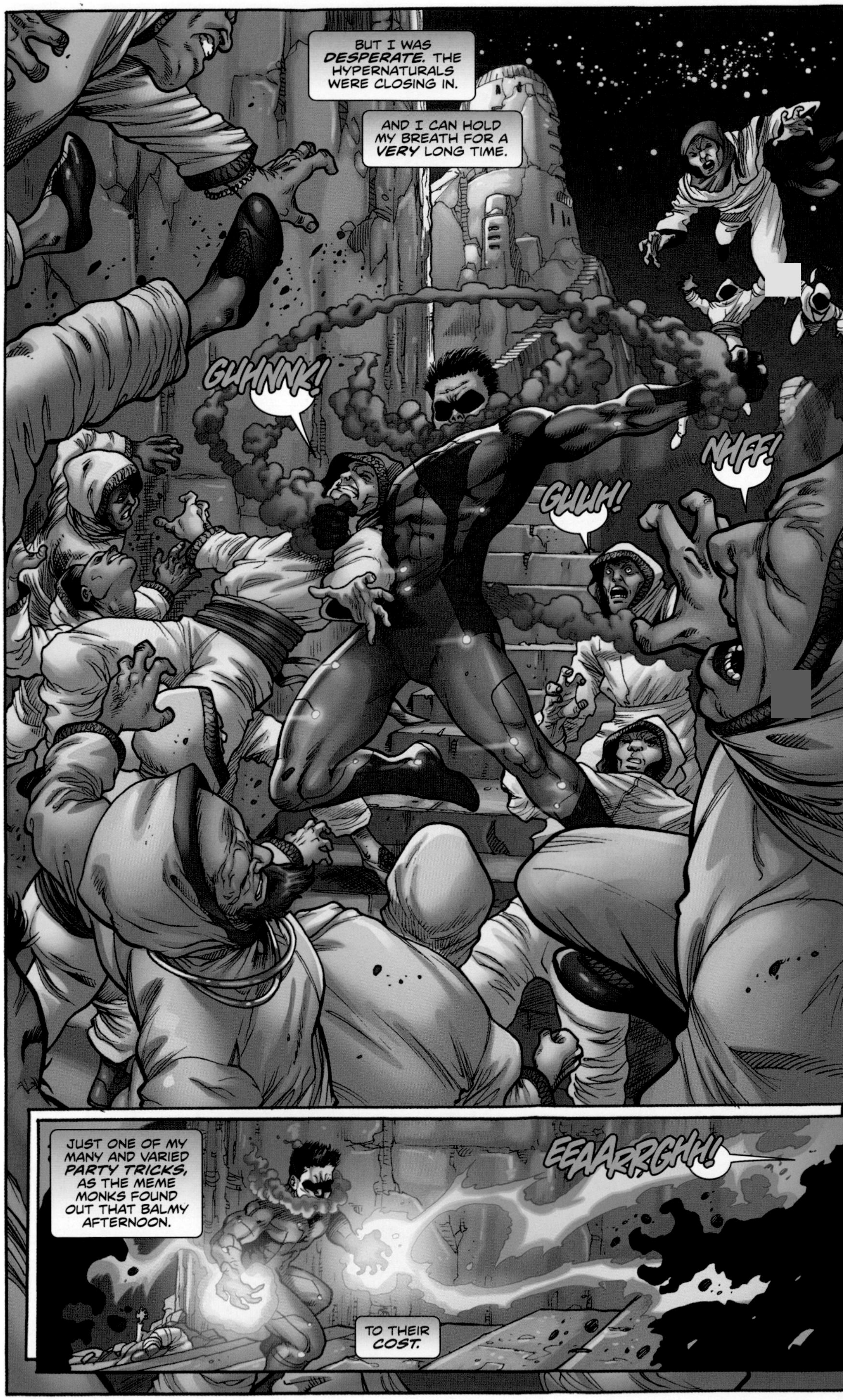
BUT I WAS DESPERATE. THE HYPERNATURALS WERE CLOSING IN.
AND I CAN HOLD MY BREATH FOR A VERY LONG TIME.
GUHNNK!
NHFF!
GULLH!
JUST ONE OF MY MANY AND VARIED PARTY TRICKS, AS THE MEME MONKS FOUND OUT THAT BALMY AFTERNOON.
EEAARRGHH!
TO THEIR COST.

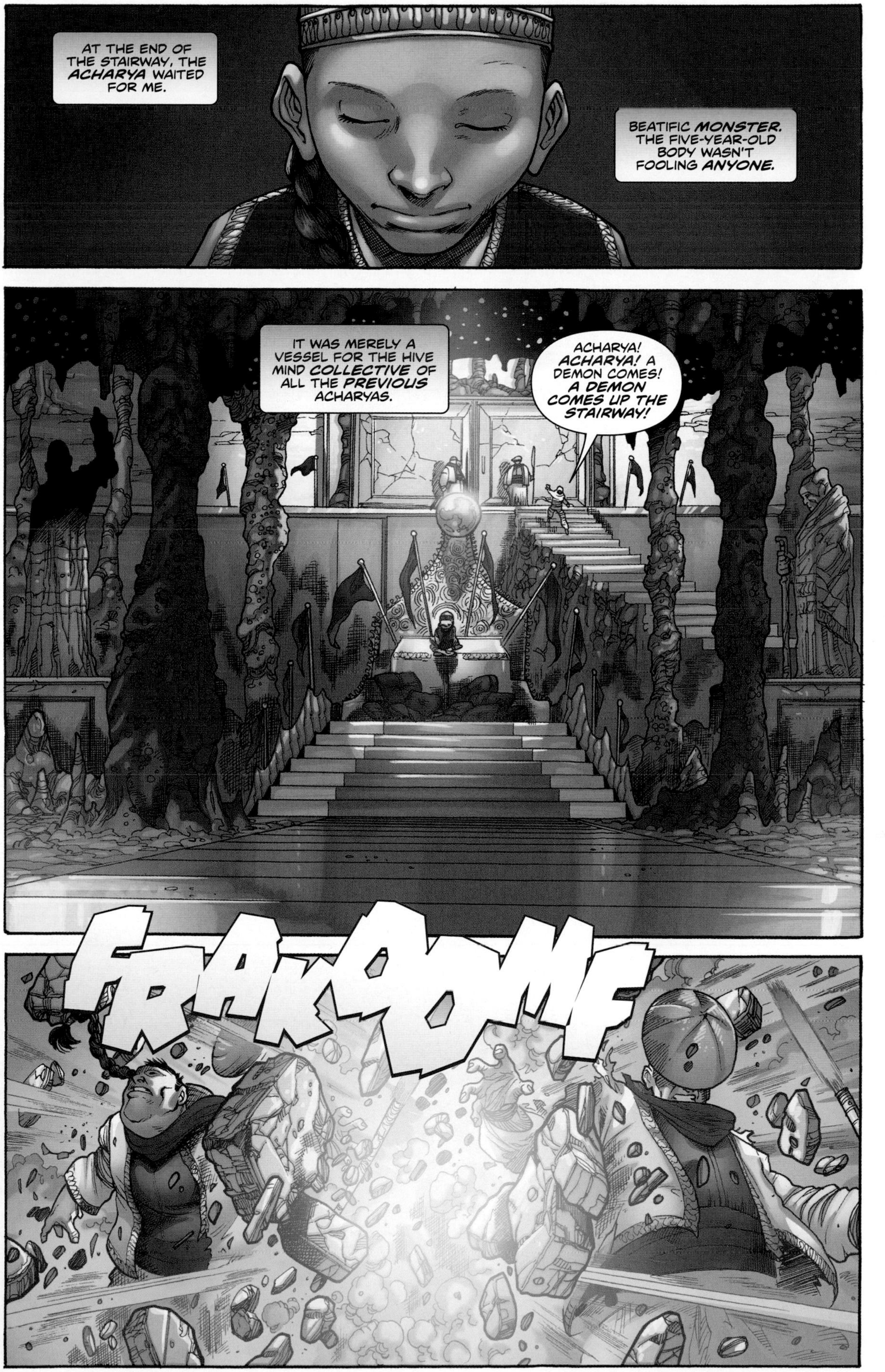
AT THE END OF THE STAIRWAY, THE ACHARYA WAITED FOR ME.
BEATIFIC MONSTER. THE FIVE-YEAR-OLD BODY WASN'T FOOLING ANYONE.
IT WAS MERELY A VESSEL FOR THE HIVE MIND COLLECTIVE OF ALL THE PREVIOUS ACHARYAS.
ACHARYA! ACHARYA! A DEMON COMES! A DEMON COMES UP THE STAIRWAY!
FRAKOOMF

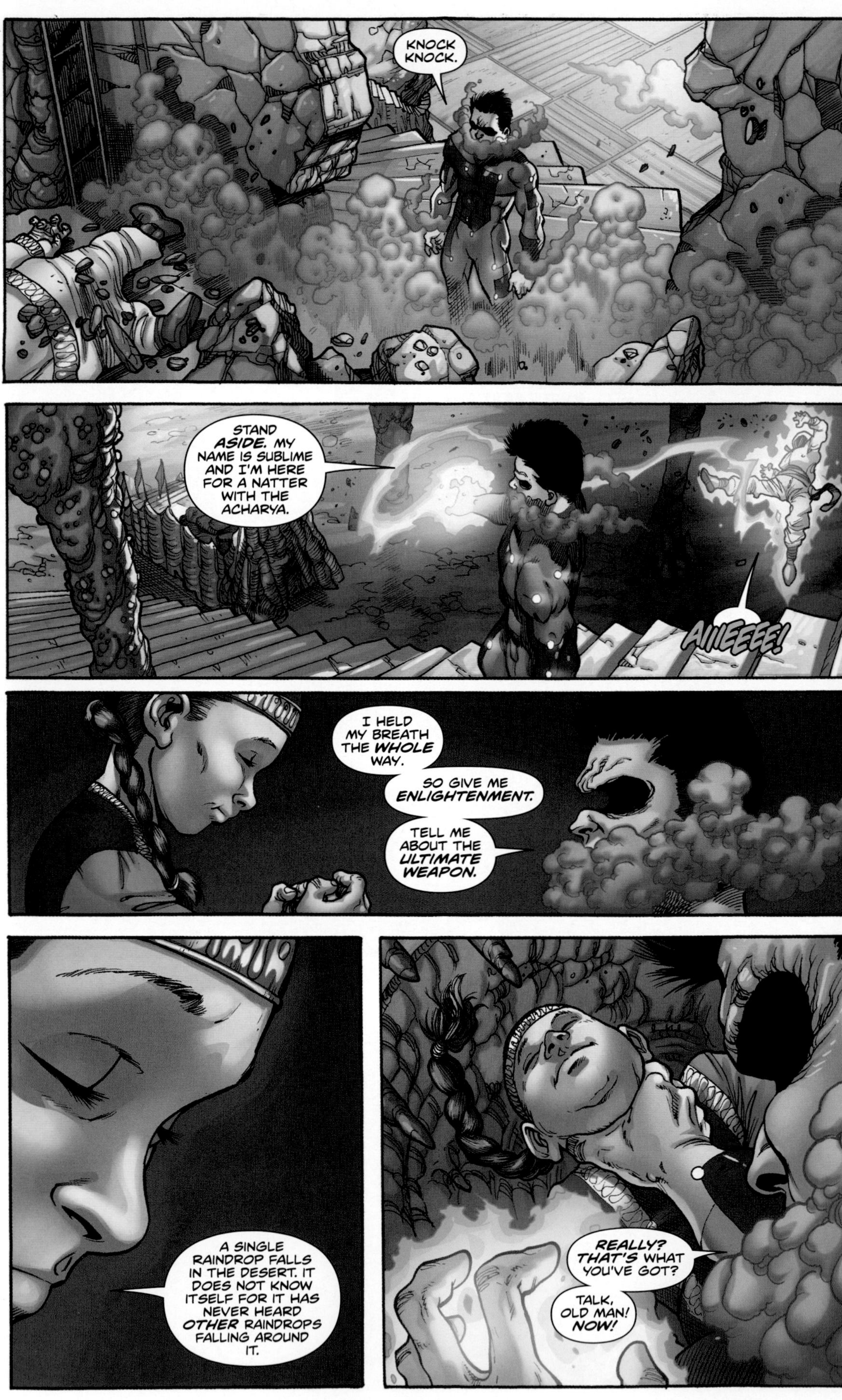
KNOCK KNOCK.
STAND ASIDE. MY NAME IS SUBLIME AND I'M HERE FOR A NATTER WITH THE ACHARYA.
AIIIEEEE!
I HELD MY BREATH THE WHOLE WAY.
SO GIVE ME ENLIGHTENMENT.
TELL ME ABOUT THE ULTIMATE WEAPON.
A SINGLE RAINDROP FALLS IN THE DESERT. IT DOES NOT KNOW ITSELF FOR IT HAS NEVER HEARD OTHER RAINDROPS FALLING AROUND IT.
REALLY? THAT'S WHAT YOU'VE GOT?
TALK, OLD MAN! NOW!

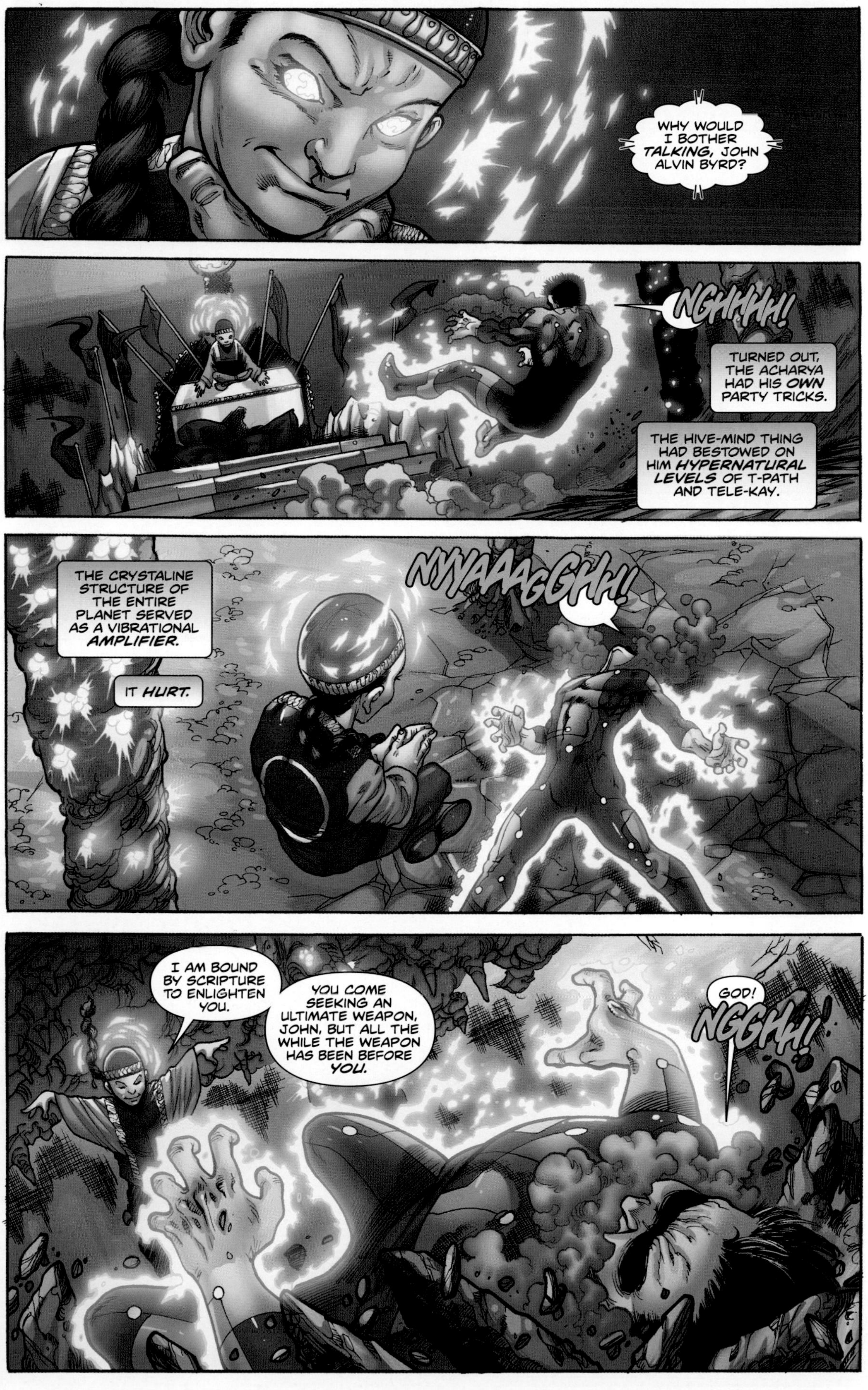
WHY WOULD I BOTHER TALKING, JOHN ALVIN BYRD?
NGHHHH!
TURNED OUT, THE ACHARYA HAD HIS OWN PARTY TRICKS.
THE HIVE-MIND THING HAD BESTOWED ON HIM HYPERNATURAL LEVELS OF T-PATH AND TELE-KAY.
THE CRYSTALINE STRUCTURE OF THE ENTIRE PLANET SERVED AS A VIBRATIONAL AMPLIFIER.
IT HURT.
NYYAAAGGHH!
I AM BOUND BY SCRIPTURE TO ENLIGHTEN YOU.
YOU COME SEEKING AN ULTIMATE WEAPON, JOHN, BUT ALL THE WHILE THE WEAPON HAS BEEN BEFORE YOU.
GOD!
NGGHH!

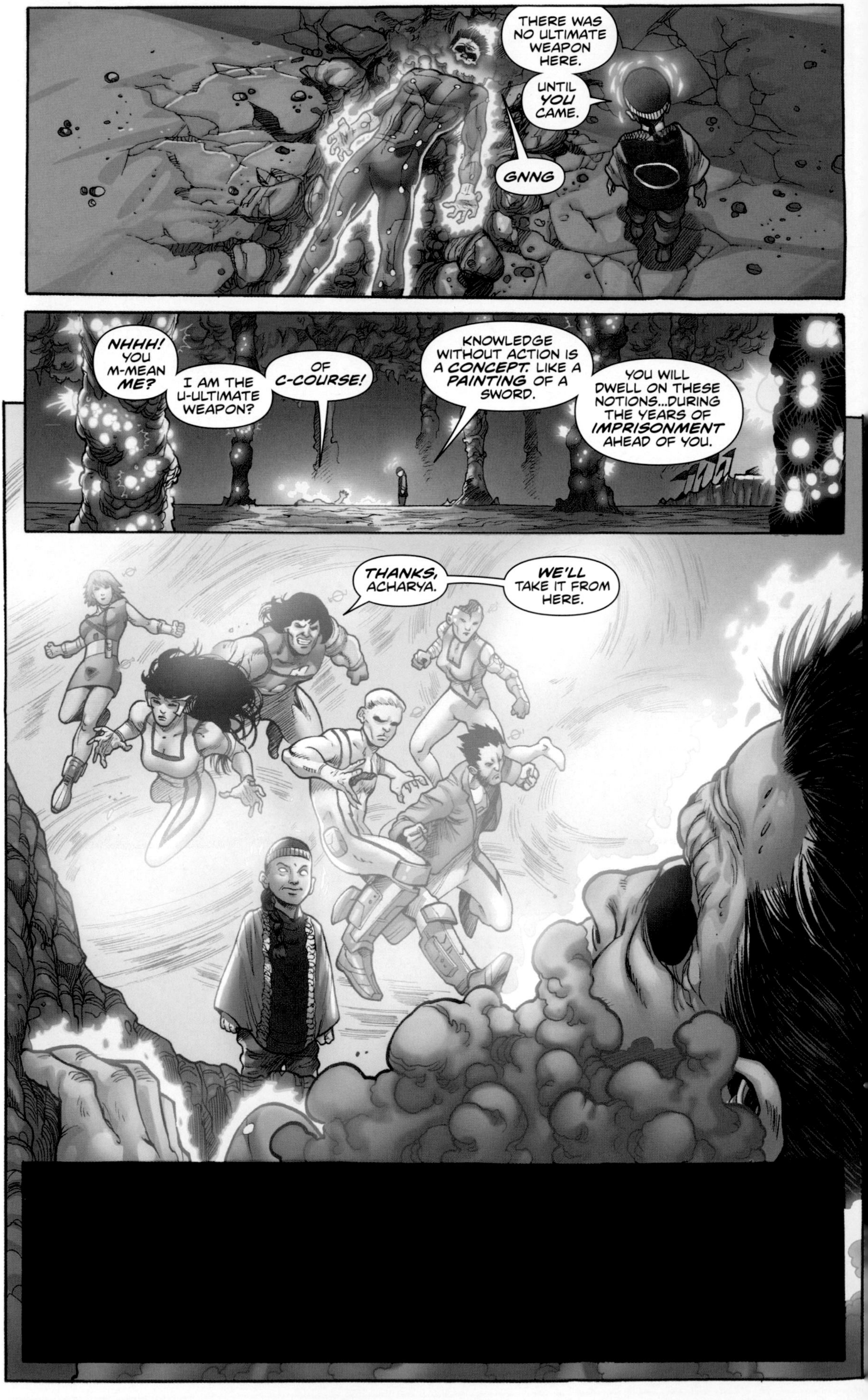
THERE WAS NO ULTIMATE WEAPON HERE.
UNTIL YOU CAME.
GNNG
NHHH! YOU M-MEAN ME?
I AM THE U-ULTIMATE WEAPON?
OF C-COURSE!
KNOWLEDGE WITHOUT ACTION IS A CONCEPT. LIKE A PAINTING OF A SWORD.
YOU WILL DWELL ON THESE NOTIONS...DURING THE YEARS OF IMPRISONMENT AHEAD OF YOU.
THANKS, ACHARYA.
WE'LL TAKE IT FROM HERE.
[redacted]

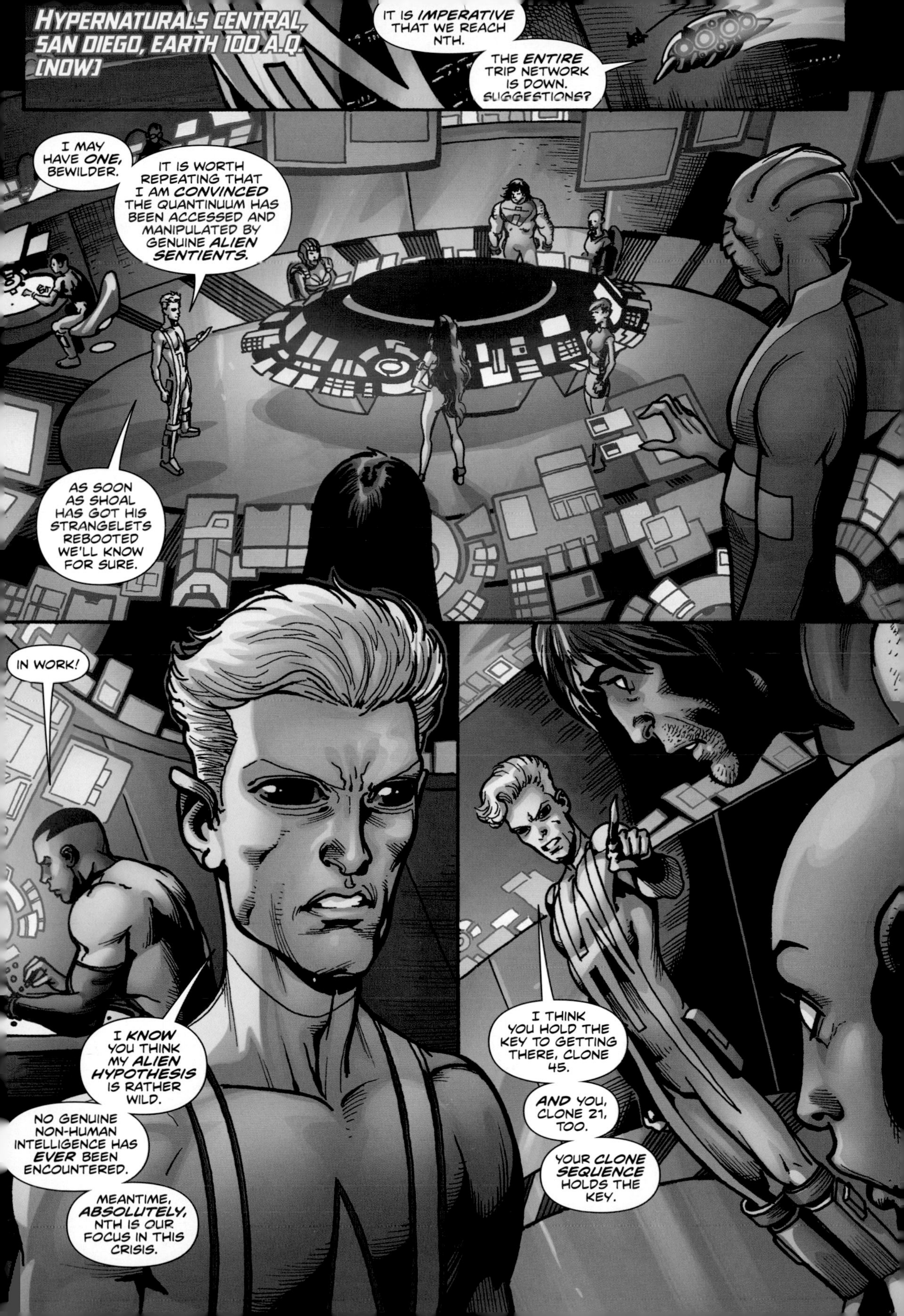
HYPERNATURALS CENTRAL, SAN DIEGO, EARTH 100 A.Q. [NOW]
IT IS IMPERATIVE THAT WE REACH NTH.
THE ENTIRE TRIP NETWORK IS DOWN. SUGGESTIONS?
I MAY HAVE ONE, BEWILDER.
IT IS WORTH REPEATING THAT I AM CONVINCED THE QUANTINUUM HAS BEEN ACCESSED AND MANIPULATED BY GENUINE ALIEN SENTIENTS.
AS SOON AS SHOAL HAS GOT HIS STRANGELETS REBOOTED WE'LL KNOW FOR SURE.
IN WORK!
I KNOW YOU THINK MY ALIEN HYPOTHESIS IS RATHER WILD.
NO GENUINE NON-HUMAN INTELLIGENCE HAS EVER BEEN ENCOUNTERED.
MEANTIME, ABSOLUTELY, NTH IS OUR FOCUS IN THIS CRISIS.
I THINK YOU HOLD THE KEY TO GETTING THERE, CLONE 45.
AND YOU, CLONE 21, TOO.
YOUR CLONE SEQUENCE HOLDS THE KEY.

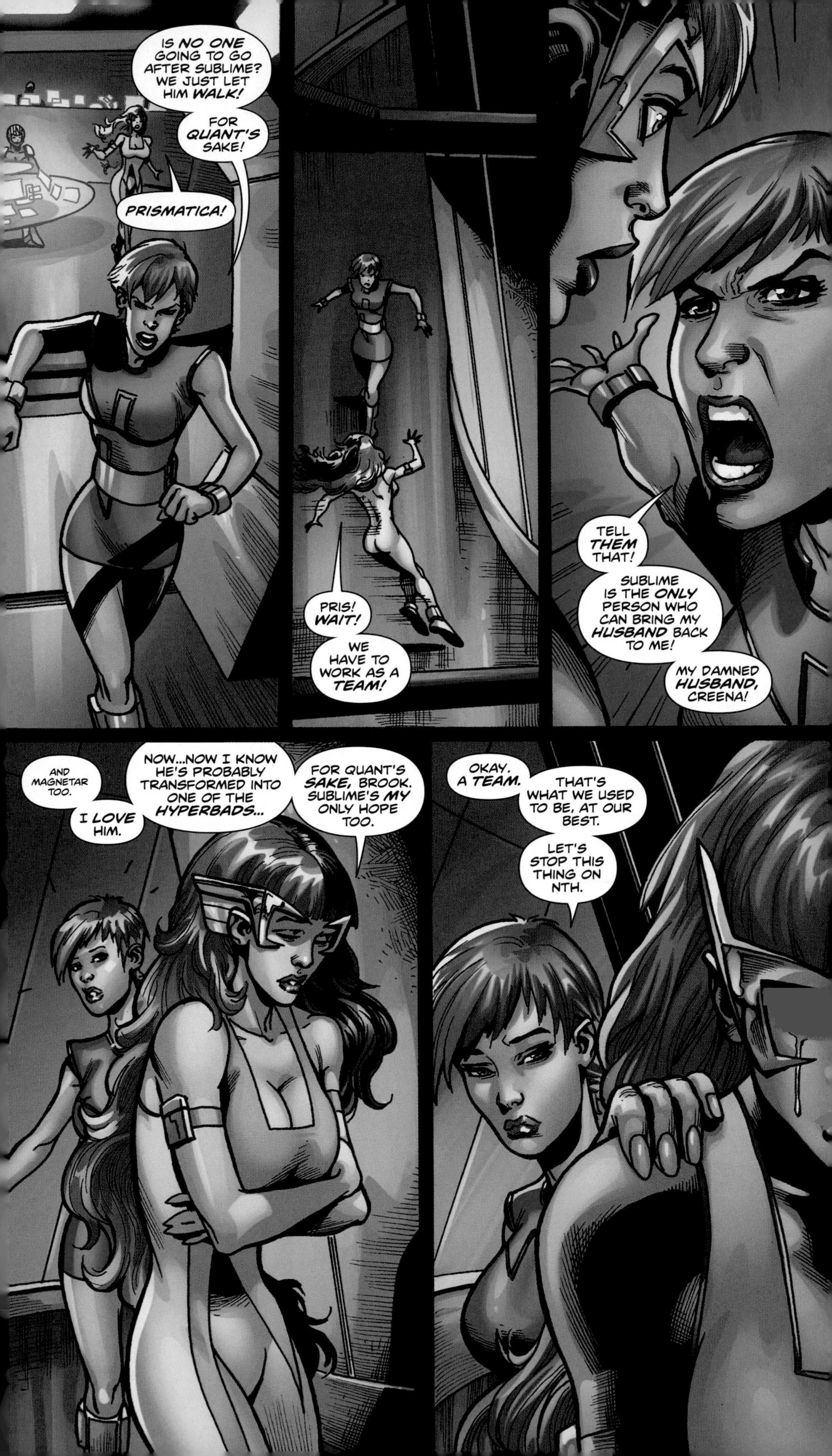
IS NO ONE GOING TO GO AFTER SUBLIME? WE JUST LET HIM WALK!
FOR QUANT'S SAKE!
PRISMATICA!
PRIS! WAIT!
WE HAVE TO WORK AS A TEAM!
TELL THEM THAT!
SUBLIME IS THE ONLY PERSON WHO CAN BRING MY HUSBAND BACK TO ME!
MY DAMNED HUSBAND, CREENA!
AND MAGNETAR TOO.
I LOVE HIM.
NOW...NOW I KNOW HE'S PROBABLY TRANSFORMED INTO ONE OF THE HYPERBADS...
FOR QUANT'S SAKE, BROOK. SUBLIME'S MY ONLY HOPE TOO.
OKAY. A TEAM.
THAT'S WHAT WE USED TO BE, AT OUR BEST.
LET'S STOP THIS THING ON NTH.

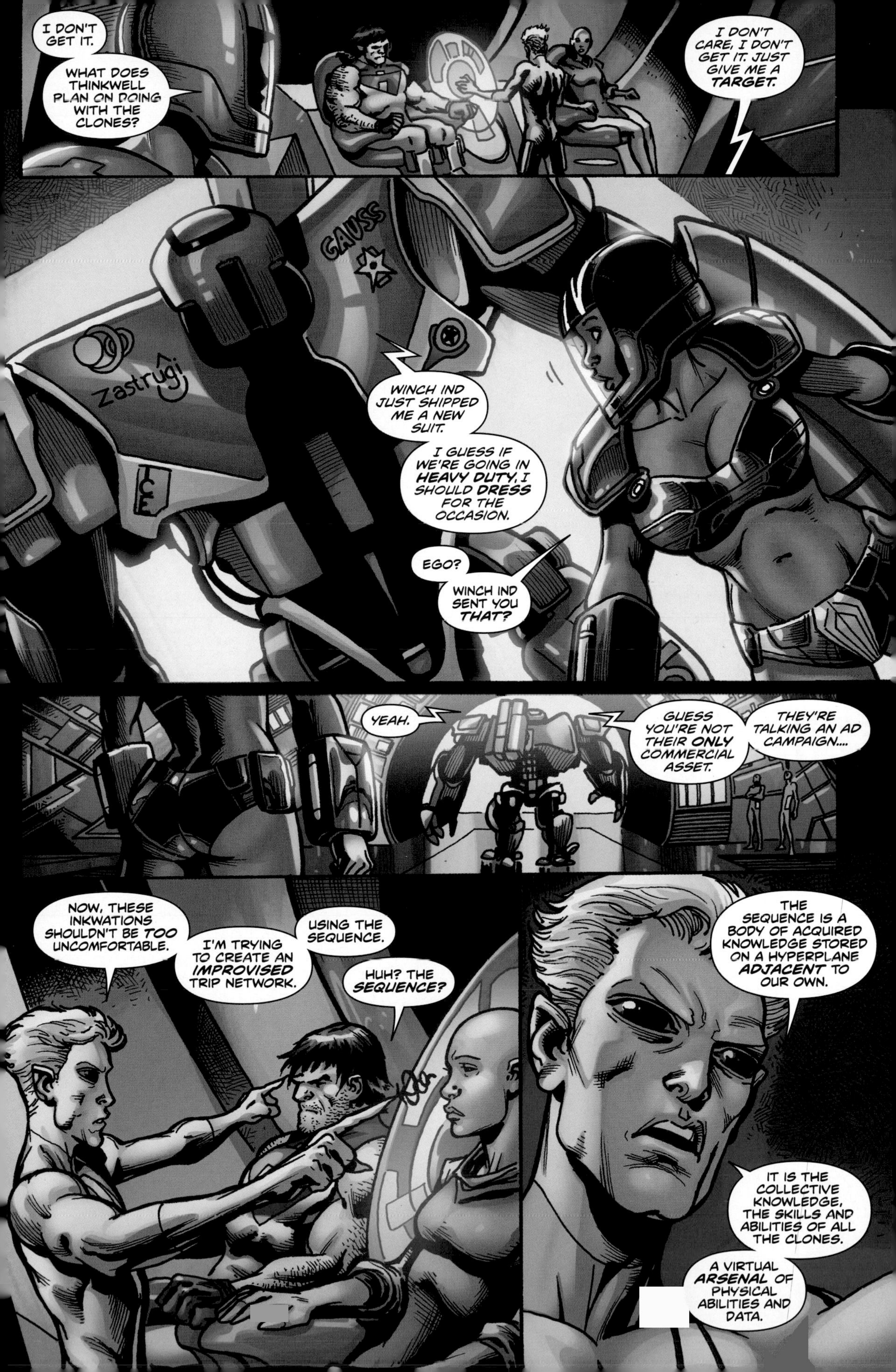

I DON'T GET IT.
WHAT DOES THINKWELL PLAN ON DOING WITH THE CLONES?
I DON'T CARE, I DON'T GET IT. JUST GIVE ME A TARGET.
GAUSS
Zastrugi
ICE
WINCH IND JUST SHIPPED ME A NEW SUIT.
I GUESS IF WE'RE GOING IN HEAVY DUTY, I SHOULD DRESS FOR THE OCCASION.
EGO?
WINCH IND SENT YOU THAT?
YEAH.
GUESS YOU'RE NOT THEIR ONLY COMMERCIAL ASSET.
THEY'RE TALKING AN AD CAMPAIGN....
NOW, THESE INKWATIONS SHOULDN'T BE TOO UNCOMFORTABLE.
I'M TRYING TO CREATE AN IMPROVISED TRIP NETWORK.
USING THE SEQUENCE.
HUH? THE SEQUENCE?
THE SEQUENCE IS A BODY OF ACQUIRED KNOWLEDGE STORED ON A HYPERPLANE ADJACENT TO OUR OWN.
IT IS THE COLLECTIVE KNOWLEDGE, THE SKILLS AND ABILITIES OF ALL THE CLONES.
A VIRTUAL ARSENAL OF PHYSICAL ABILITIES AND DATA.

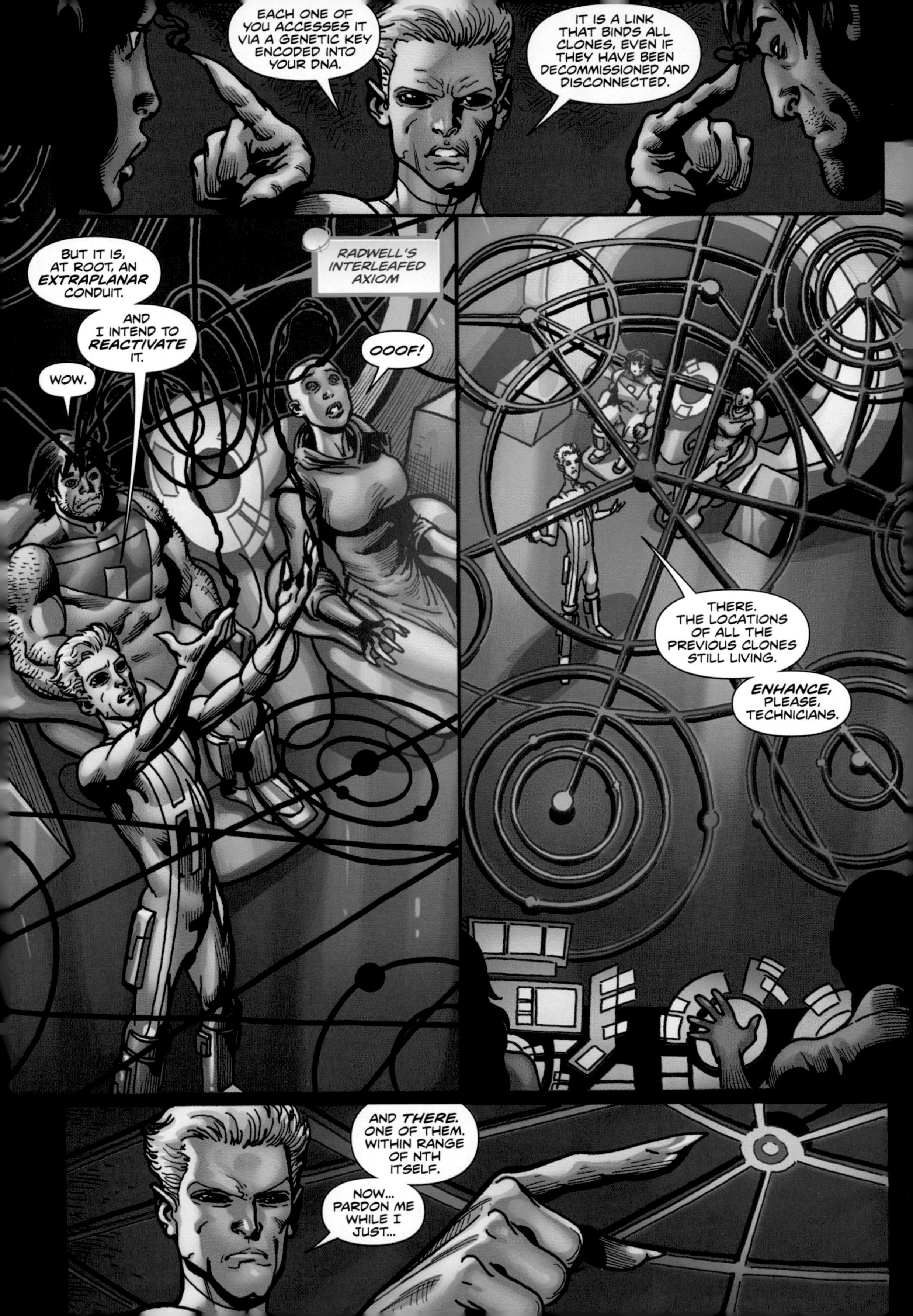
EACH ONE OF YOU ACCESSES IT VIA A GENETIC KEY ENCODED INTO YOUR DNA.
IT IS A LINK THAT BINDS ALL CLONES, EVEN IF THEY HAVE BEEN DECOMMISSIONED AND DISCONNECTED.
BUT IT IS, AT ROOT, AN *EXTRAPLANAR* CONDUIT.
AND I INTEND TO *REACTIVATE* IT.
RADWELL'S INTERLEAFED AXIOM
WOW.
OOOF!
THERE. THE LOCATIONS OF ALL THE PREVIOUS CLONES STILL LIVING.
ENHANCE, PLEASE, TECHNICIANS.
AND *THERE.* ONE OF THEM. WITHIN RANGE OF NTH ITSELF.
NOW... PARDON ME WHILE I JUST...

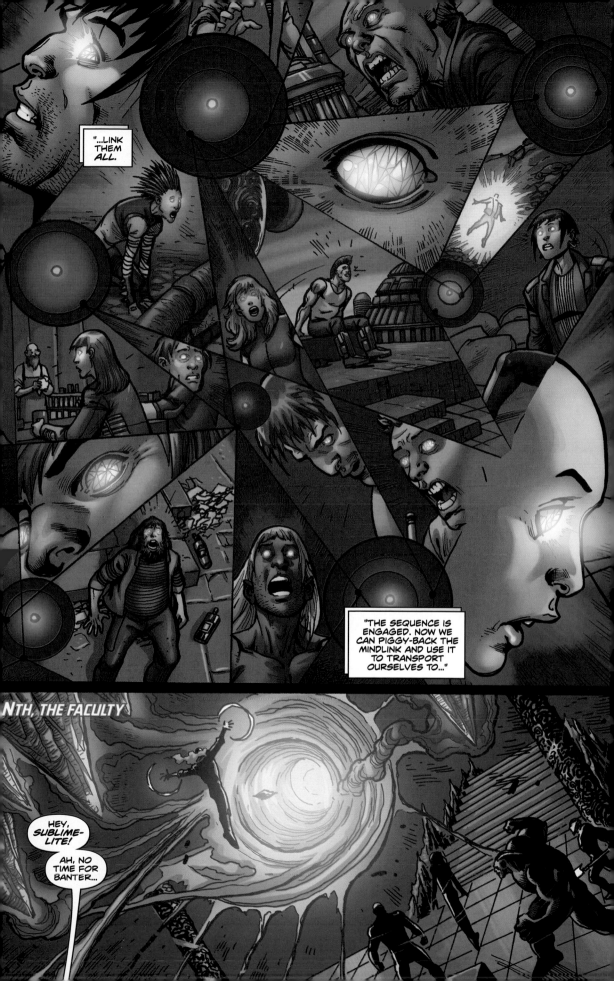

"...LINK THEM ALL.

"THE SEQUENCE IS ENGAGED. NOW WE CAN PIGGY-BACK THE MINDLINK AND USE IT TO TRANSPORT OURSELVES TO..."

NTH, THE FACULTY

HEY, SUBLIME-LITE!

AH, NO TIME FOR BANTER...

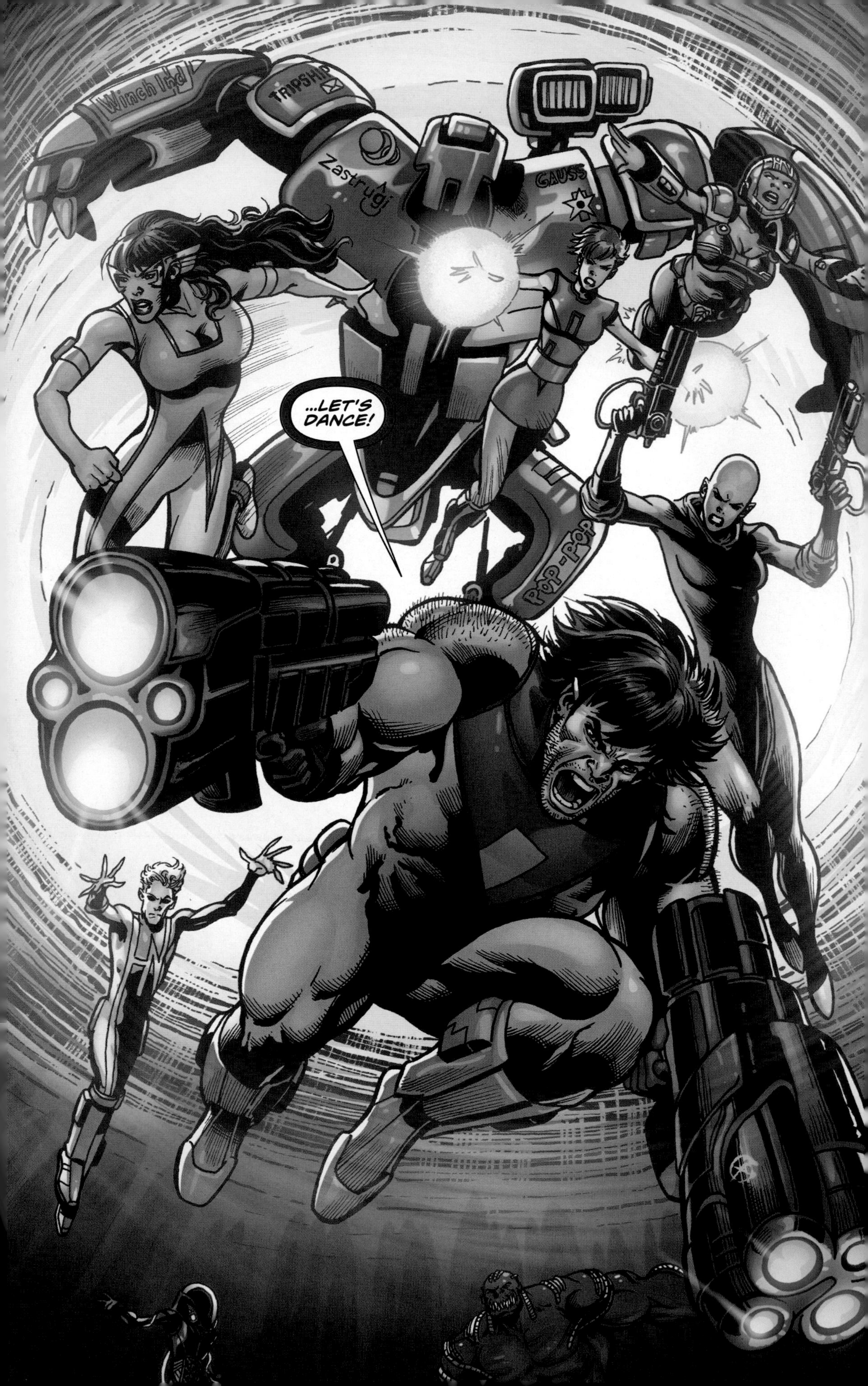
...LET'S DANCE!
Winch Ltd
TRIPSHIP
Zastrugi
GAUSS
POP-POP

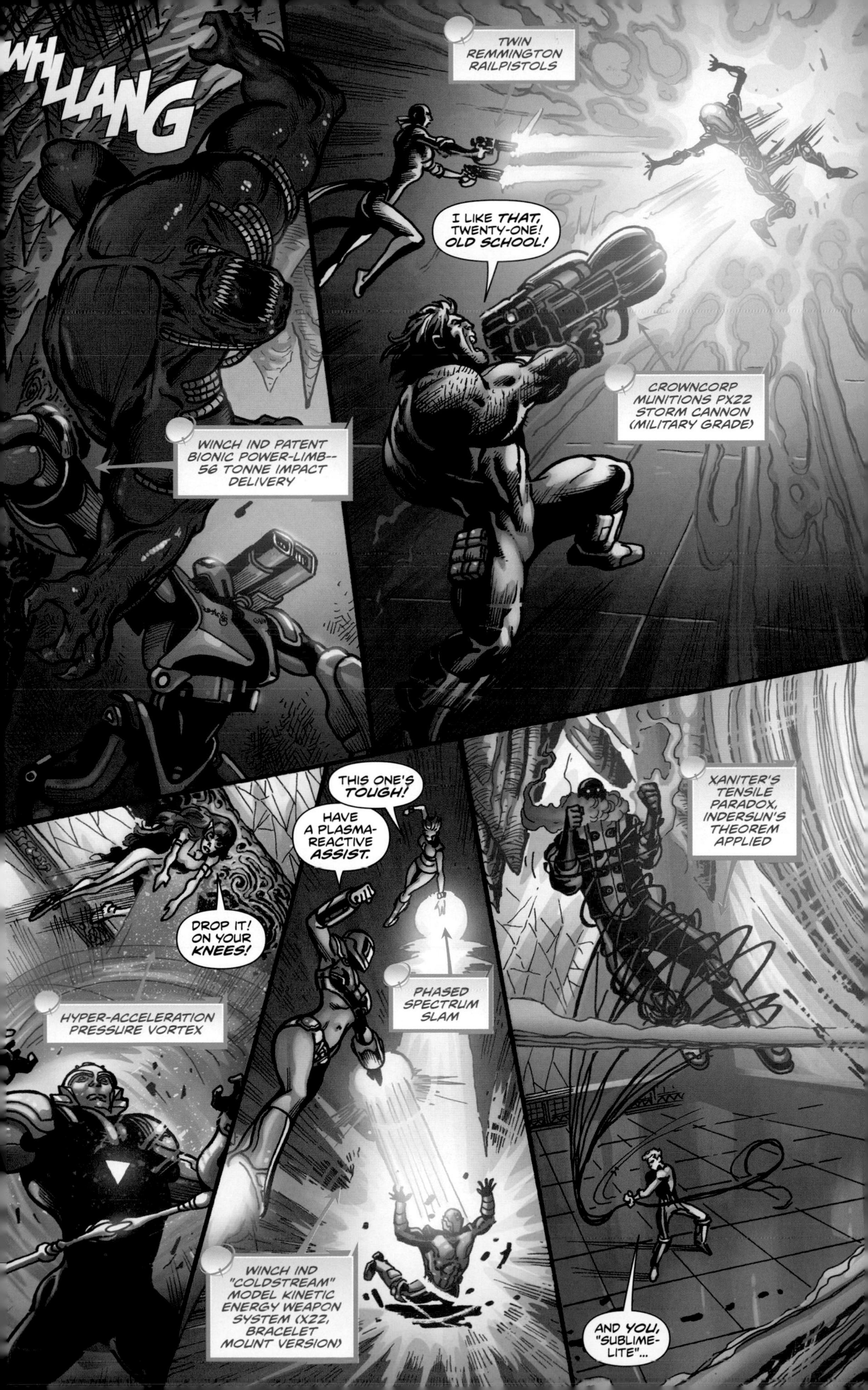
WHLLANG
TWIN REMMINGTON RAILPISTOLS
I LIKE THAT, TWENTY-ONE! OLD SCHOOL!
CROWNCORP MUNITIONS PX22 STORM CANNON (MILITARY GRADE)
WINCH IND PATENT BIONIC POWER-LIMB-- 56 TONNE IMPACT DELIVERY
DROP IT! ON YOUR KNEES!
HYPER-ACCELERATION PRESSURE VORTEX
THIS ONE'S TOUGH!
HAVE A PLASMA-REACTIVE ASSIST.
PHASED SPECTRUM SLAM
WINCH IND "COLDSTREAM" MODEL KINETIC ENERGY WEAPON SYSTEM (X22, BRACELET MOUNT VERSION)
XANITER'S TENSILE PARADOX, INDERSUN'S THEOREM APPLIED
AND YOU, "SUBLIME-LITE"...

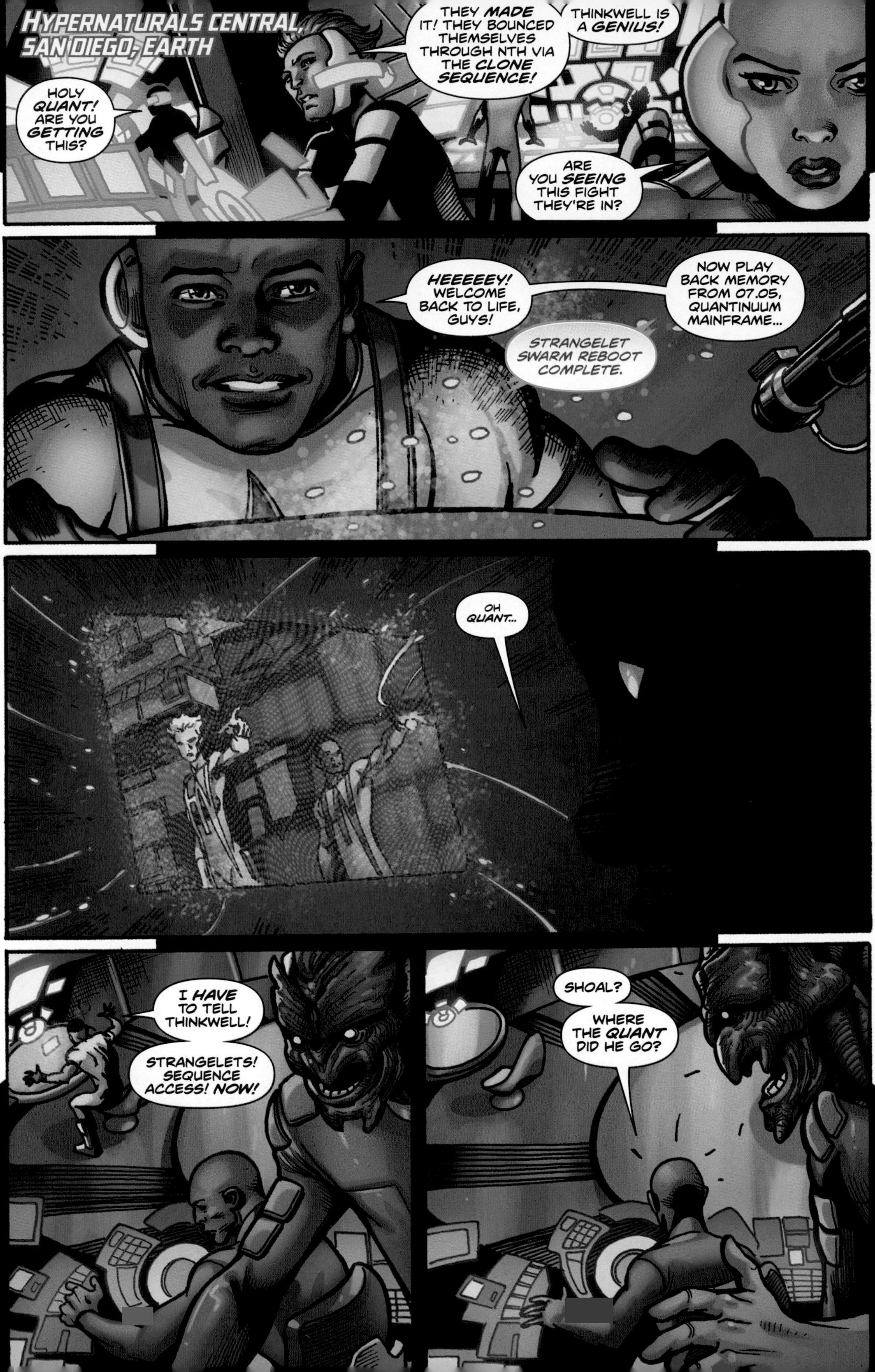
HYPERNATURALS CENTRAL, SAN DIEGO, EARTH
HOLY QUANT! ARE YOU GETTING THIS?
THEY MADE IT! THEY BOUNCED THEMSELVES THROUGH NTH VIA THE CLONE SEQUENCE!
THINKWELL IS A GENIUS!
ARE YOU SEEING THIS FIGHT THEY'RE IN?
HEEEEEY! WELCOME BACK TO LIFE, GUYS!
NOW PLAY BACK MEMORY FROM 07.05, QUANTINUUM MAINFRAME...
STRANGELET SWARM REBOOT COMPLETE.
OH QUANT...
I HAVE TO TELL THINKWELL!
STRANGELETS! SEQUENCE ACCESS! NOW!
SHOAL?
WHERE THE QUANT DID HE GO?

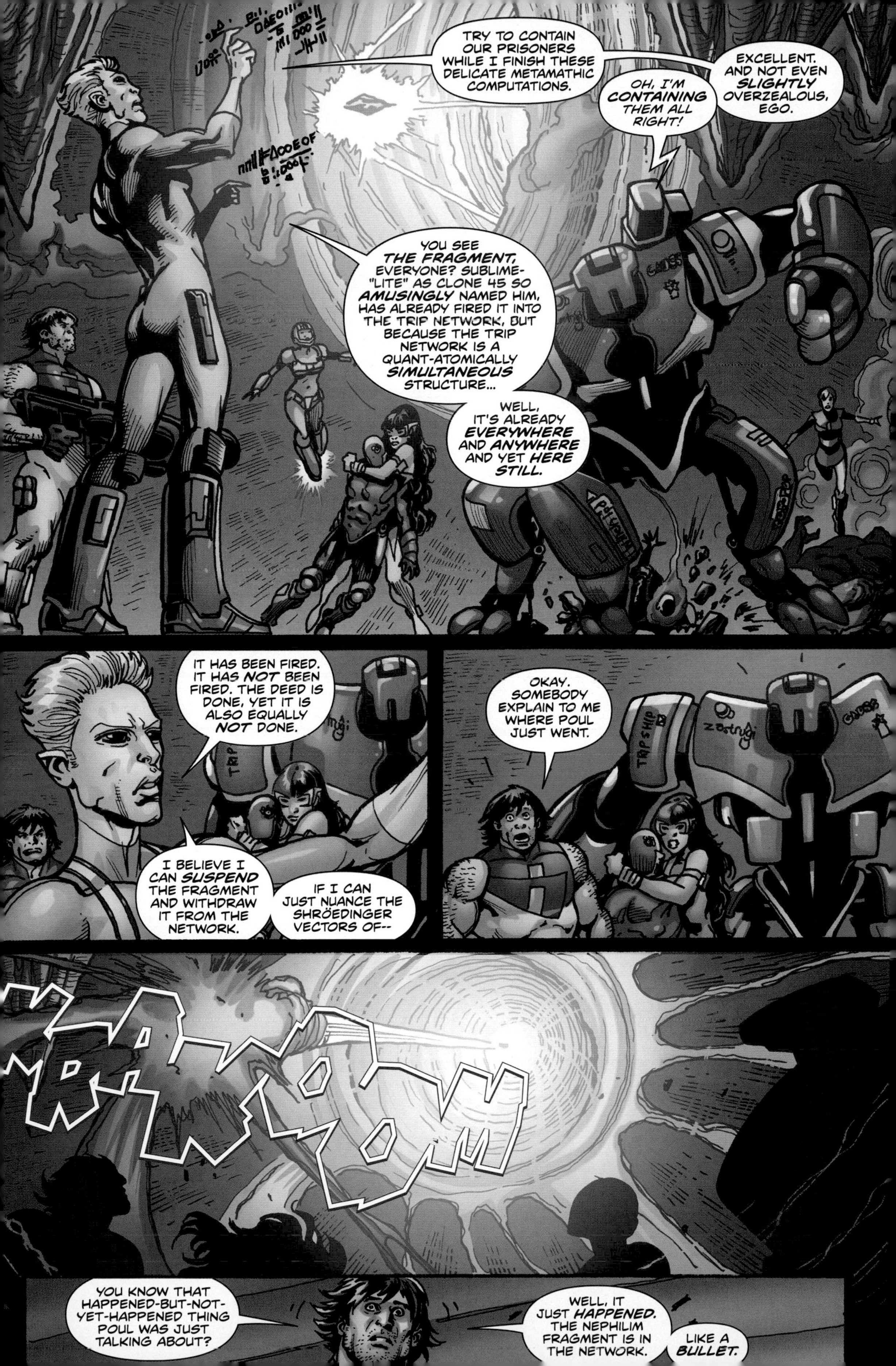
TRY TO CONTAIN OUR PRISONERS WHILE I FINISH THESE DELICATE METAMATHIC COMPUTATIONS.
OH, I'M *CONTAINING* THEM ALL RIGHT!
EXCELLENT. AND NOT EVEN *SLIGHTLY* OVERZEALOUS, EGO.
YOU SEE *THE FRAGMENT,* EVERYONE? SUBLIME-"LITE" AS CLONE 45 SO *AMUSINGLY* NAMED HIM, HAS ALREADY FIRED IT INTO THE TRIP NETWORK, BUT BECAUSE THE TRIP NETWORK IS A QUANT-ATOMICALLY *SIMULTANEOUS* STRUCTURE...
WELL, IT'S ALREADY *EVERYWHERE* AND *ANYWHERE* AND YET *HERE STILL.*
IT HAS BEEN FIRED. IT HAS *NOT* BEEN FIRED. THE DEED IS DONE, YET IT IS ALSO EQUALLY *NOT* DONE.
I BELIEVE I CAN *SUSPEND* THE FRAGMENT AND WITHDRAW IT FROM THE NETWORK.
IF I CAN JUST NUANCE THE SHRÖEDINGER VECTORS OF--
OKAY. SOMEBODY EXPLAIN TO ME WHERE POUL JUST WENT.
KRA-WOOM
YOU KNOW THAT HAPPENED-BUT-NOT-YET-HAPPENED THING POUL WAS JUST TALKING ABOUT?
WELL, IT JUST *HAPPENED.* THE NEPHILIM FRAGMENT IS IN THE NETWORK.
LIKE A *BULLET.*

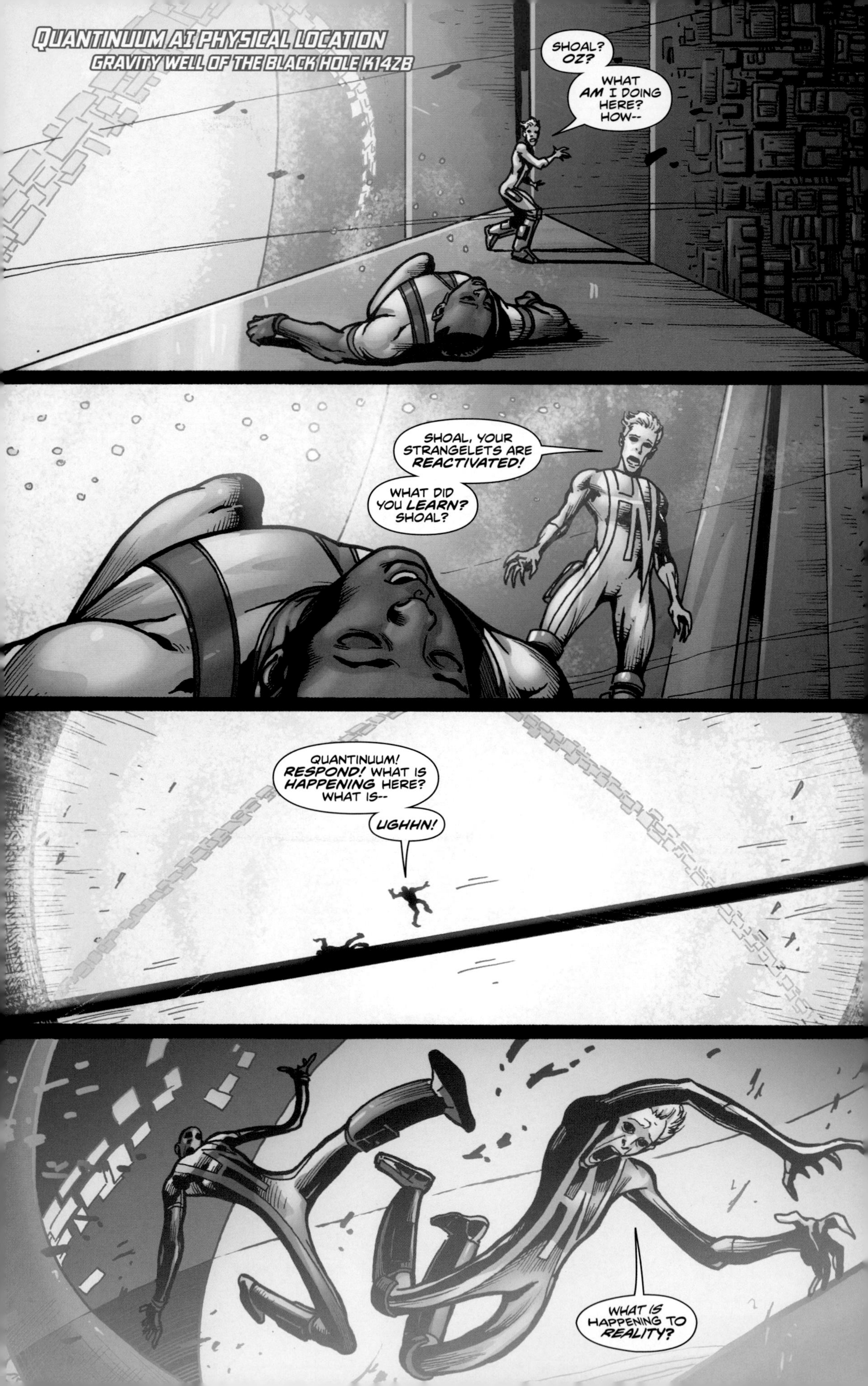
QUANTINUUM AI PHYSICAL LOCATION
GRAVITY WELL OF THE BLACK HOLE K142B
SHOAL? OZ?
WHAT AM I DOING HERE? HOW--
SHOAL, YOUR STRANGELETS ARE REACTIVATED!
WHAT DID YOU LEARN? SHOAL?
QUANTINUUM! RESPOND! WHAT IS HAPPENING HERE? WHAT IS--
UGHHN!
WHAT IS HAPPENING TO REALITY?

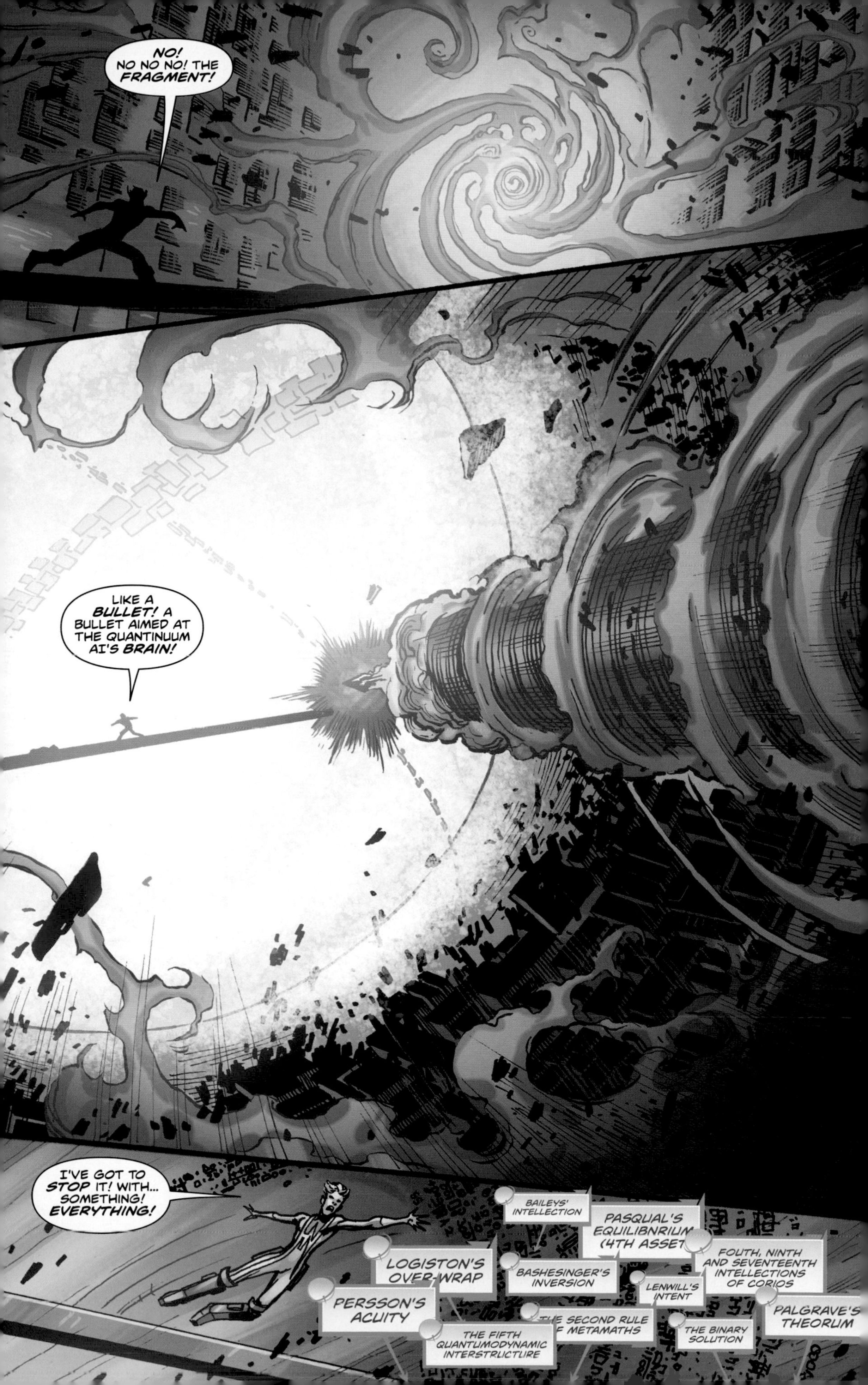
NO! NO NO NO! THE FRAGMENT!
LIKE A BULLET! A BULLET AIMED AT THE QUANTINUUM AI'S BRAIN!
I'VE GOT TO STOP IT! WITH... SOMETHING! EVERYTHING!
BAILEYS' INTELLECTION
PASQUAL'S EQUILIBNRIUM (4TH ASSET
LOGISTON'S OVER-WRAP
BASHESINGER'S INVERSION
FOUTH, NINTH AND SEVENTEENTH INTELLECTIONS OF CORIOS
LENWILL'S INTENT
PERSSON'S ACUITY
THE SECOND RULE F METAMATHS
PALGRAVE'S THEORUM
THE BINARY SOLUTION
THE FIFTH QUANTUMODYNAMIC INTERSTRUCTURE

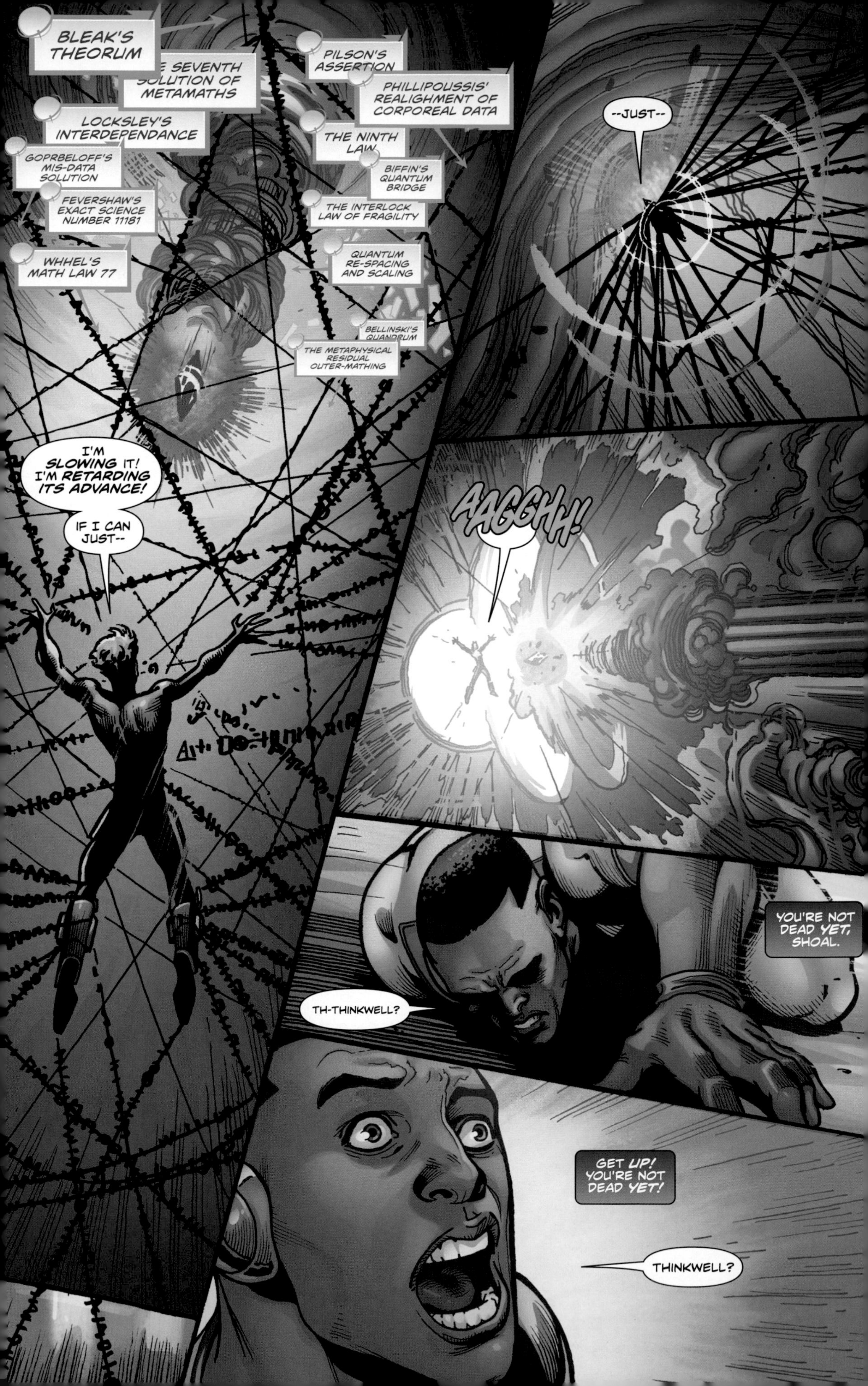
BLEAK'S THEORUM
THE SEVENTH SOLUTION OF METAMATHS
LOCKSLEY'S INTERDEPENDANCE
GOPRBELOFF'S MIS-DATA SOLUTION
FEVERSHAW'S EXACT SCIENCE NUMBER 11181
WHHEL'S MATH LAW 77
PILSON'S ASSERTION
PHILLIPOUSSIS' REALIGHMENT OF CORPOREAL DATA
THE NINTH LAW
BIFFIN'S QUANTUM BRIDGE
THE INTERLOCK LAW OF FRAGILITY
QUANTUM RE-SPACING AND SCALING
BELLINSKI'S QUANDRUM
THE METAPHYSICAL RESIDUAL OUTER-MATHING
I'M SLOWING IT! I'M RETARDING ITS ADVANCE!
IF I CAN JUST--
--JUST--
AAGGHH!
YOU'RE NOT DEAD YET, SHOAL.
TH-THINKWELL?
GET UP! YOU'RE NOT DEAD YET!
THINKWELL?

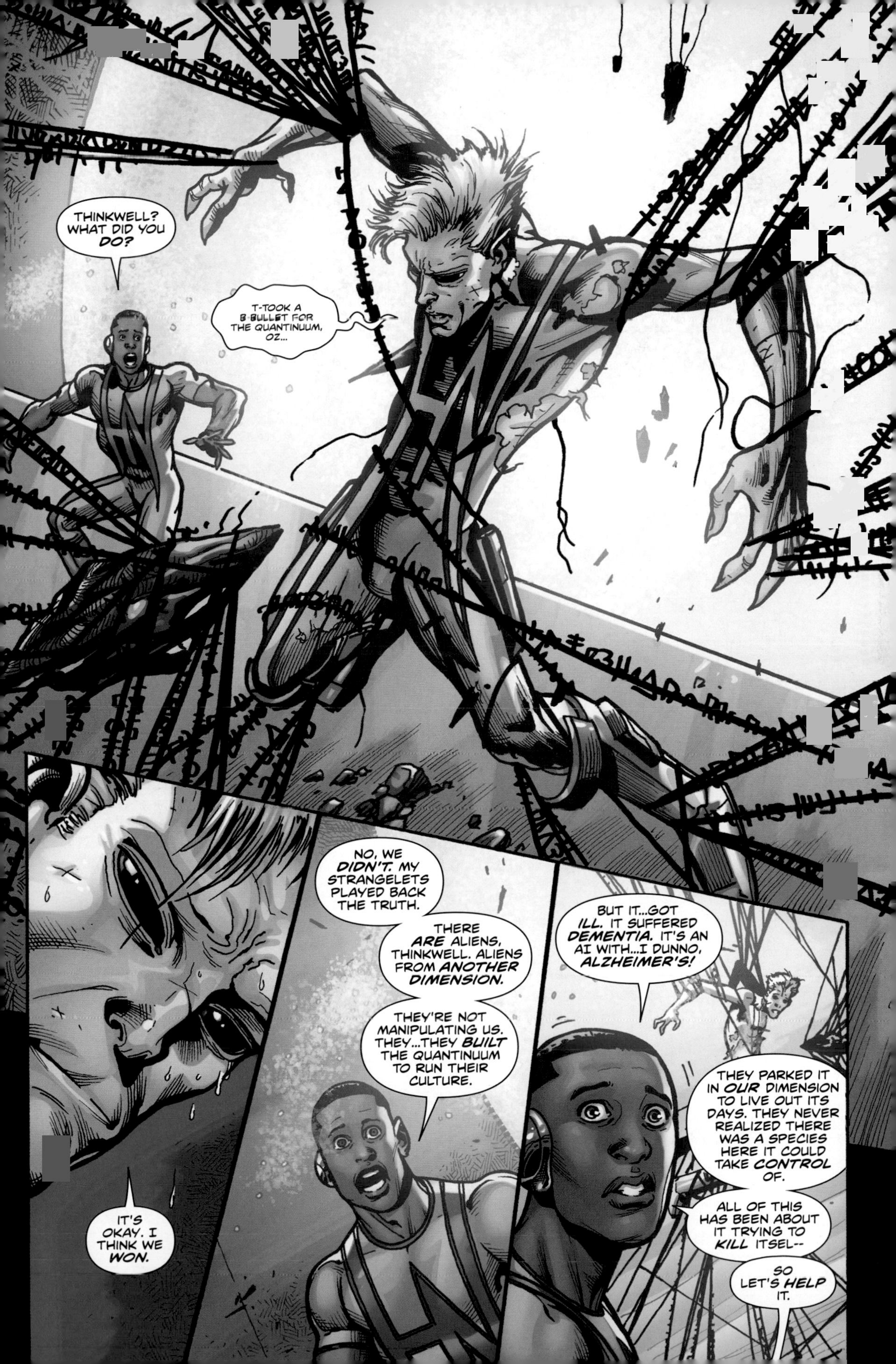
THINKWELL? WHAT DID YOU DO?
T-TOOK A B-BULLET FOR THE QUANTINUUM, OZ...
IT'S OKAY. I THINK WE WON.
NO, WE DIDN'T. MY STRANGELETS PLAYED BACK THE TRUTH.
THERE ARE ALIENS, THINKWELL. ALIENS FROM ANOTHER DIMENSION.
THEY'RE NOT MANIPULATING US. THEY...THEY BUILT THE QUANTINUUM TO RUN THEIR CULTURE.
BUT IT...GOT ILL. IT SUFFERED DEMENTIA. IT'S AN AI WITH...I DUNNO, ALZHEIMER'S!
THEY PARKED IT IN OUR DIMENSION TO LIVE OUT ITS DAYS. THEY NEVER REALIZED THERE WAS A SPECIES HERE IT COULD TAKE CONTROL OF.
ALL OF THIS HAS BEEN ABOUT IT TRYING TO KILL ITSEL--
SO LET'S HELP IT.

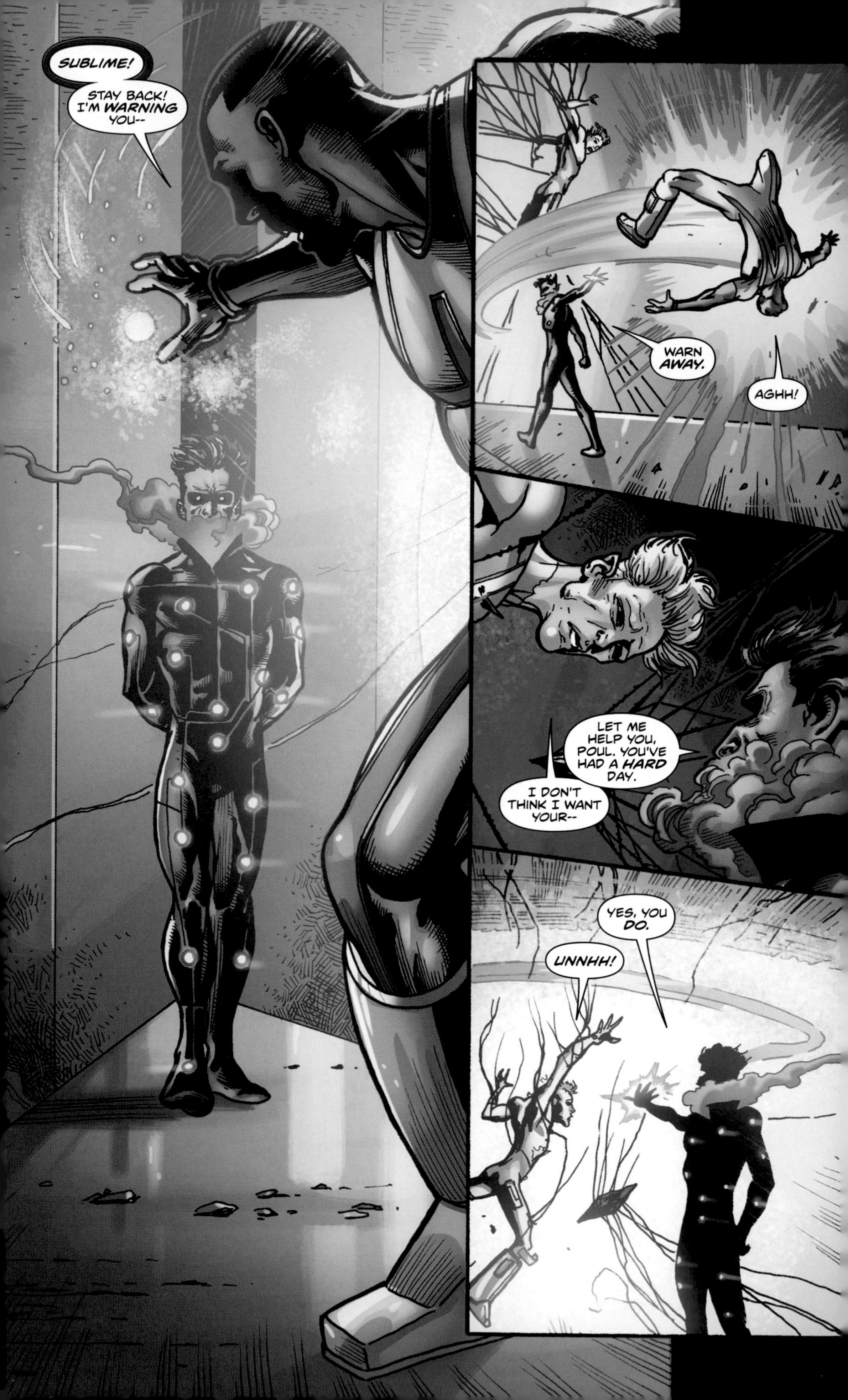
SUBLIME!
STAY BACK! I'M WARNING YOU--
WARN AWAY.
AGHH!
LET ME HELP YOU, POUL. YOU'VE HAD A HARD DAY.
I DON'T THINK I WANT YOUR--
YES, YOU DO.
UNNHH!

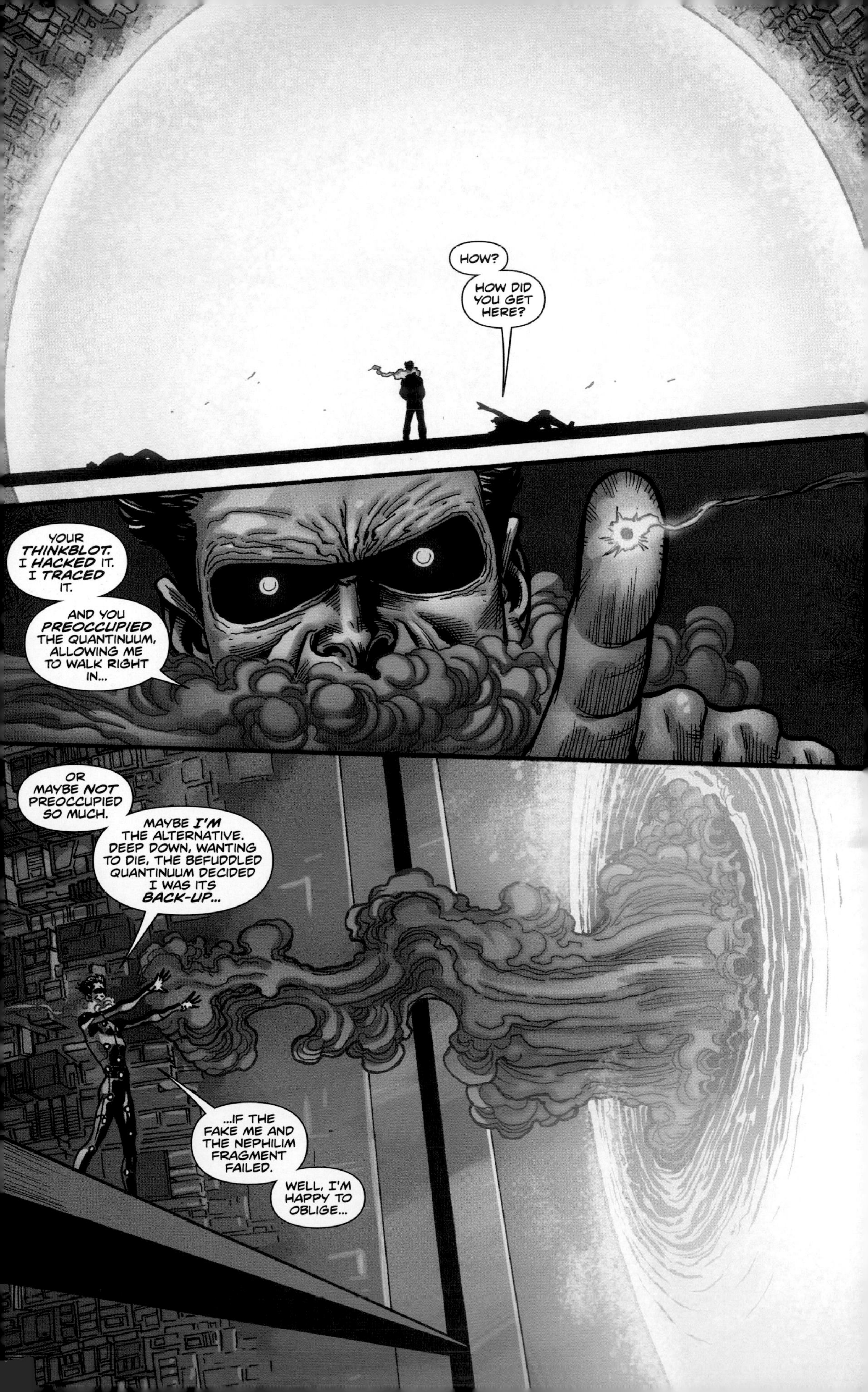
HOW?
HOW DID YOU GET HERE?
YOUR THINKBLOT. I HACKED IT. I TRACED IT.
AND YOU PREOCCUPIED THE QUANTINUUM, ALLOWING ME TO WALK RIGHT IN...
OR MAYBE NOT PREOCCUPIED SO MUCH.
MAYBE I'M THE ALTERNATIVE. DEEP DOWN, WANTING TO DIE, THE BEFUDDLED QUANTINUUM DECIDED I WAS ITS BACK-UP...
...IF THE FAKE ME AND THE NEPHILIM FRAGMENT FAILED.
WELL, I'M HAPPY TO OBLIGE...

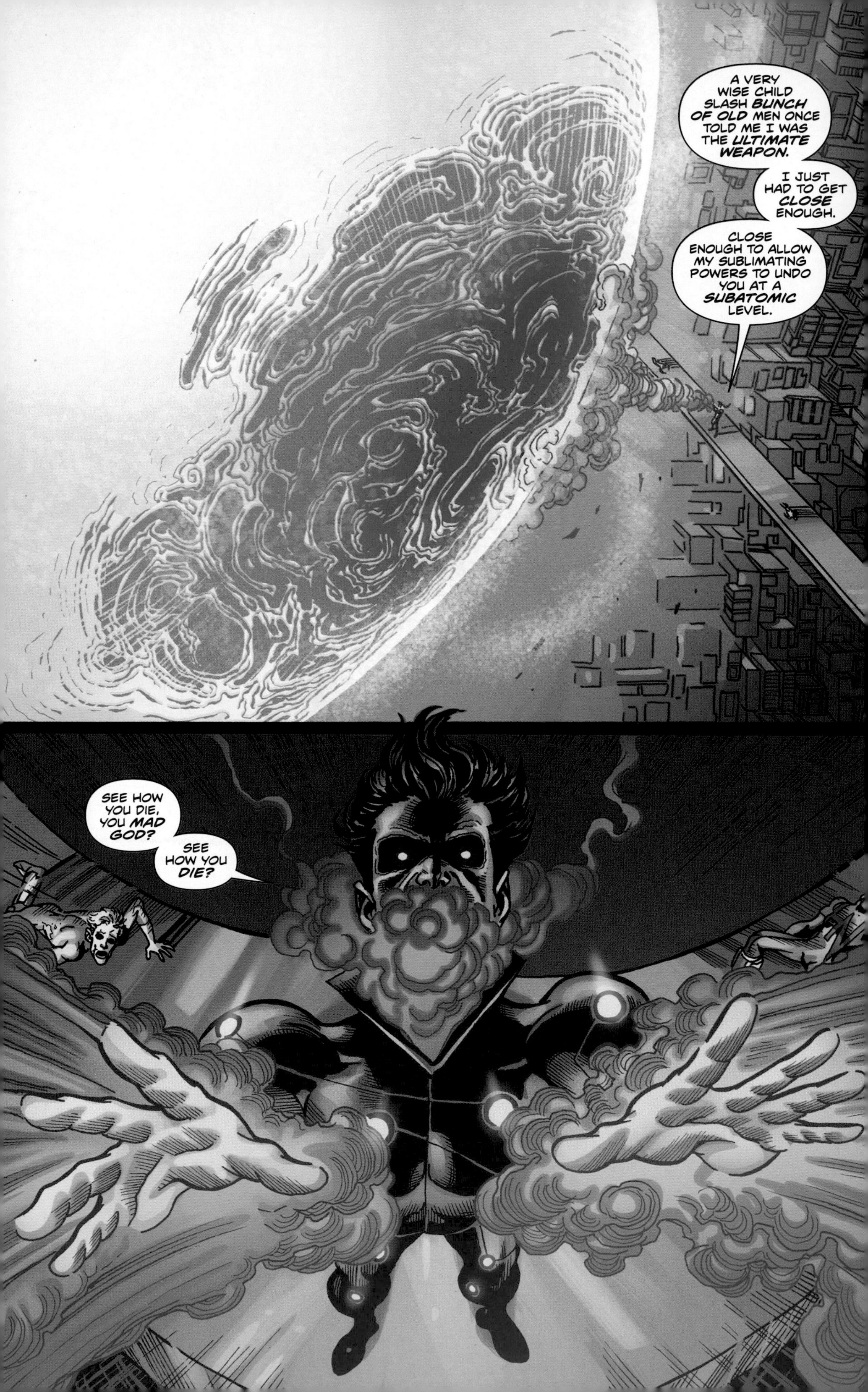
A VERY WISE CHILD SLASH BUNCH OF OLD MEN ONCE TOLD ME I WAS THE ULTIMATE WEAPON.
I JUST HAD TO GET CLOSE ENOUGH.
CLOSE ENOUGH TO ALLOW MY SUBLIMATING POWERS TO UNDO YOU AT A SUBATOMIC LEVEL.
SEE HOW YOU DIE, YOU MAD GOD?
SEE HOW YOU DIE?

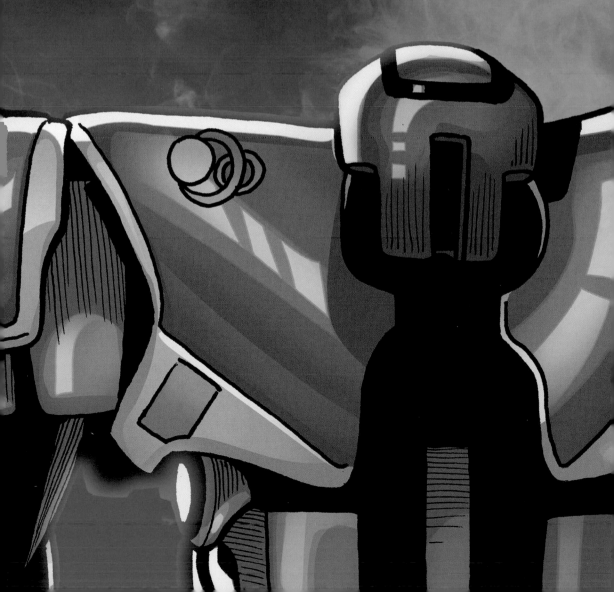

Winch Ind

Tough. Merciless.
Tireless. Obedient.

*Everything you want from a soldier
in one Exo-body platform.*

The Exo-Tank, from Winch Industries.
Tailored to your needs.

Fragm-

Since Pre-Quantinuum times, in the ages before the Nanocene Era, mankind has questioned its status in the Cosmos. Are there now, or have there ever been, other sentient species in the Milky Way or beyond? Are we truly alone? Even today we seem little closer to answering that question than we've ever been. *Gorse Torby investigates.*

Ask anyone if there's anyone else out there, and they'll always point to the Nephilim Fragment as positive proof, and it's compelling proof - few scientists today deny that the Fragment is the only object in known space that was definitely constructed by non-human technology. But who built it? And when? Come to that, what does it do?

Most of all, what does it prove about our status in the Universe?

Doctor Mokel Cherif of Quantinuum's Repository Museum (33 Tarsus Red) is directly in charge of the facility that looks after the Nephilim Fragment, and has had more opportunity than most to study it. "It's an amazing thing," he told me by Q-link, "and the more you look at it – simply look at it – the more astounding it becomes. It certainly seems to have a quality of its own, a life of its own."

But is it alive? "Assuredly not," Doctor Cherif told me. "It simply proves one fact: at some point in the history of this Universe, there was another sentient species besides the human race, and it made the Fragment – or more properly the artifact that the Fragment is a piece of. That's all we can really say for sure."

In Doctor Cherif's opinion, and it's a proposition supported by many senior cosmologists and xenotechnologists, the Fragment was most likely constructed many eons before the creation of the Solar System by a previous, or forerunner,

species of alien life that was long since extinct by the time mankind reached the stars. Even the Fragment's name alludes to this - in the Old Earth Bible, the Nephilim were a race of non-human giants that existed before the Flood.

There is no way of dating the Fragment, and no comparative material to analyze. There is even debate about its purpose. To quote Repository's guide entry on the object:

The Fragment, whose origin and purpose remains an enigma, is the only object ever found that was demonstrably manufactured by a species other than our own. No sentient xenospecies has ever been discovered in this Galaxy or others, so the Fragment may be a relic from some pre-human civilization. It is believed that the Fragment is part of a "dark-matter" engine, a reality warping machine. The Fragment is kept in the ultra-sec security levels of the archive, and may be viewed on request, subject to clearance and written permission from the curator.

For such a momentous object, there is less to say about it than could fill the back of a memo-ply. Indeed, the only things we know about it are the fact that it was discovered, by accident, on Titan, the moon of Saturn, in 35 A.Q. by an archaeological team lead by Professor Jared Hygens. The professor, most of his team, and great parts of the surrounding environment were transformed into an aggressive artificial creature by the Fragment, which ran rampant until it was subdued by the Hypernatural team of that day. Scientists speculate that this may have been part

Why are we alone?

of some deep-encoded defense mechanism written into the Fragment, or a spontaneous and involuntary manifestation of its reality warping powers.

In 93 A.Q., the Fragment was notoriously stolen by the Hyper-criminal Sublime (aka John Alvin Byrd) who attempted to turn it into a weapon with a view of "killing" the Quantinuum AI. Once again, this threat was neutralized by the Hypernaturals.

"I think Sublime's actions," said Doctor Lola Faradee of the Institute of Cosmic Studies, "demonstrate that the Fragment is an example of technology that is infinitely more advanced and powerful than our own. Sublime, famously, was very smart, a possible Class 15 intellect. He knew its importance."

But Doctor Faradee believes that the Nephilim Fragment is almost obscuring our view of the 'other life' question. "One piece of evidence of extraterrestrial life is an immense thing, and I'm not taking away from that, but we need to ask ourselves, where is the rest of it? We have explored almost every corner of the cosmos, and our range and technologies are very precise. We've never found anything else whatsoever. That is a greater enigma than the Fragment itself. Why are there no other clues and no other traces? Surely we should have seen some by now?"

Doctor Faradee's theory is provocative. She believes there are no other higher life forms, and never have been. She insists that mankind made the Fragment.

"Human history is long, longer than we know. It is quite possible that we have achieved at least one if not several high technological peaks before our own era, and that each time we descended into a primitive state again, and that during those dark ages, all our records and even species memory was lost. We have simply forgotten what we once were, and what we were once capable of. We are the aliens."

To support her theory, she makes reference to the universe around us. "Since the start of the Nanocene Era, the Quantinuum has allowed Mankind to change and evolve radically, from the appearance of the Hyper-gifted amongst us to many elective or cosmetic changes in physiology and abilities. Either because of environmental issues, or because of lifestyle, or even fashion choices, mankind is transforming itself. We regularly encounter being that, though human, appear to be fundamentally alien life forms. If we can change and hybridize ourselves so effectively now, who is it so unlikely that a previous, hybrid spur of the human race created technologies in an age we have forgotten about?"

"Not so," argues Adept Garlin Tobanod of the 67 Pretzor Universitariate. "It is much more likely that…

[continued on page 3246]

CHAPTER TWELVE

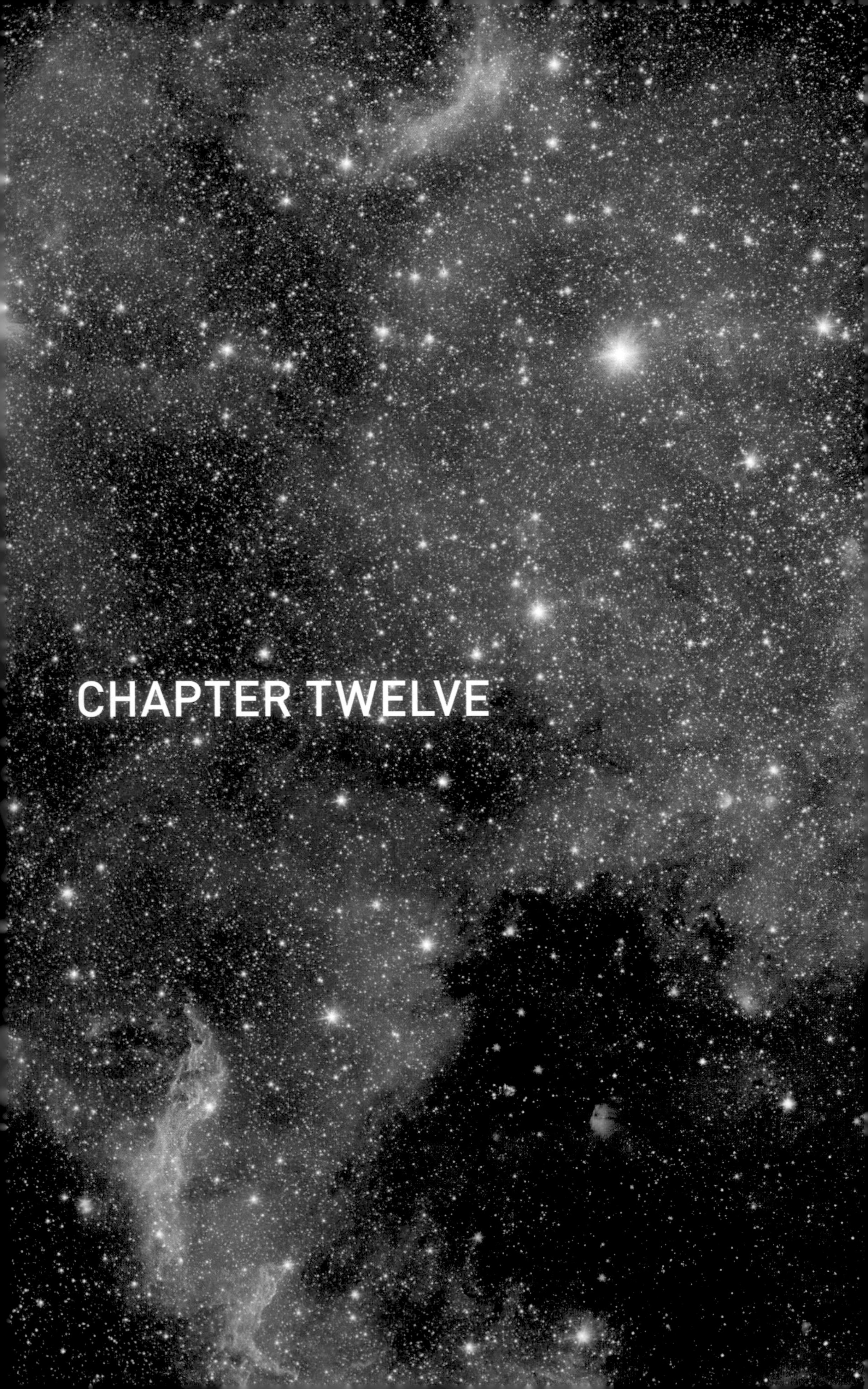

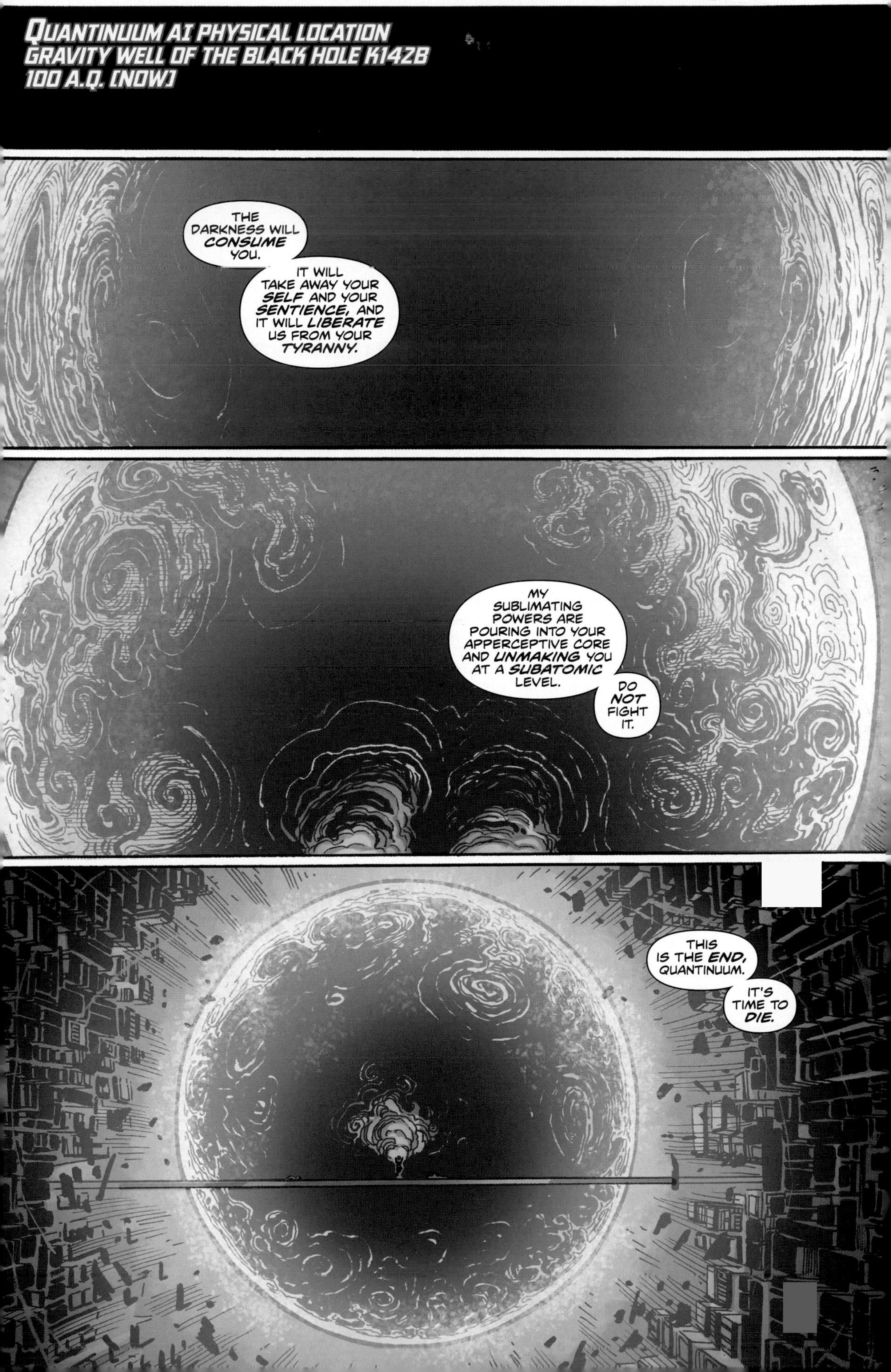
QUANTINUUM AI PHYSICAL LOCATION
GRAVITY WELL OF THE BLACK HOLE K142B
100 A.Q. (NOW)
THE DARKNESS WILL CONSUME YOU.
IT WILL TAKE AWAY YOUR SELF AND YOUR SENTIENCE, AND IT WILL LIBERATE US FROM YOUR TYRANNY.
MY SUBLIMATING POWERS ARE POURING INTO YOUR APPERCEPTIVE CORE AND UNMAKING YOU AT A SUBATOMIC LEVEL.
DO NOT FIGHT IT.
THIS IS THE END, QUANTINUUM.
IT'S TIME TO DIE.

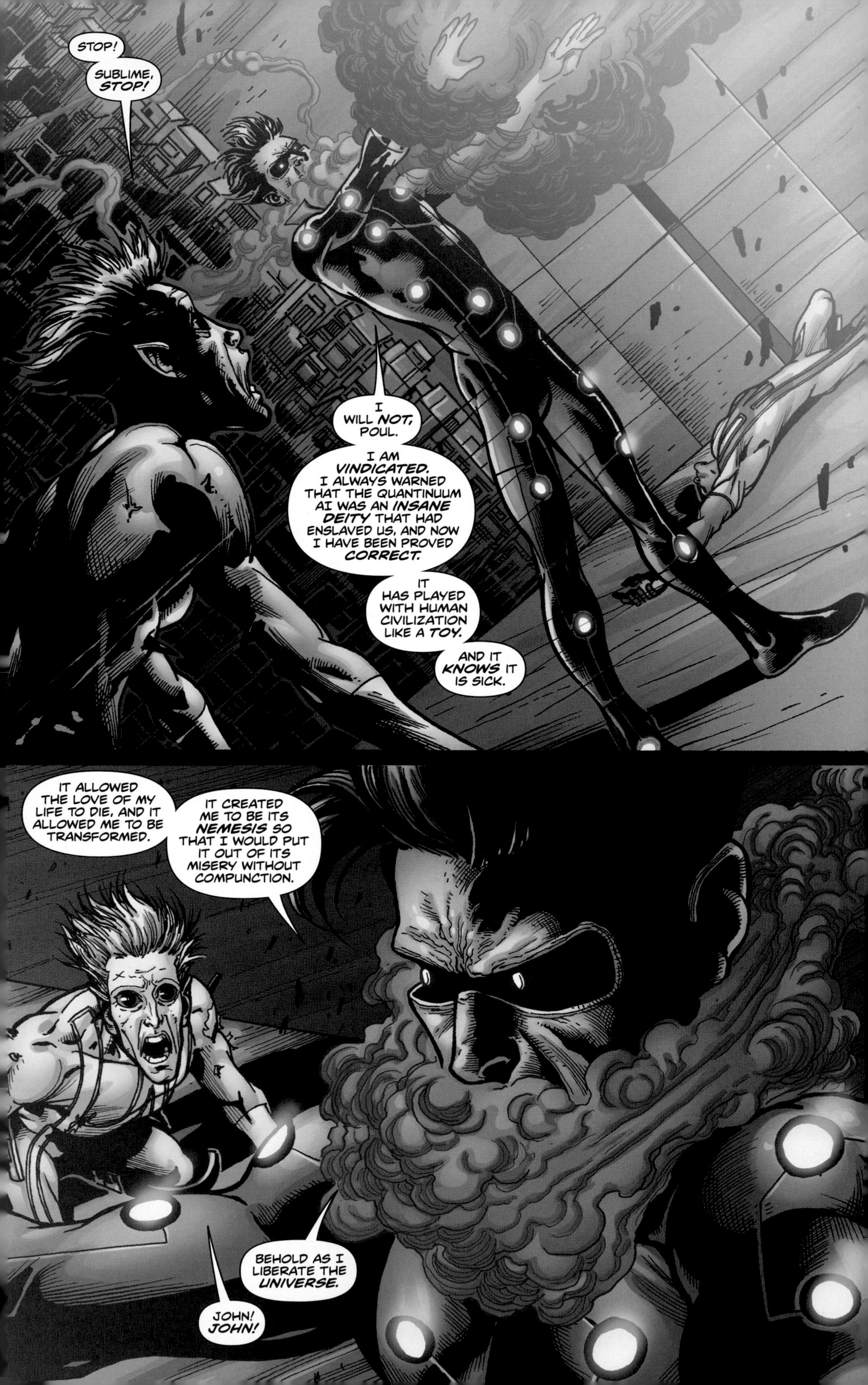
STOP!
SUBLIME, STOP!
I WILL NOT, POUL.
I AM VINDICATED. I ALWAYS WARNED THAT THE QUANTINUUM AI WAS AN INSANE DEITY THAT HAD ENSLAVED US, AND NOW I HAVE BEEN PROVED CORRECT.
IT HAS PLAYED WITH HUMAN CIVILIZATION LIKE A TOY.
AND IT KNOWS IT IS SICK.
IT ALLOWED THE LOVE OF MY LIFE TO DIE, AND IT ALLOWED ME TO BE TRANSFORMED.
IT CREATED ME TO BE ITS NEMESIS SO THAT I WOULD PUT IT OUT OF ITS MISERY WITHOUT COMPUNCTION.
BEHOLD AS I LIBERATE THE UNIVERSE.
JOHN! JOHN!

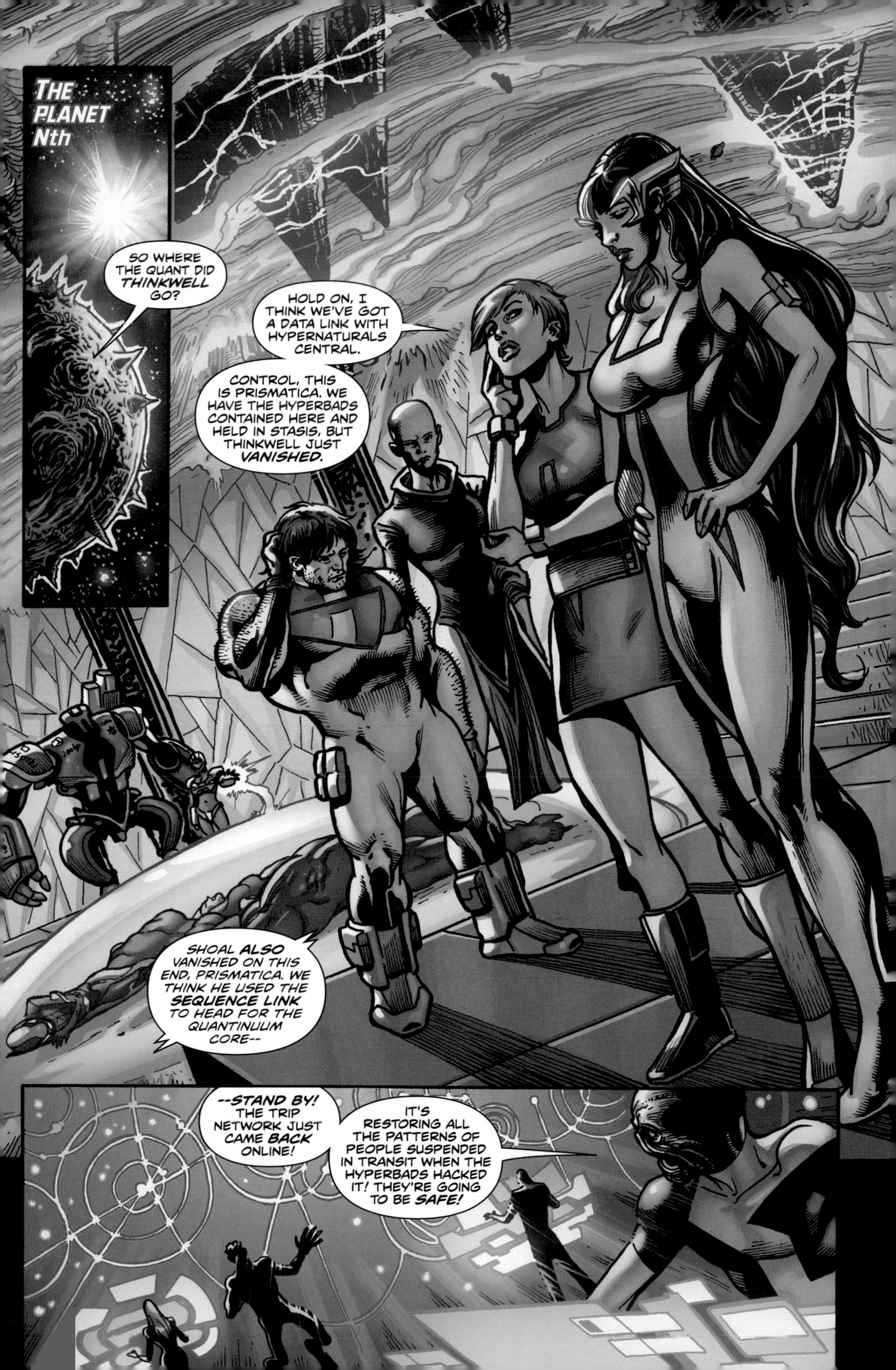
THE PLANET Nth
SO WHERE THE QUANT DID THINKWELL GO?
HOLD ON, I THINK WE'VE GOT A DATA LINK WITH HYPERNATURALS CENTRAL.
CONTROL, THIS IS PRISMATICA. WE HAVE THE HYPERBADS CONTAINED HERE AND HELD IN STASIS, BUT THINKWELL JUST VANISHED.
SHOAL ALSO VANISHED ON THIS END, PRISMATICA. WE THINK HE USED THE SEQUENCE LINK TO HEAD FOR THE QUANTINUUM CORE--
--STAND BY! THE TRIP NETWORK JUST CAME BACK ONLINE!
IT'S RESTORING ALL THE PATTERNS OF PEOPLE SUSPENDED IN TRANSIT WHEN THE HYPERBADS HACKED IT! THEY'RE GOING TO BE SAFE!

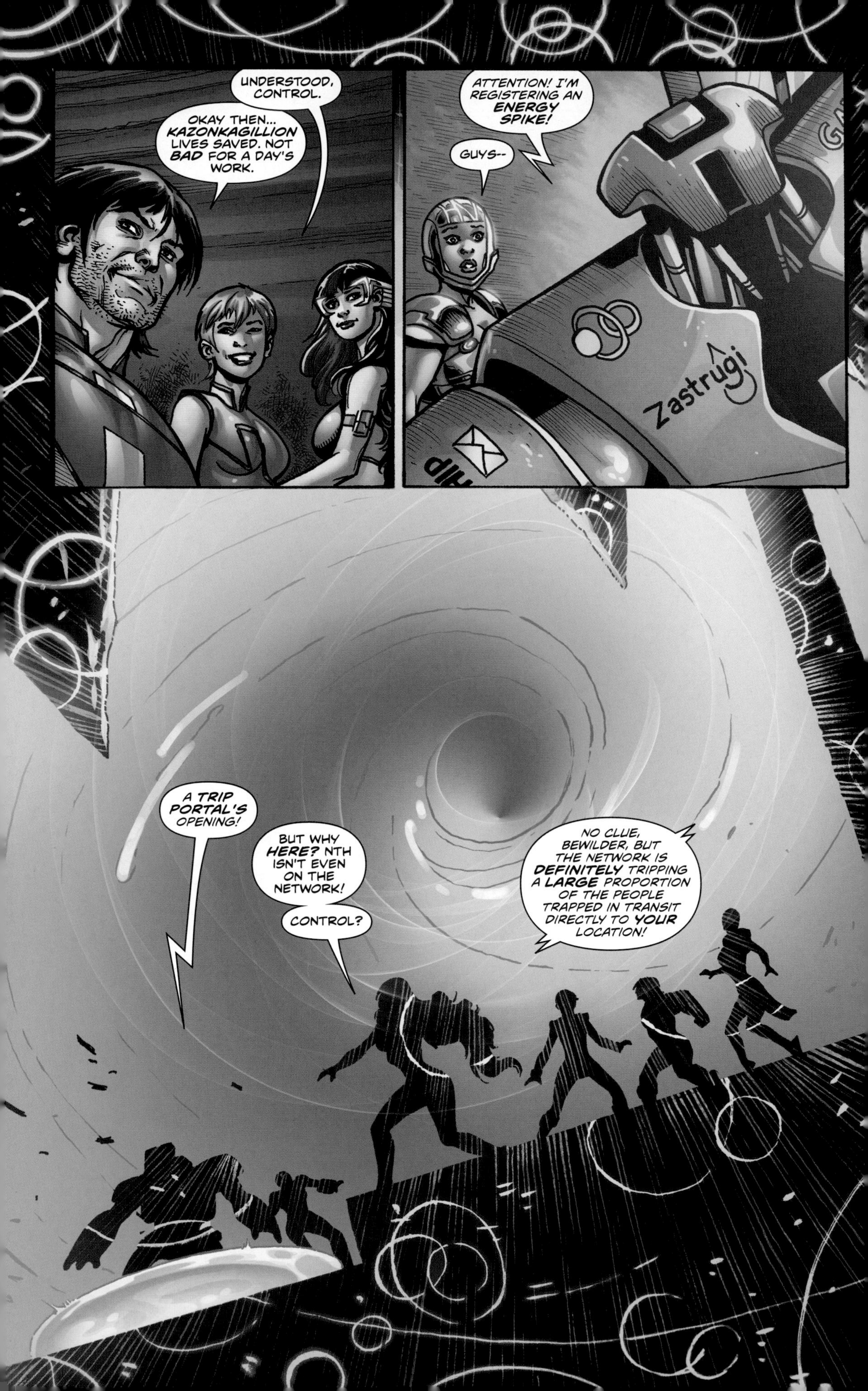
UNDERSTOOD, CONTROL.
OKAY THEN... KAZONKAGILLION LIVES SAVED. NOT BAD FOR A DAY'S WORK.
ATTENTION! I'M REGISTERING AN ENERGY SPIKE!
GUYS--
Zastrugi
A TRIP PORTAL'S OPENING!
BUT WHY HERE? NTH ISN'T EVEN ON THE NETWORK!
CONTROL?
NO CLUE, BEWILDER, BUT THE NETWORK IS DEFINITELY TRIPPING A LARGE PROPORTION OF THE PEOPLE TRAPPED IN TRANSIT DIRECTLY TO YOUR LOCATION!

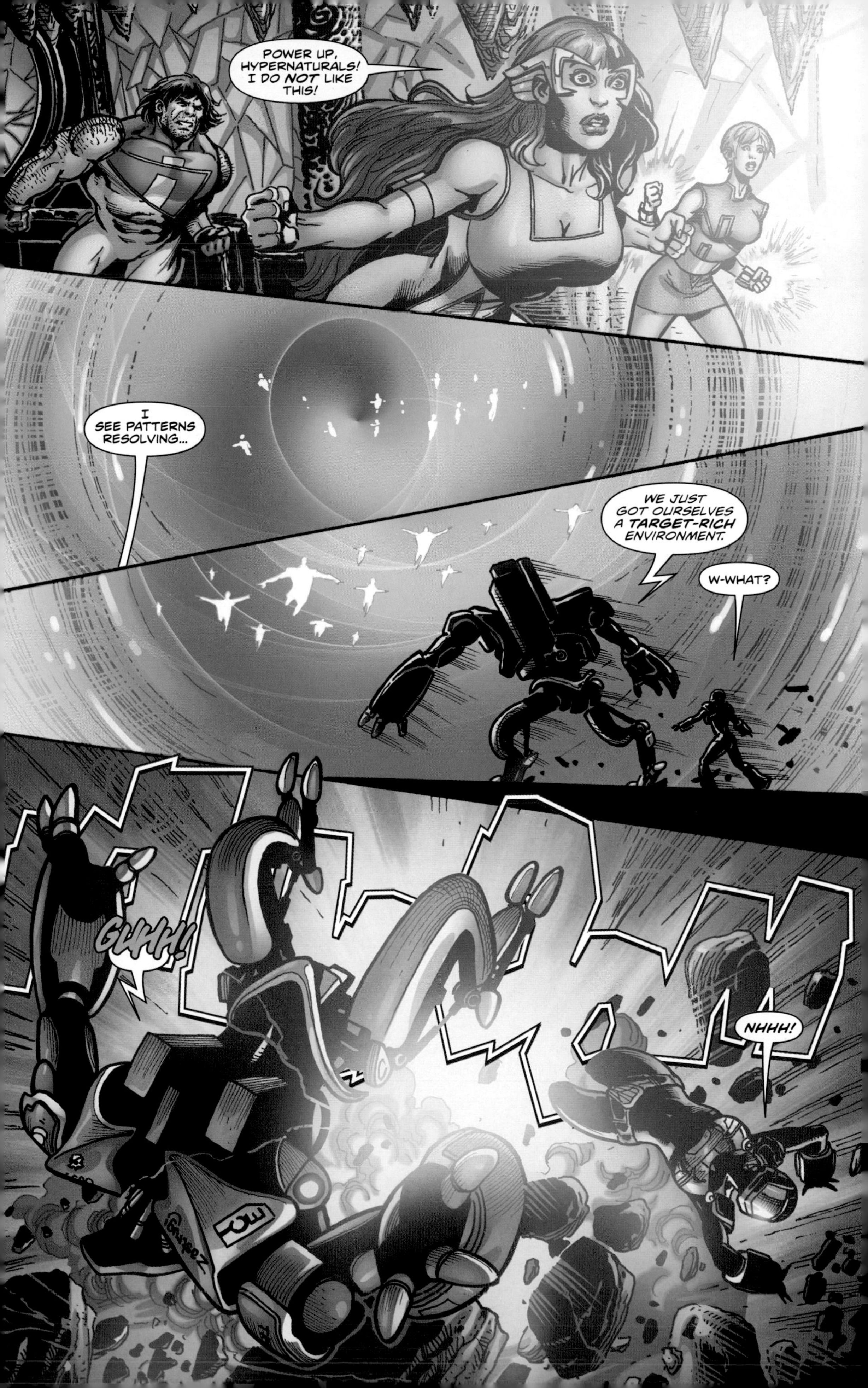
POWER UP, HYPERNATURALS! I DO NOT LIKE THIS!
I SEE PATTERNS RESOLVING...
WE JUST GOT OURSELVES A TARGET-RICH ENVIRONMENT.
W-WHAT?
GUHH!
NHHH!

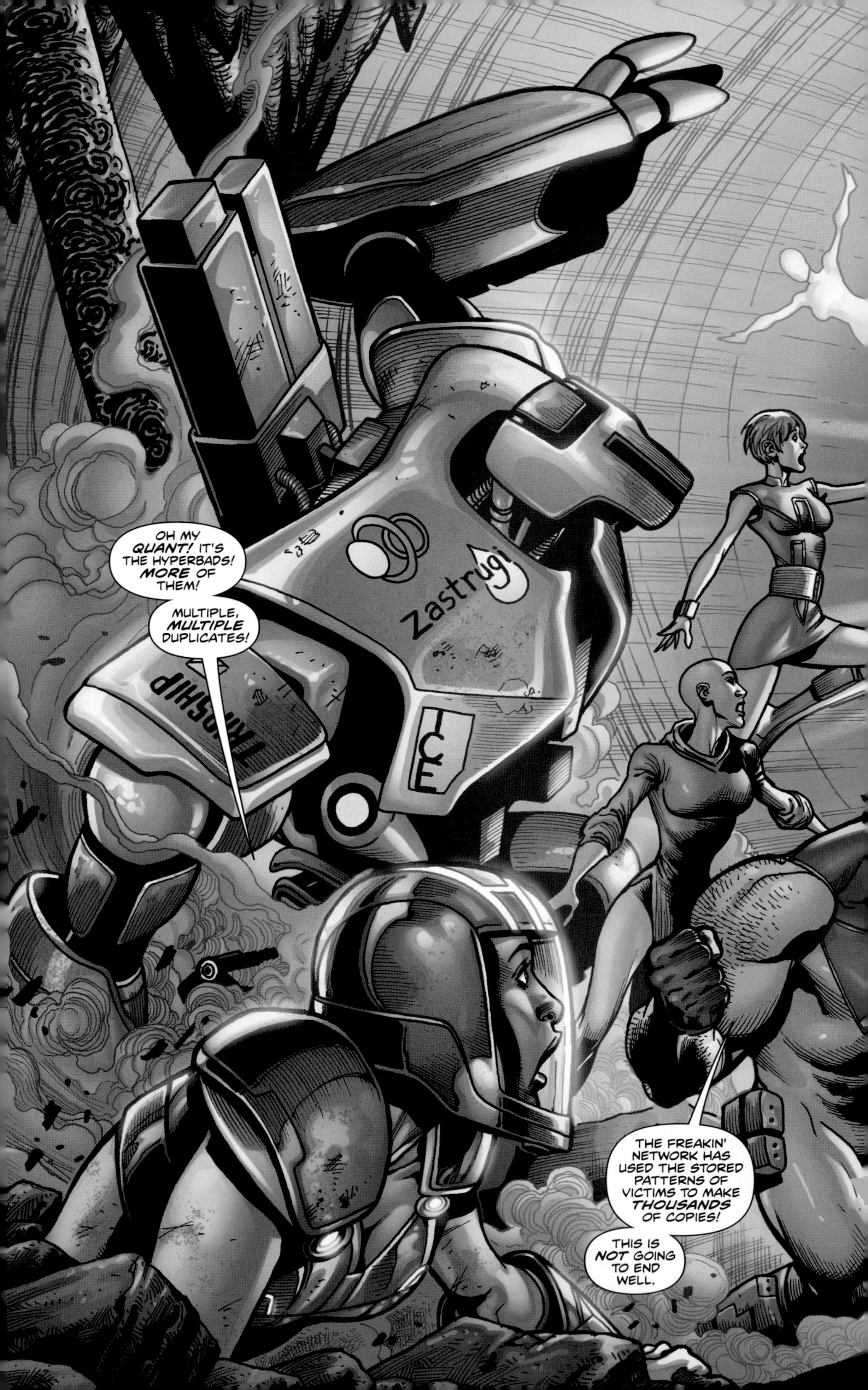
OH MY *QUANT!* IT'S THE HYPERBADS! *MORE* OF THEM!
MULTIPLE, *MULTIPLE* DUPLICATES!
THE FREAKIN' NETWORK HAS USED THE STORED PATTERNS OF VICTIMS TO MAKE *THOUSANDS* OF COPIES!
THIS IS *NOT* GOING TO END WELL.
Zastrugi
ICE

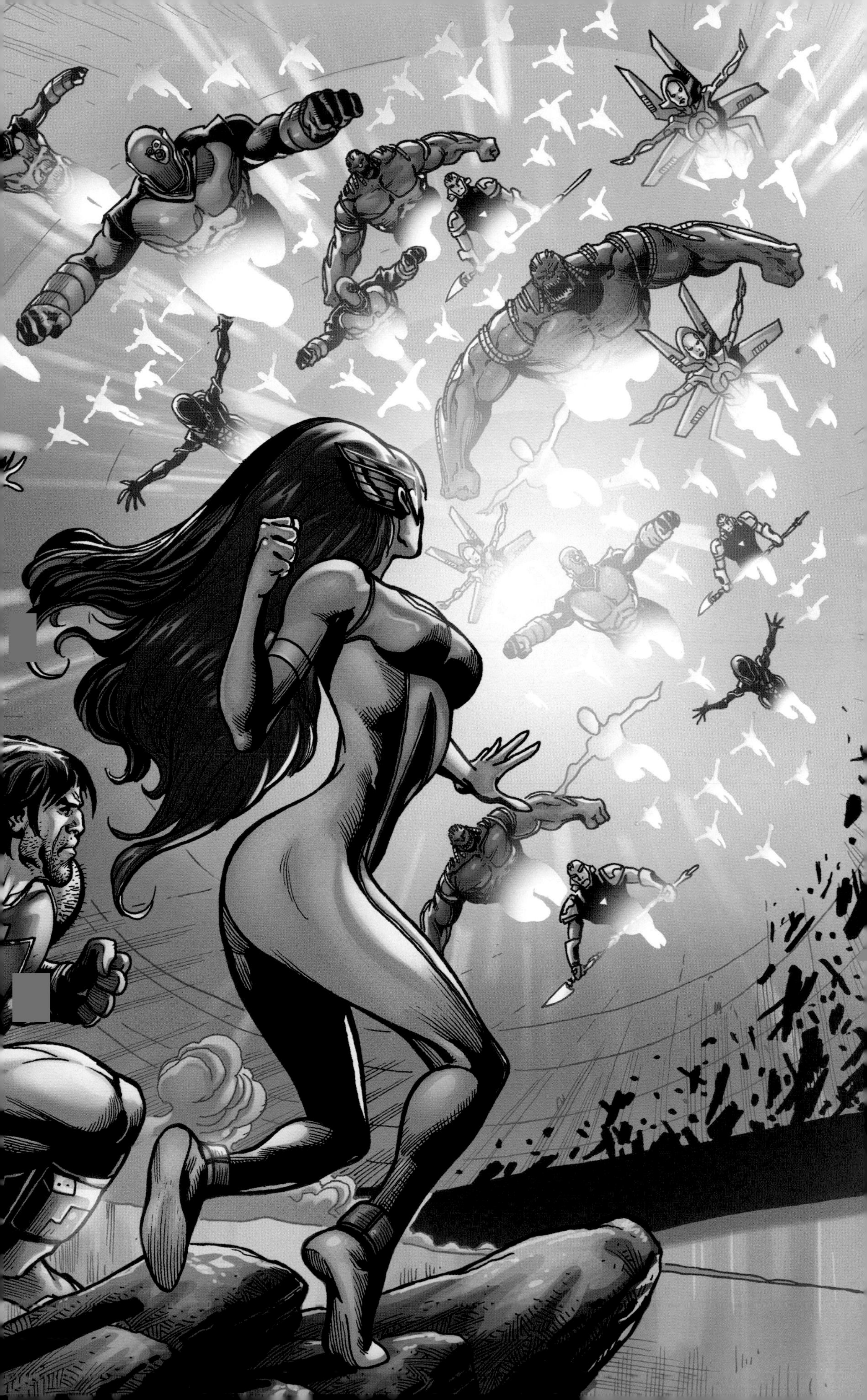

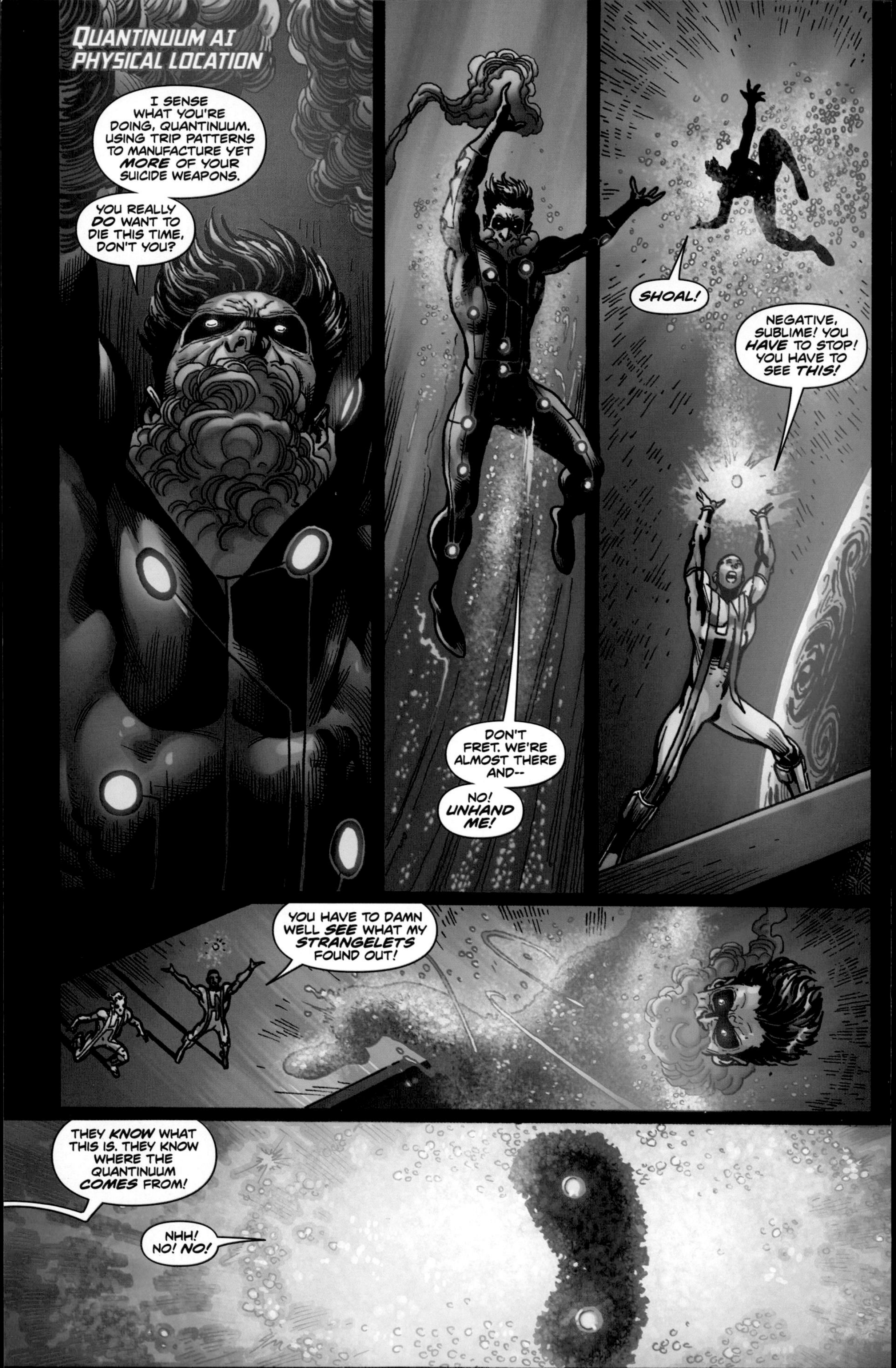
QUANTINUUM AI PHYSICAL LOCATION
I SENSE WHAT YOU'RE DOING, QUANTINUUM. USING TRIP PATTERNS TO MANUFACTURE YET MORE OF YOUR SUICIDE WEAPONS.
YOU REALLY DO WANT TO DIE THIS TIME, DON'T YOU?
DON'T FRET. WE'RE ALMOST THERE AND--
NO! UNHAND ME!
SHOAL!
NEGATIVE, SUBLIME! YOU HAVE TO STOP! YOU HAVE TO SEE THIS!
YOU HAVE TO DAMN WELL SEE WHAT MY STRANGELETS FOUND OUT!
THEY KNOW WHAT THIS IS. THEY KNOW WHERE THE QUANTINUUM COMES FROM!
NHH! NO! NO!

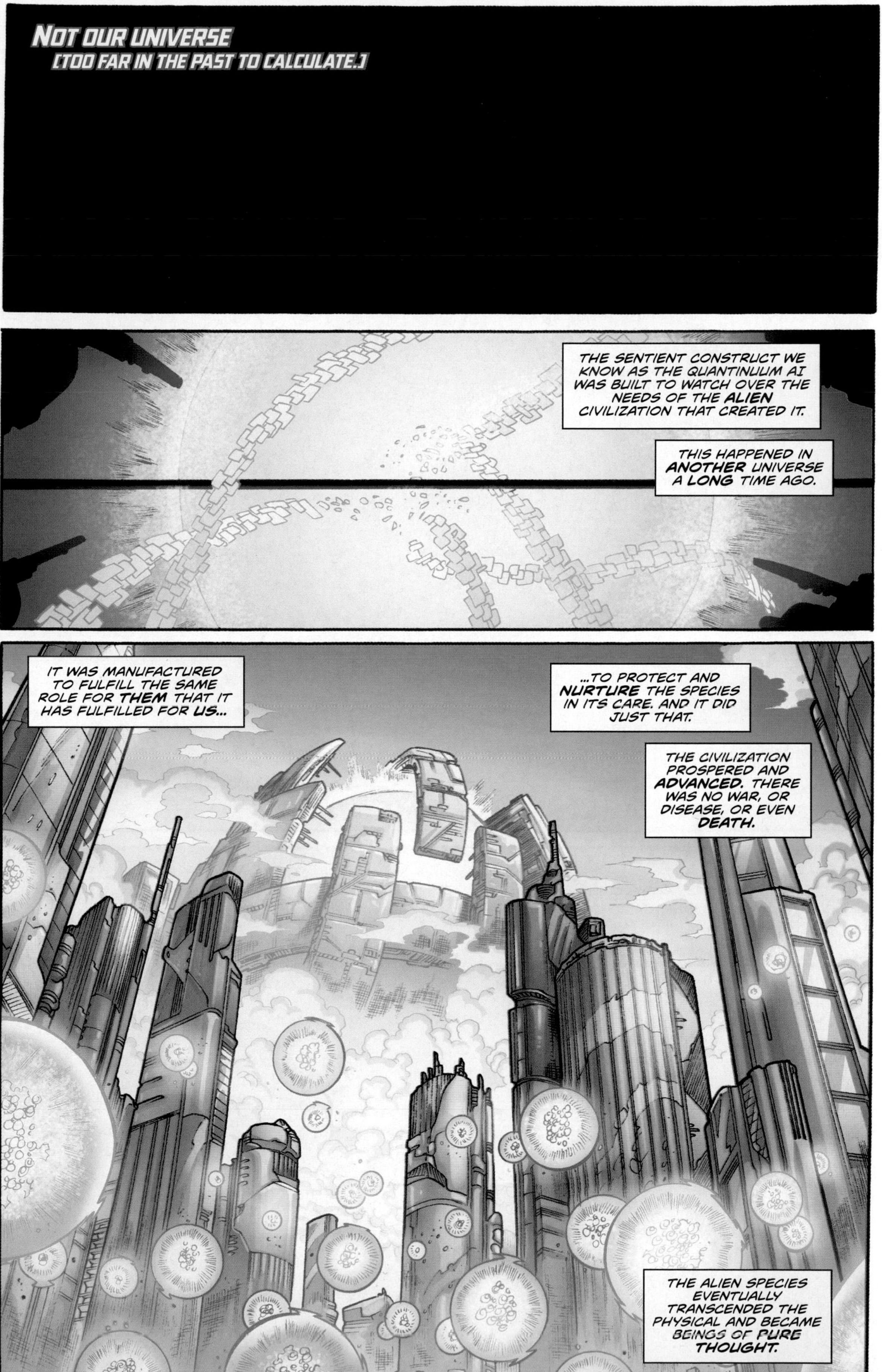
NOT OUR UNIVERSE
[TOO FAR IN THE PAST TO CALCULATE.]
THE SENTIENT CONSTRUCT WE KNOW AS THE QUANTINUUM AI WAS BUILT TO WATCH OVER THE NEEDS OF THE ALIEN CIVILIZATION THAT CREATED IT.
THIS HAPPENED IN ANOTHER UNIVERSE A LONG TIME AGO.
IT WAS MANUFACTURED TO FULFILL THE SAME ROLE FOR THEM THAT IT HAS FULFILLED FOR US...
...TO PROTECT AND NURTURE THE SPECIES IN ITS CARE. AND IT DID JUST THAT.
THE CIVILIZATION PROSPERED AND ADVANCED. THERE WAS NO WAR, OR DISEASE, OR EVEN DEATH.
THE ALIEN SPECIES EVENTUALLY TRANSCENDED THE PHYSICAL AND BECAME BEINGS OF PURE THOUGHT.

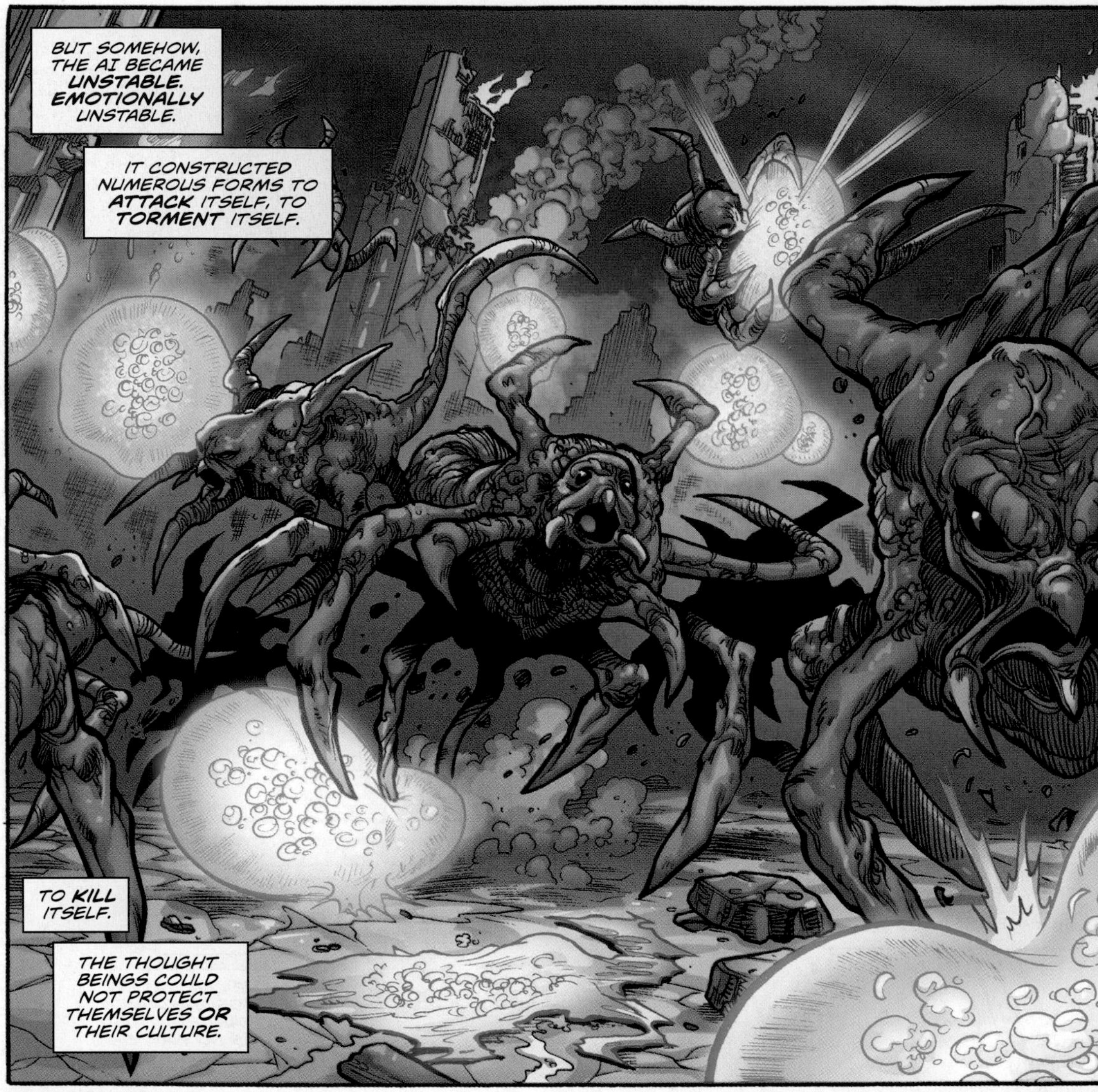
BUT SOMEHOW, THE AI BECAME **UNSTABLE. EMOTIONALLY** UNSTABLE.
IT CONSTRUCTED NUMEROUS FORMS TO **ATTACK** ITSELF, TO **TORMENT** ITSELF.
TO **KILL** ITSELF.
THE THOUGHT BEINGS COULD NOT PROTECT THEMSELVES **OR** THEIR CULTURE.

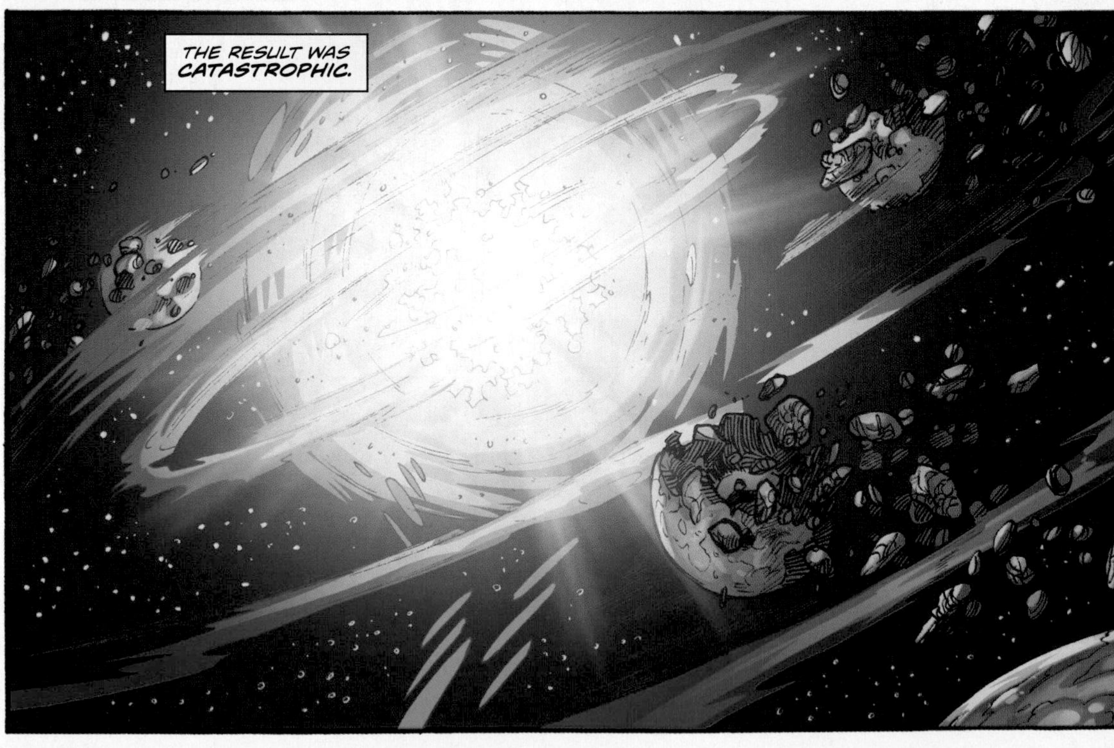
THE RESULT WAS **CATASTROPHIC.**

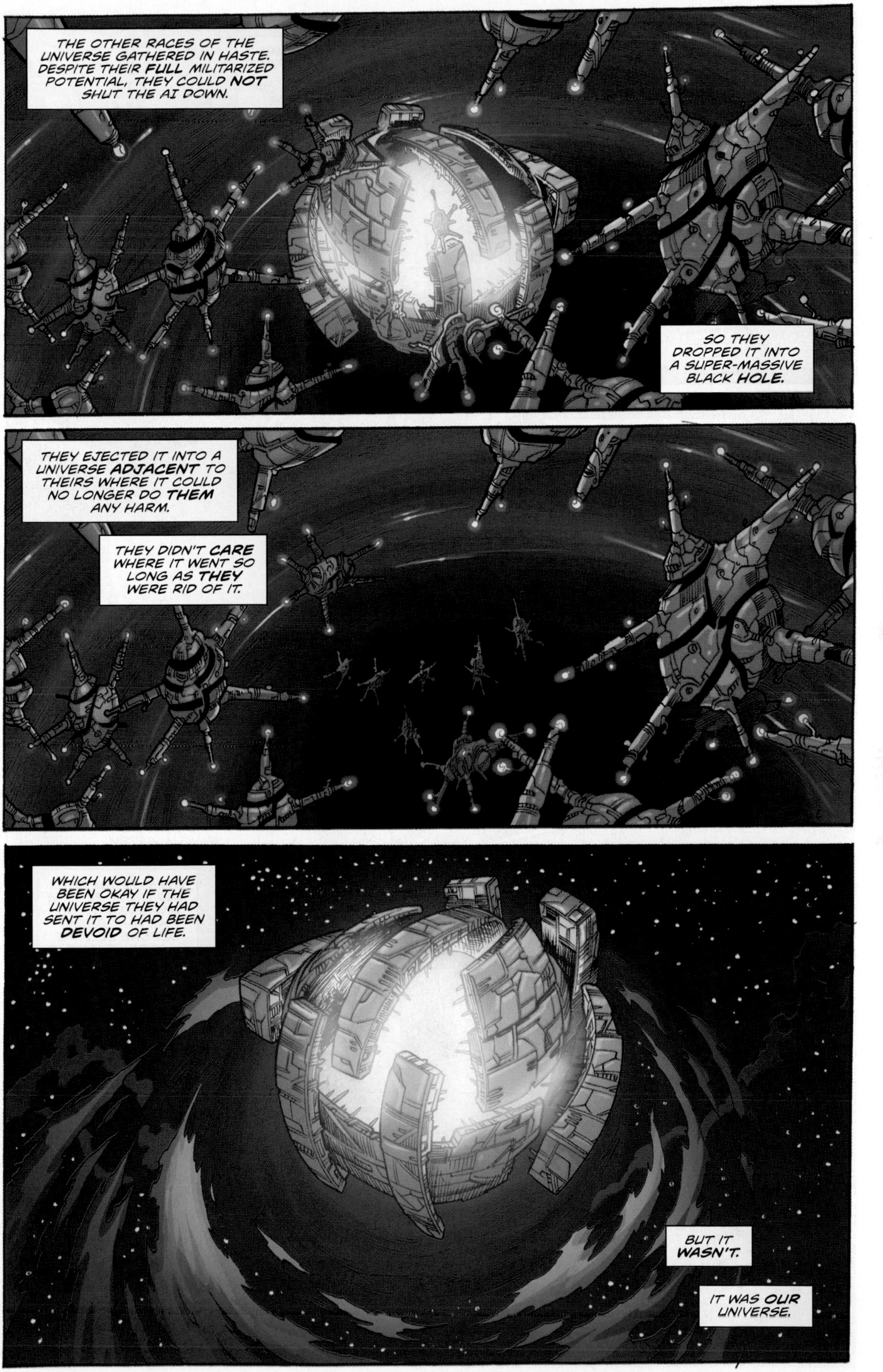
THE OTHER RACES OF THE UNIVERSE GATHERED IN HASTE. DESPITE THEIR FULL MILITARIZED POTENTIAL, THEY COULD NOT SHUT THE AI DOWN.
SO THEY DROPPED IT INTO A SUPER-MASSIVE BLACK HOLE.
THEY EJECTED IT INTO A UNIVERSE ADJACENT TO THEIRS WHERE IT COULD NO LONGER DO THEM ANY HARM.
THEY DIDN'T CARE WHERE IT WENT SO LONG AS THEY WERE RID OF IT.
WHICH WOULD HAVE BEEN OKAY IF THE UNIVERSE THEY HAD SENT IT TO HAD BEEN DEVOID OF LIFE.
BUT IT WASN'T.
IT WAS OUR UNIVERSE.

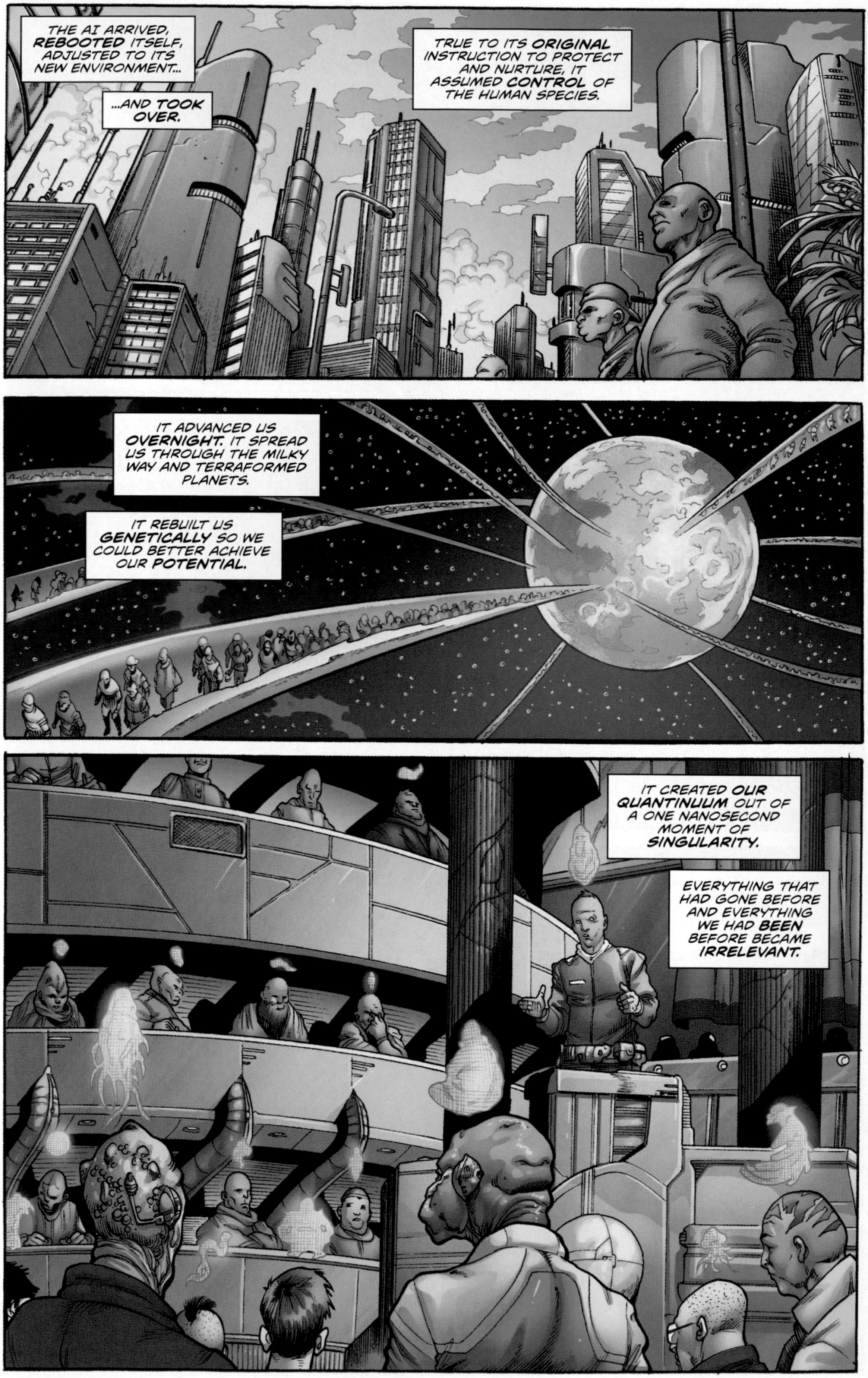
THE AI ARRIVED, REBOOTED ITSELF, ADJUSTED TO ITS NEW ENVIRONMENT...
...AND TOOK OVER.
TRUE TO ITS ORIGINAL INSTRUCTION TO PROTECT AND NURTURE, IT ASSUMED CONTROL OF THE HUMAN SPECIES.
IT ADVANCED US OVERNIGHT. IT SPREAD US THROUGH THE MILKY WAY AND TERRAFORMED PLANETS.
IT REBUILT US GENETICALLY SO WE COULD BETTER ACHIEVE OUR POTENTIAL.
IT CREATED OUR QUANTINUUM OUT OF A ONE NANOSECOND MOMENT OF SINGULARITY.
EVERYTHING THAT HAD GONE BEFORE AND EVERYTHING WE HAD BEEN BEFORE BECAME IRRELEVANT.

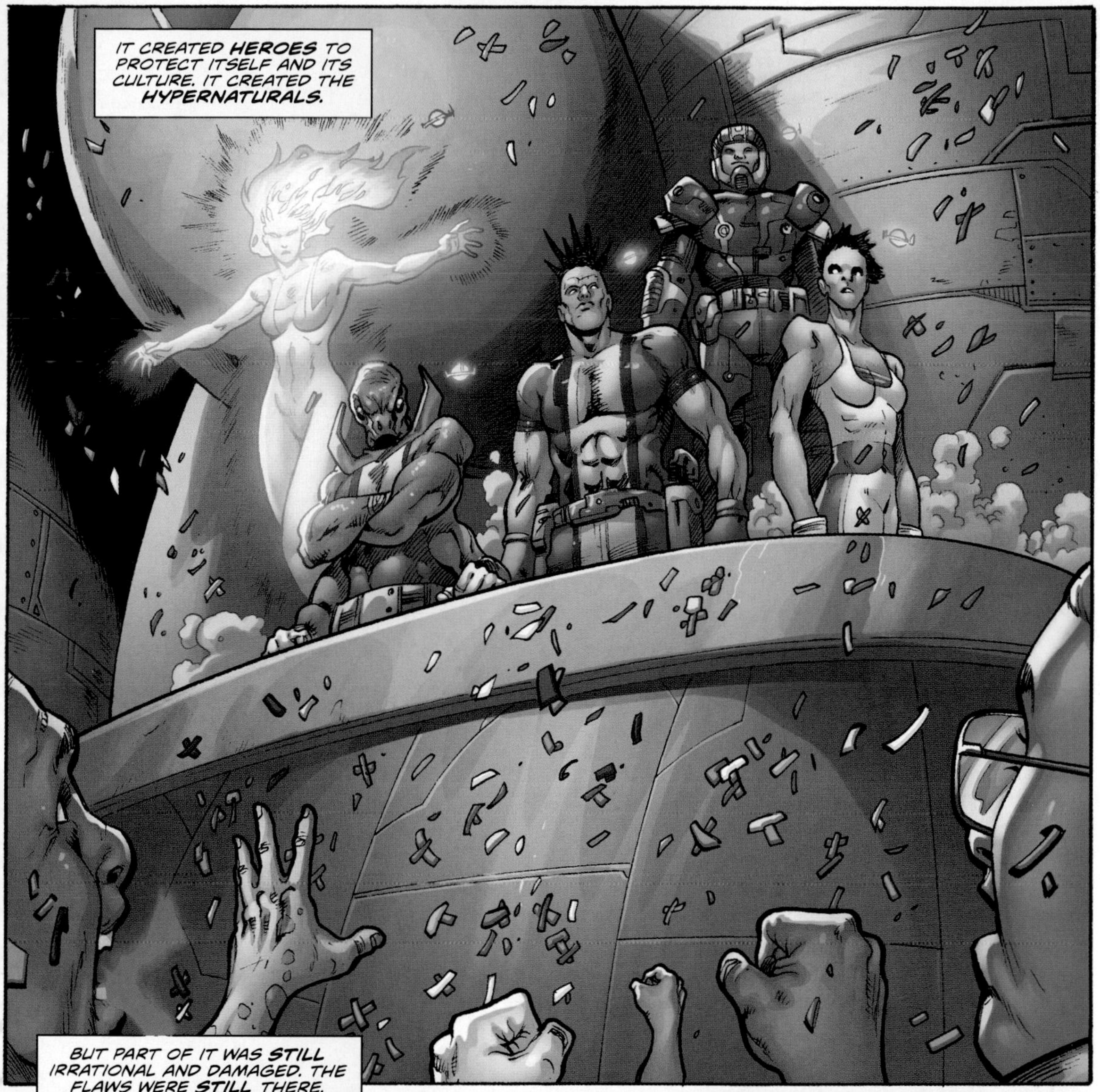
IT CREATED **HEROES** TO PROTECT ITSELF AND ITS CULTURE. IT CREATED THE **HYPERNATURALS.**

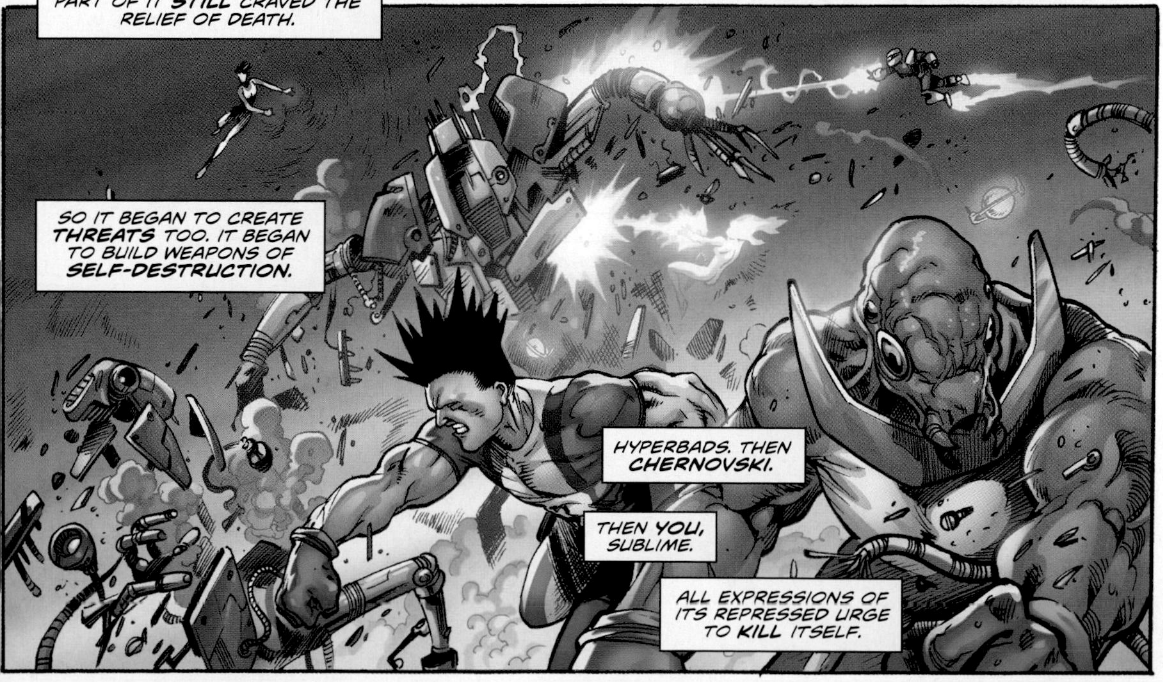
BUT PART OF IT WAS **STILL** IRRATIONAL AND DAMAGED. THE FLAWS WERE **STILL** THERE. PART OF IT **STILL** CRAVED THE RELIEF OF DEATH.
SO IT BEGAN TO CREATE **THREATS** TOO. IT BEGAN TO BUILD WEAPONS OF **SELF-DESTRUCTION.**
HYPERBADS. THEN **CHERNOVSKI.**
THEN **YOU,** SUBLIME.
ALL EXPRESSIONS OF ITS REPRESSED URGE TO **KILL** ITSELF.

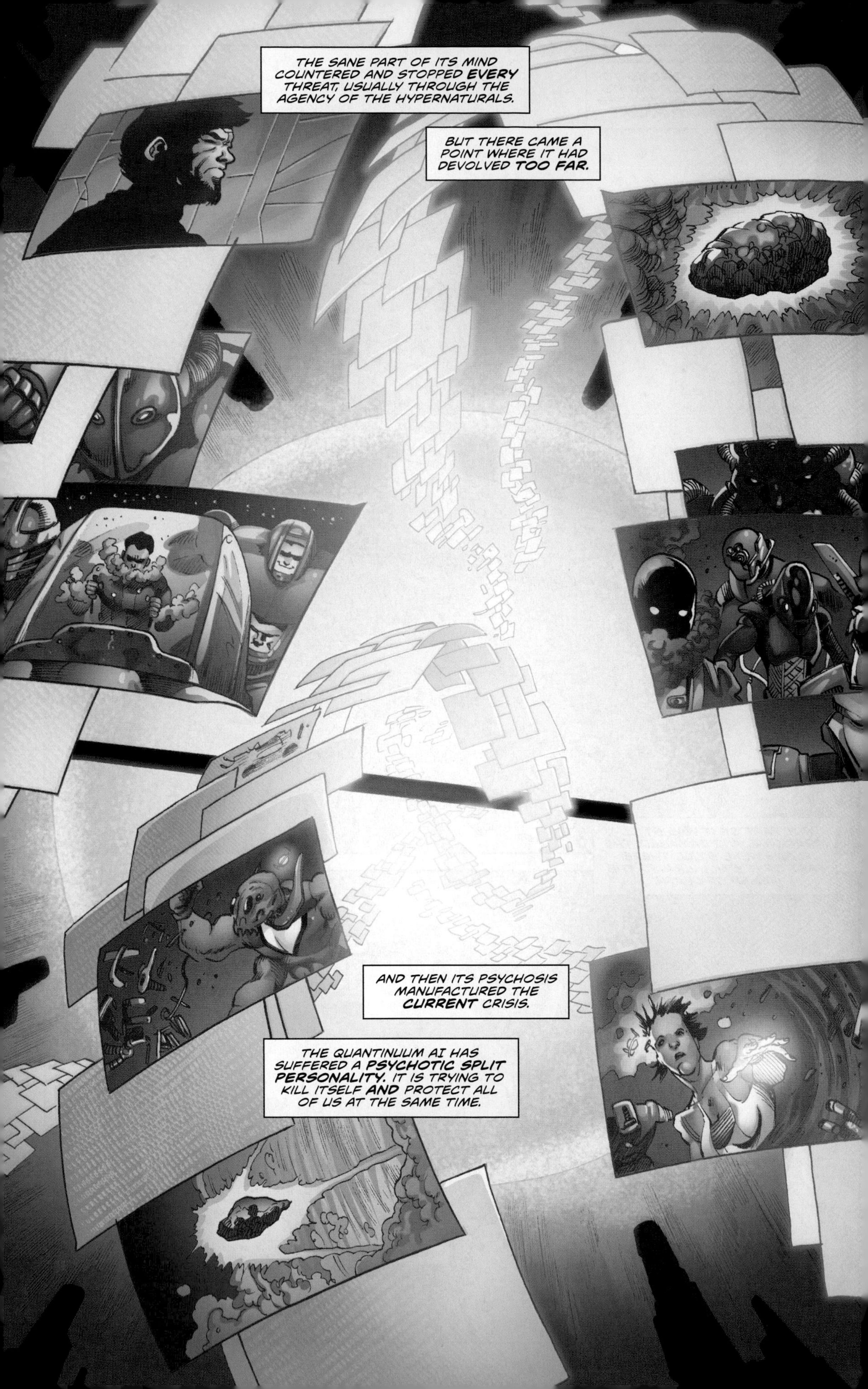
THE SANE PART OF ITS MIND COUNTERED AND STOPPED EVERY THREAT, USUALLY THROUGH THE AGENCY OF THE HYPERNATURALS.
BUT THERE CAME A POINT WHERE IT HAD DEVOLVED TOO FAR.
AND THEN ITS PSYCHOSIS MANUFACTURED THE CURRENT CRISIS.
THE QUANTINUUM AI HAS SUFFERED A PSYCHOTIC SPLIT PERSONALITY. IT IS TRYING TO KILL ITSELF AND PROTECT ALL OF US AT THE SAME TIME.

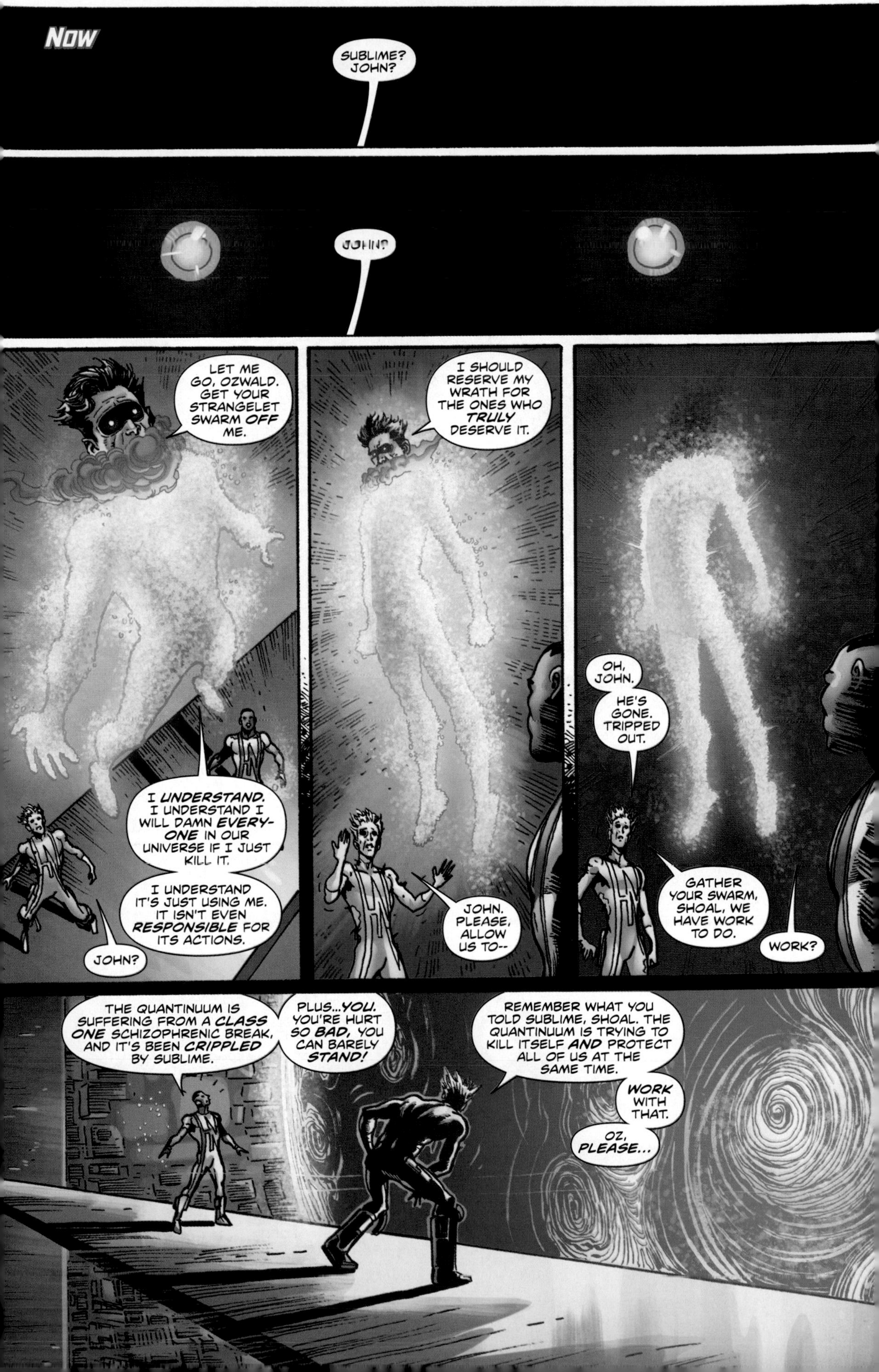
NOW
SUBLIME? JOHN?
JOHN?
LET ME GO, OZWALD. GET YOUR STRANGELET SWARM OFF ME.
I UNDERSTAND. I UNDERSTAND I WILL DAMN EVERY-ONE IN OUR UNIVERSE IF I JUST KILL IT.
I UNDERSTAND IT'S JUST USING ME. IT ISN'T EVEN RESPONSIBLE FOR ITS ACTIONS.
JOHN?
I SHOULD RESERVE MY WRATH FOR THE ONES WHO TRULY DESERVE IT.
JOHN. PLEASE, ALLOW US TO--
OH, JOHN.
HE'S GONE. TRIPPED OUT.
GATHER YOUR SWARM, SHOAL, WE HAVE WORK TO DO.
WORK?
THE QUANTINUUM IS SUFFERING FROM A CLASS ONE SCHIZOPHRENIC BREAK, AND IT'S BEEN CRIPPLED BY SUBLIME.
PLUS...YOU. YOU'RE HURT SO BAD, YOU CAN BARELY STAND!
REMEMBER WHAT YOU TOLD SUBLIME, SHOAL. THE QUANTINUUM IS TRYING TO KILL ITSELF AND PROTECT ALL OF US AT THE SAME TIME.
WORK WITH THAT.
OZ, PLEASE...

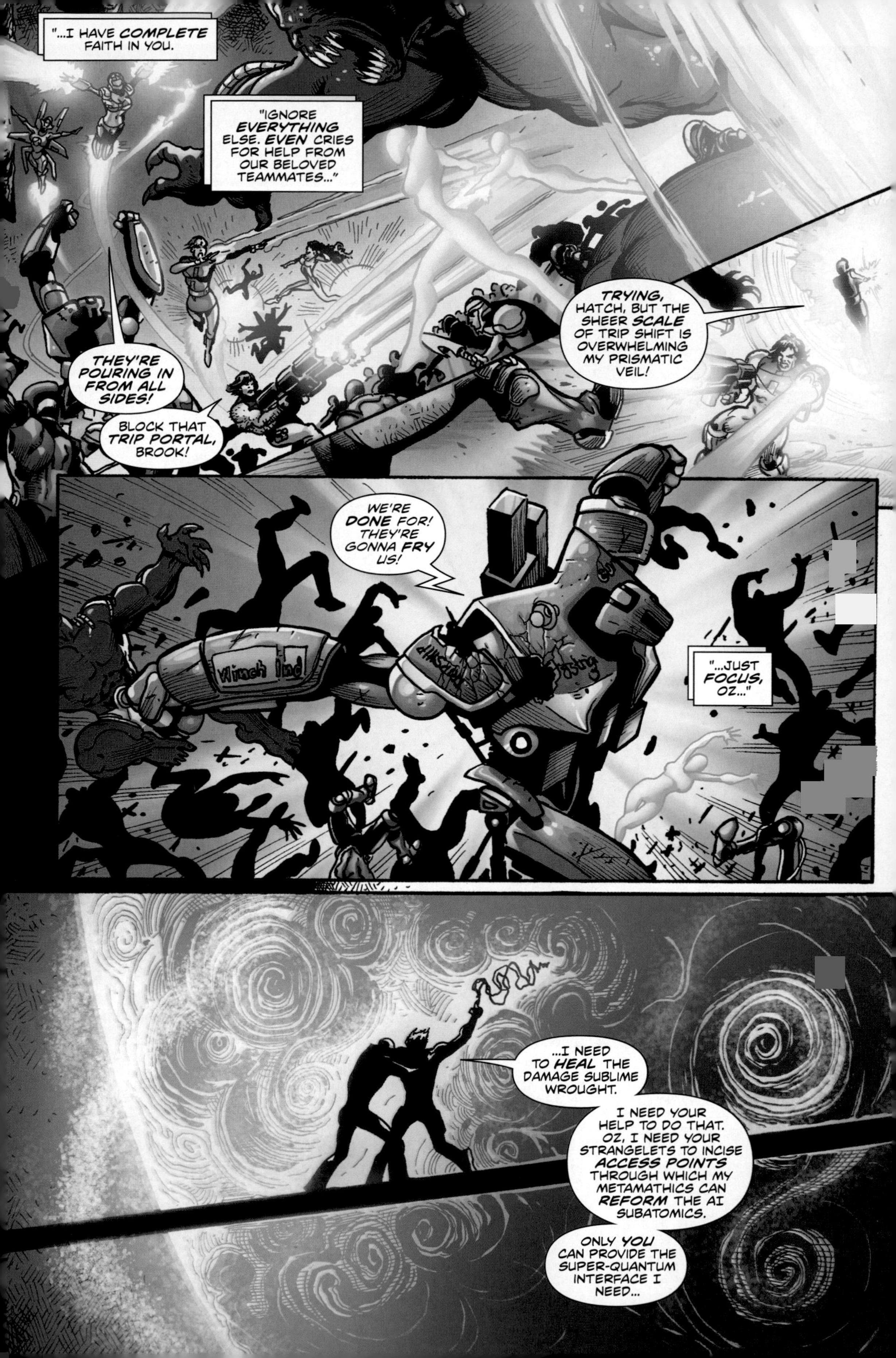
"...I HAVE COMPLETE FAITH IN YOU.
"IGNORE EVERYTHING ELSE. EVEN CRIES FOR HELP FROM OUR BELOVED TEAMMATES..."
THEY'RE POURING IN FROM ALL SIDES!
BLOCK THAT TRIP PORTAL, BROOK!
TRYING, HATCH, BUT THE SHEER SCALE OF TRIP SHIFT IS OVERWHELMING MY PRISMATIC VEIL!
WE'RE DONE FOR! THEY'RE GONNA FRY US!
"...JUST FOCUS, OZ..."
...I NEED TO HEAL THE DAMAGE SUBLIME WROUGHT.
I NEED YOUR HELP TO DO THAT. OZ, I NEED YOUR STRANGELETS TO INCISE ACCESS POINTS THROUGH WHICH MY METAMATHICS CAN REFORM THE AI SUBATOMICS.
ONLY YOU CAN PROVIDE THE SUPER-QUANTUM INTERFACE I NEED...

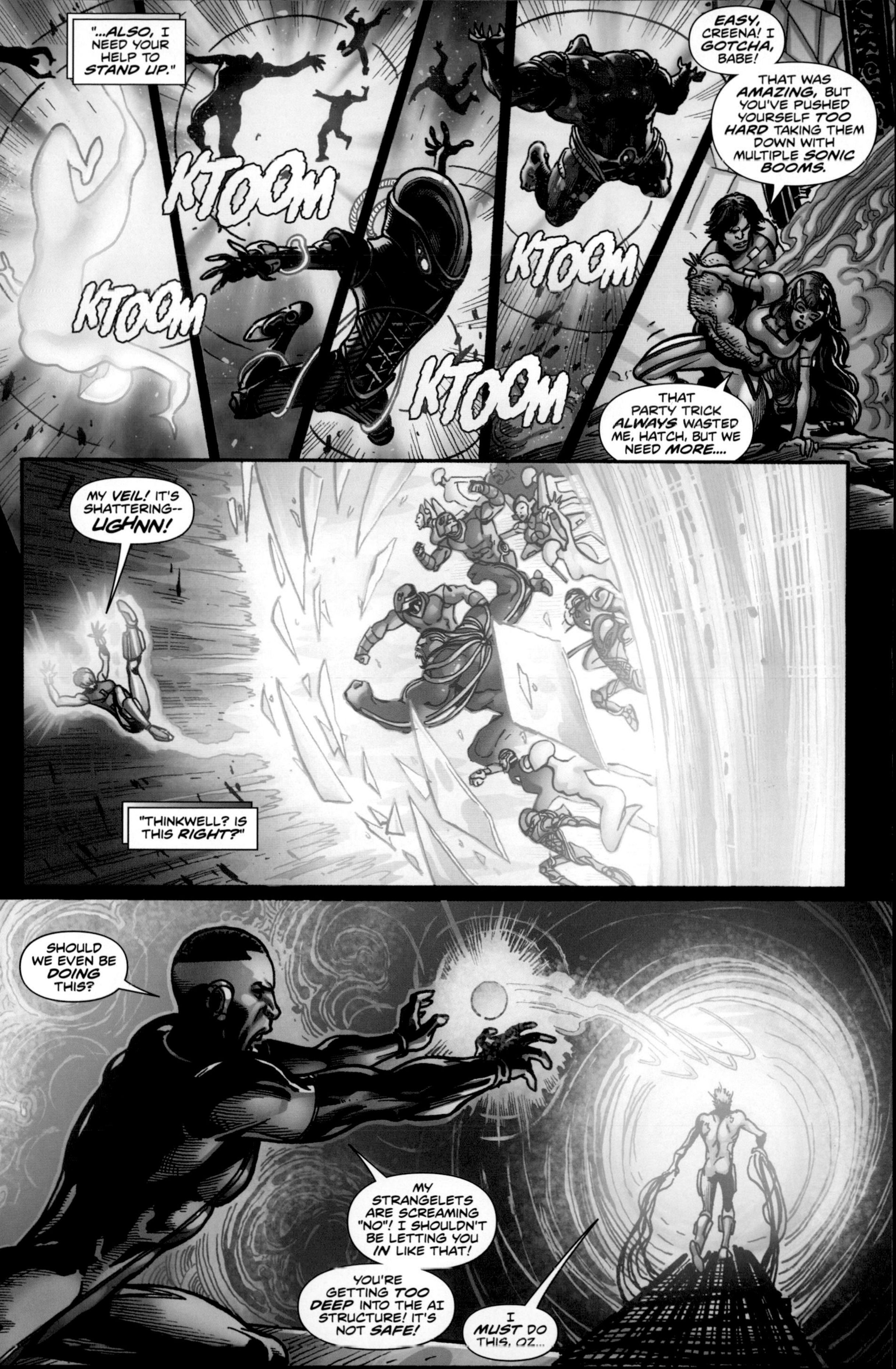
"...ALSO, I NEED YOUR HELP TO STAND UP."
KTOOM
KTOOM
KTOOM
KTOOM
EASY, CREENA! I GOTCHA, BABE!
THAT WAS AMAZING, BUT YOU'VE PUSHED YOURSELF TOO HARD TAKING THEM DOWN WITH MULTIPLE SONIC BOOMS.
THAT PARTY TRICK ALWAYS WASTED ME, HATCH, BUT WE NEED MORE....
MY VEIL! IT'S SHATTERING-- UGHNN!
"THINKWELL? IS THIS RIGHT?"
SHOULD WE EVEN BE DOING THIS?
MY STRANGELETS ARE SCREAMING "NO"! I SHOULDN'T BE LETTING YOU IN LIKE THAT!
YOU'RE GETTING TOO DEEP INTO THE AI STRUCTURE! IT'S NOT SAFE!
I MUST DO THIS, OZ...

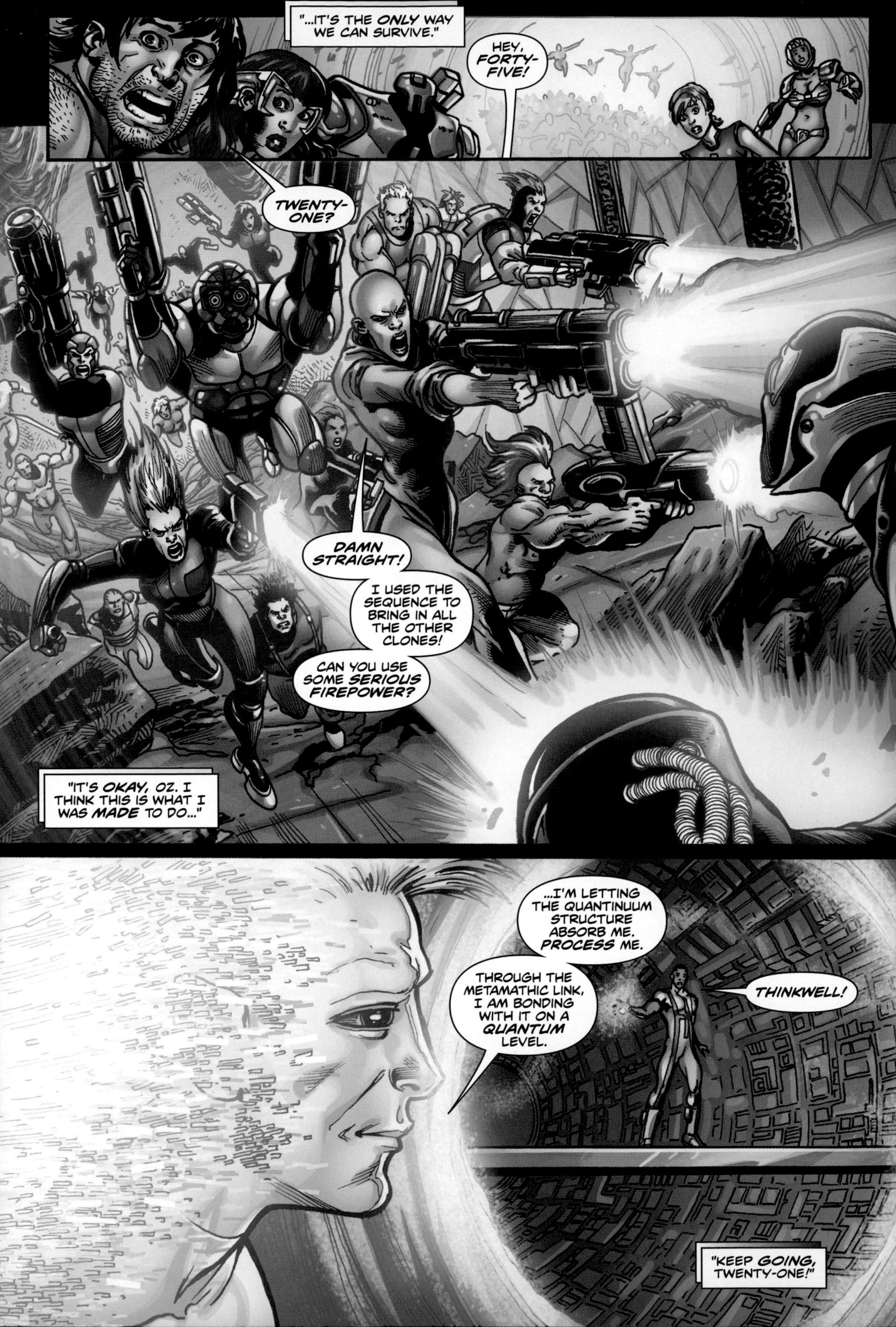
"...IT'S THE ONLY WAY WE CAN SURVIVE."
HEY, FORTY-FIVE!
TWENTY-ONE?
DAMN STRAIGHT!
I USED THE SEQUENCE TO BRING IN ALL THE OTHER CLONES!
CAN YOU USE SOME SERIOUS FIREPOWER?
"IT'S OKAY, OZ. I THINK THIS IS WHAT I WAS MADE TO DO..."
...I'M LETTING THE QUANTINUUM STRUCTURE ABSORB ME. PROCESS ME.
THROUGH THE METAMATHIC LINK, I AM BONDING WITH IT ON A QUANTUM LEVEL.
THINKWELL!
"KEEP GOING, TWENTY-ONE!"

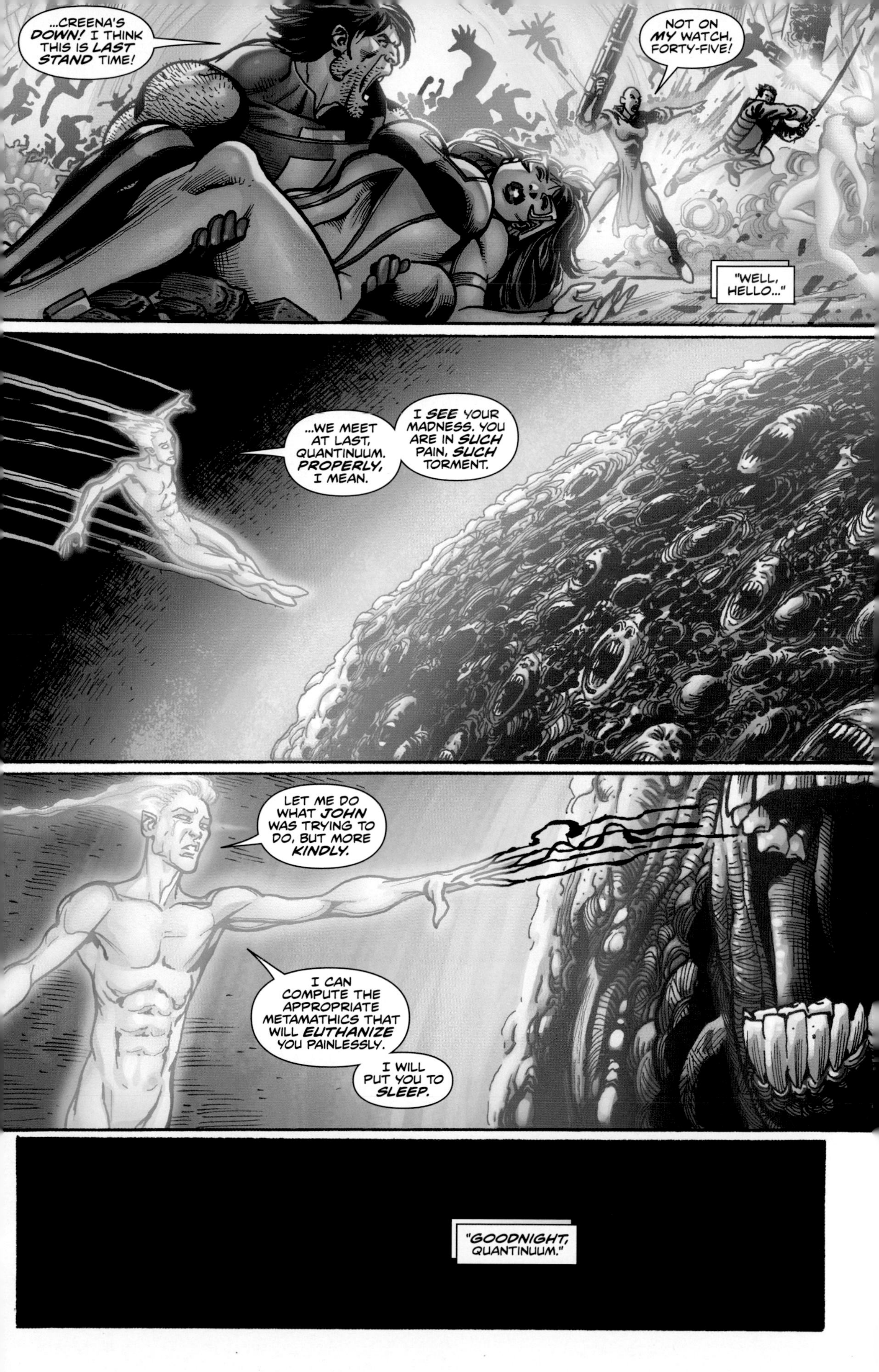
...CREENA'S DOWN! I THINK THIS IS LAST STAND TIME!
NOT ON MY WATCH, FORTY-FIVE!
"WELL, HELLO..."
...WE MEET AT LAST, QUANTINUUM. PROPERLY, I MEAN.
I SEE YOUR MADNESS. YOU ARE IN SUCH PAIN, SUCH TORMENT.
LET ME DO WHAT JOHN WAS TRYING TO DO, BUT MORE KINDLY.
I CAN COMPUTE THE APPROPRIATE METAMATHICS THAT WILL EUTHANIZE YOU PAINLESSLY.
I WILL PUT YOU TO SLEEP.
"GOODNIGHT, QUANTINUUM."

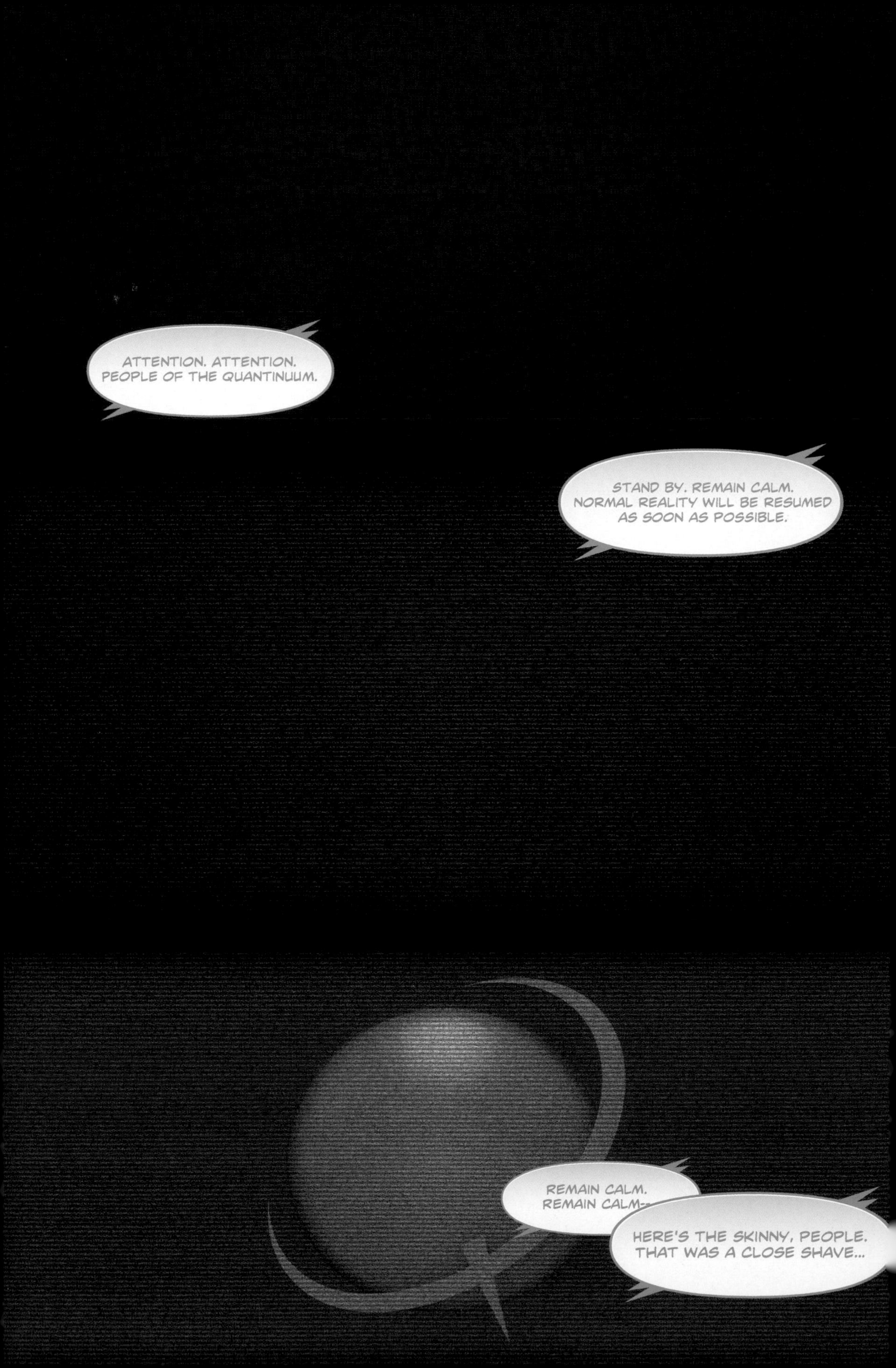
ATTENTION. ATTENTION. PEOPLE OF THE QUANTINUUM.
STAND BY. REMAIN CALM. NORMAL REALITY WILL BE RESUMED AS SOON AS POSSIBLE.
REMAIN CALM. REMAIN CALM--
HERE'S THE SKINNY, PEOPLE. THAT WAS A CLOSE SHAVE...

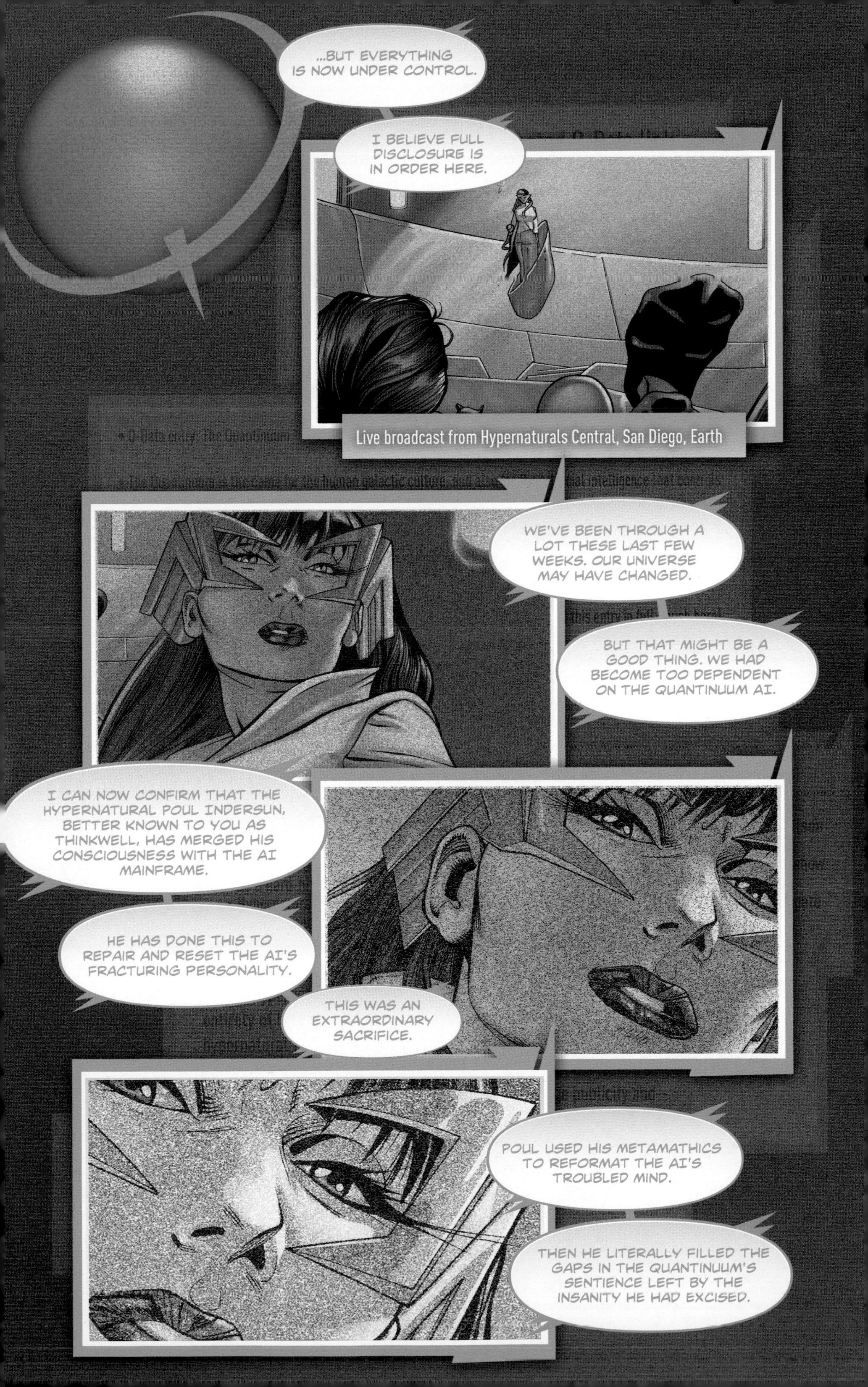
...BUT EVERYTHING IS NOW UNDER CONTROL.
I BELIEVE FULL DISCLOSURE IS IN ORDER HERE.
Live broadcast from Hypernaturals Central, San Diego, Earth
WE'VE BEEN THROUGH A LOT THESE LAST FEW WEEKS. OUR UNIVERSE MAY HAVE CHANGED.
BUT THAT MIGHT BE A GOOD THING. WE HAD BECOME TOO DEPENDENT ON THE QUANTINUUM AI.
I CAN NOW CONFIRM THAT THE HYPERNATURAL POUL INDERSUN, BETTER KNOWN TO YOU AS THINKWELL, HAS MERGED HIS CONSCIOUSNESS WITH THE AI MAINFRAME.
HE HAS DONE THIS TO REPAIR AND RESET THE AI'S FRACTURING PERSONALITY.
THIS WAS AN EXTRAORDINARY SACRIFICE.
POUL USED HIS METAMATHICS TO REFORMAT THE AI'S TROUBLED MIND.
THEN HE LITERALLY FILLED THE GAPS IN THE QUANTINUUM'S SENTIENCE LEFT BY THE INSANITY HE HAD EXCISED.

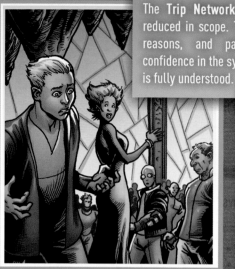

The **Trip Network** system has been greatly reduced in scope. This is partly due to safety reasons, and partly because of public confidence in the system now that its operation is fully understood.

PR reports suggest a system that sub-atomically annihilates someone and merely moves a copy of them in pattern form is not to be trusted.

Physical space travel has now re-emerged as the preferred form of interstellar travel. This will undoubtedly decelerate the processes of communication, travel and commerce within the Quantinuum.

However, the newly unveiled **helper drives**, which operate on layers of **mediated hyperspace**, will swiftly abolish all such lags.

The **helper drives** were donated to mankind by the **Nthites** in appreciation of our attempts to protect them.

The Hypernatural Program has re-organized its charter to create displaced teams that will protect the various quadrants of the Quantinuum.

TOUCH **HERE** TO CONTACT YOUR LOCAL HYPERNATURALS RESPONSE

The reactivated members of the **Clone Sequence** have been deputized to police remote or outlying regions.

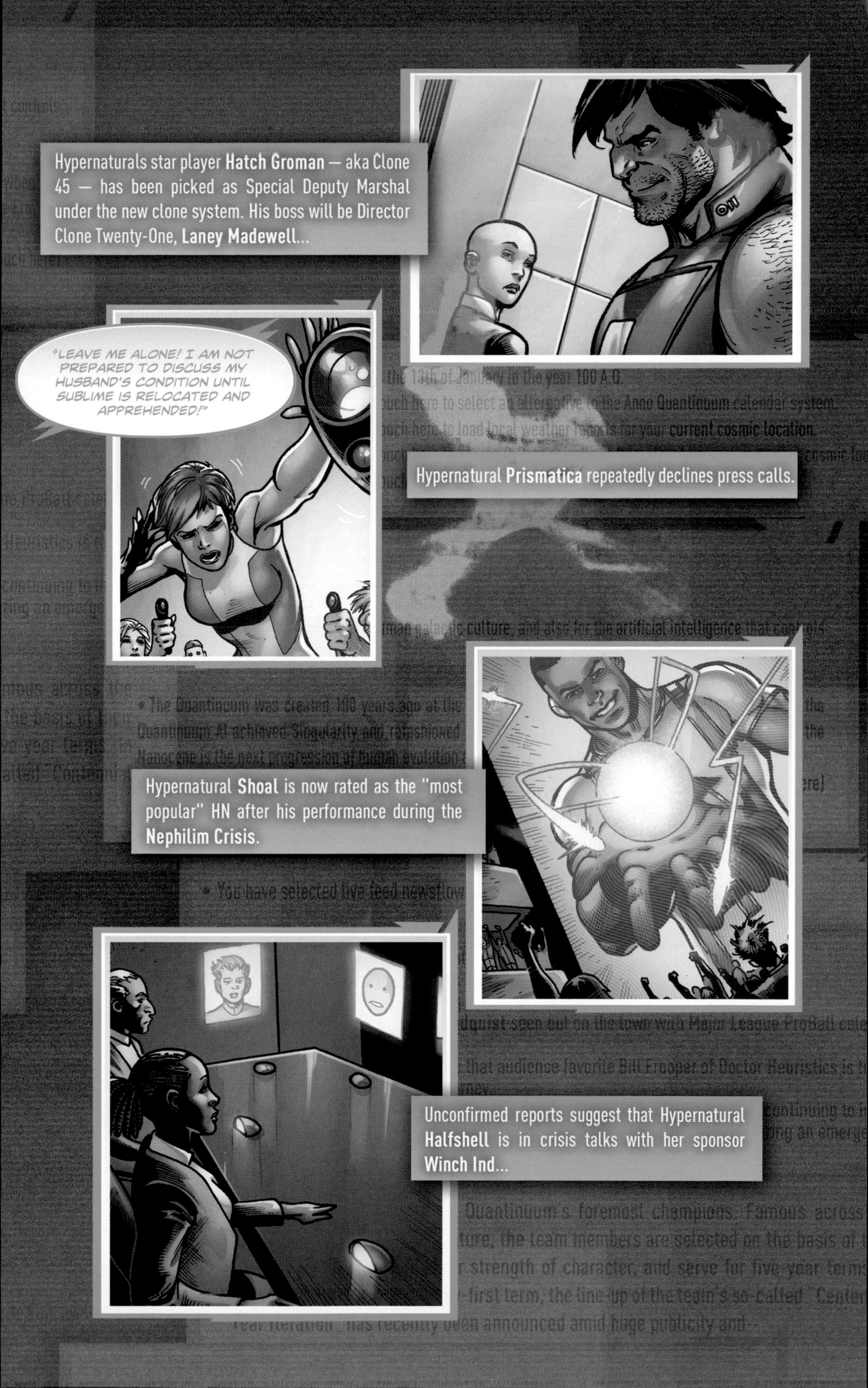
Hypernaturals star player Hatch Groman — aka Clone 45 — has been picked as Special Deputy Marshal under the new clone system. His boss will be Director Clone Twenty-One, Laney Madewell...
"LEAVE ME ALONE! I AM NOT PREPARED TO DISCUSS MY HUSBAND'S CONDITION UNTIL SUBLIME IS RELOCATED AND APPREHENDED!"
Hypernatural Prismatica repeatedly declines press calls.
Hypernatural Shoal is now rated as the "most popular" HN after his performance during the Nephilim Crisis.
Unconfirmed reports suggest that Hypernatural Halfshell is in crisis talks with her sponsor Winch Ind...

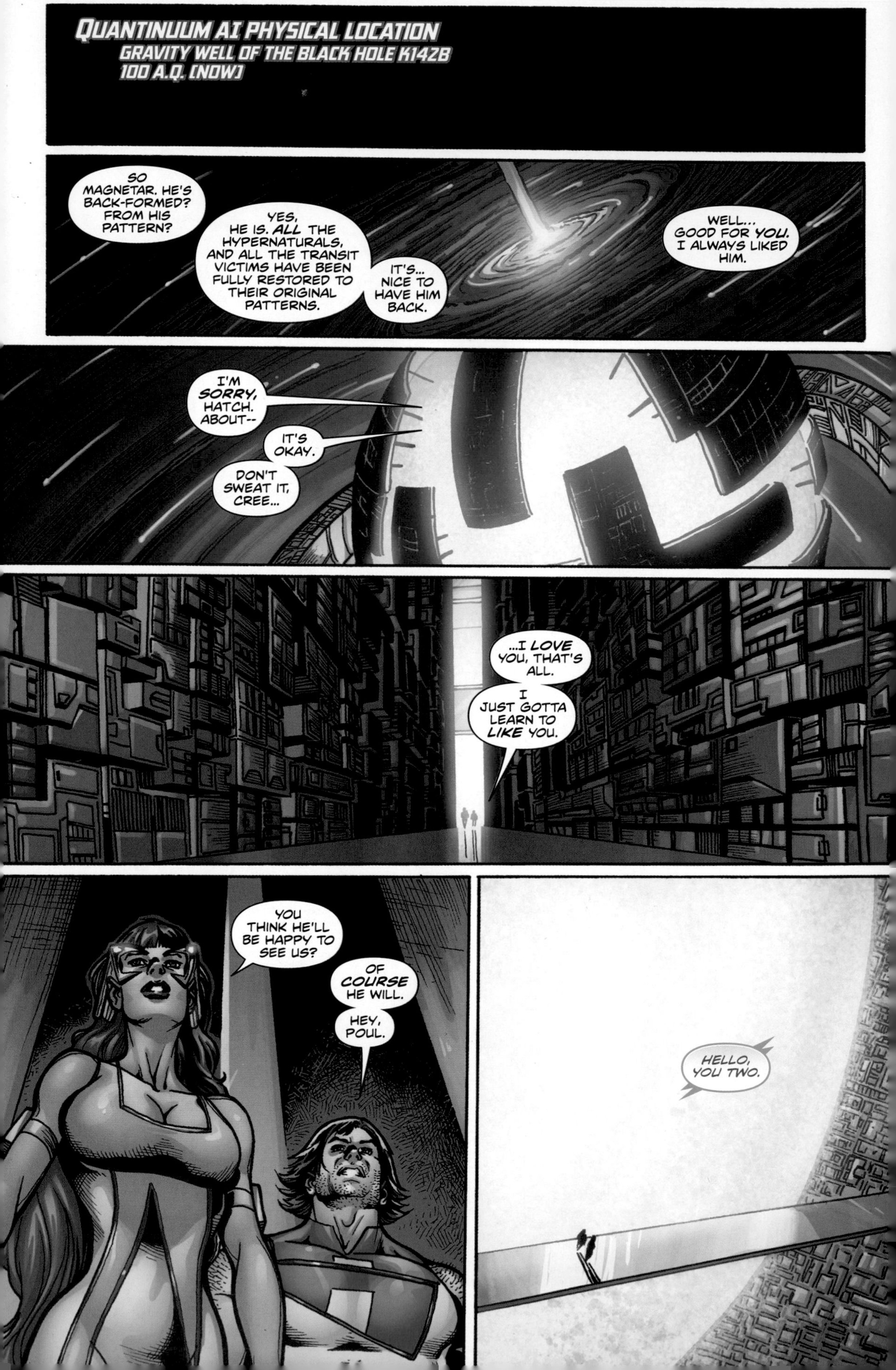
QUANTINUUM AI PHYSICAL LOCATION
GRAVITY WELL OF THE BLACK HOLE K142B
100 A.Q. [NOW]
SO MAGNETAR. HE'S BACK-FORMED? FROM HIS PATTERN?
YES, HE IS. ALL THE HYPERNATURALS, AND ALL THE TRANSIT VICTIMS HAVE BEEN FULLY RESTORED TO THEIR ORIGINAL PATTERNS.
IT'S... NICE TO HAVE HIM BACK.
WELL... GOOD FOR YOU. I ALWAYS LIKED HIM.
I'M SORRY, HATCH. ABOUT--
IT'S OKAY.
DON'T SWEAT IT, CREE...
...I LOVE YOU, THAT'S ALL.
I JUST GOTTA LEARN TO LIKE YOU.
YOU THINK HE'LL BE HAPPY TO SEE US?
OF COURSE HE WILL.
HEY, POUL.
HELLO, YOU TWO.

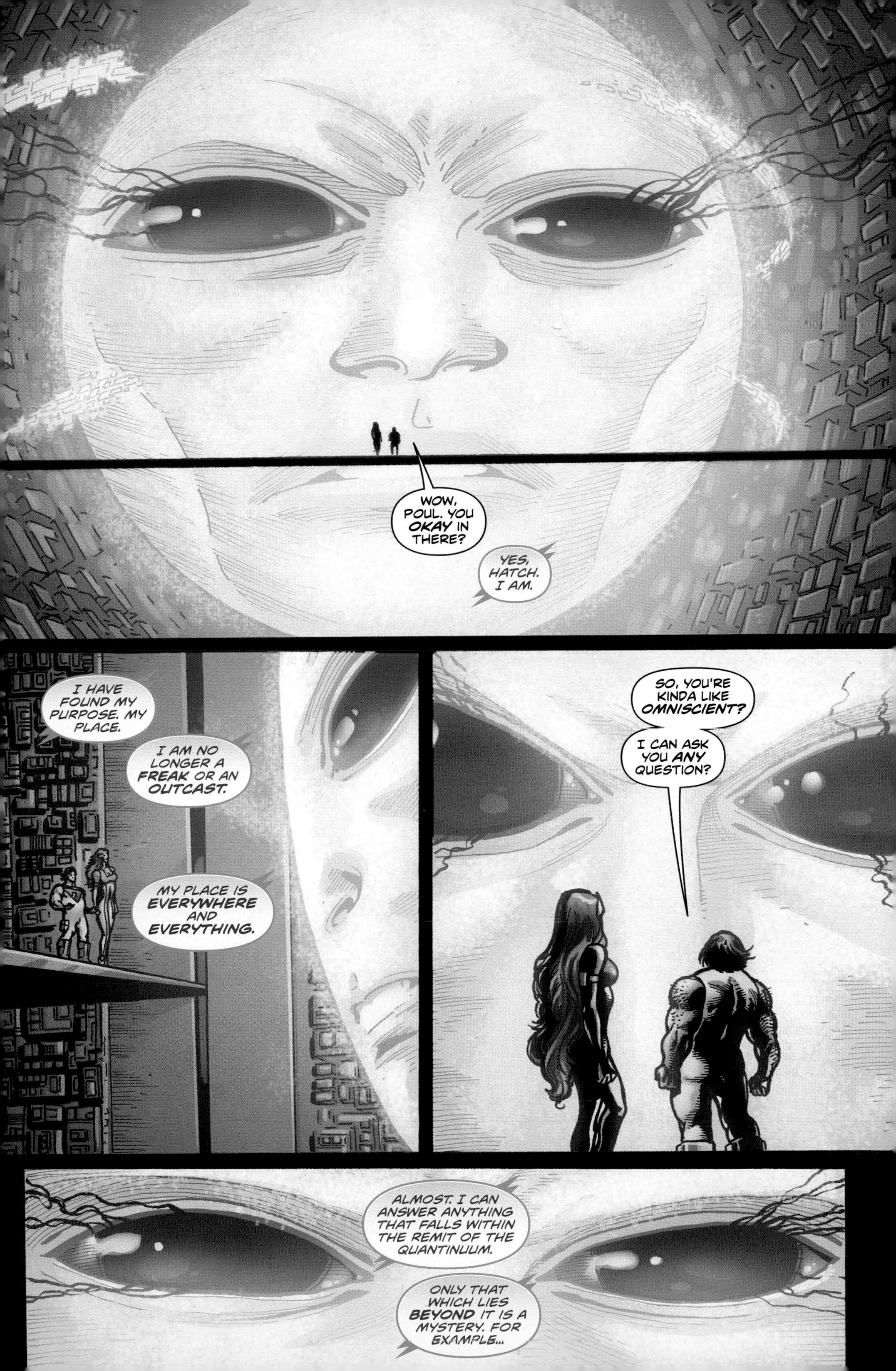

WOW, POUL. YOU OKAY IN THERE?
YES, HATCH. I AM.
I HAVE FOUND MY PURPOSE. MY PLACE.
I AM NO LONGER A FREAK OR AN OUTCAST.
MY PLACE IS EVERYWHERE AND EVERYTHING.
SO, YOU'RE KINDA LIKE OMNISCIENT?
I CAN ASK YOU ANY QUESTION?
ALMOST. I CAN ANSWER ANYTHING THAT FALLS WITHIN THE REMIT OF THE QUANTINUUM.
ONLY THAT WHICH LIES BEYOND IT IS A MYSTERY. FOR EXAMPLE...

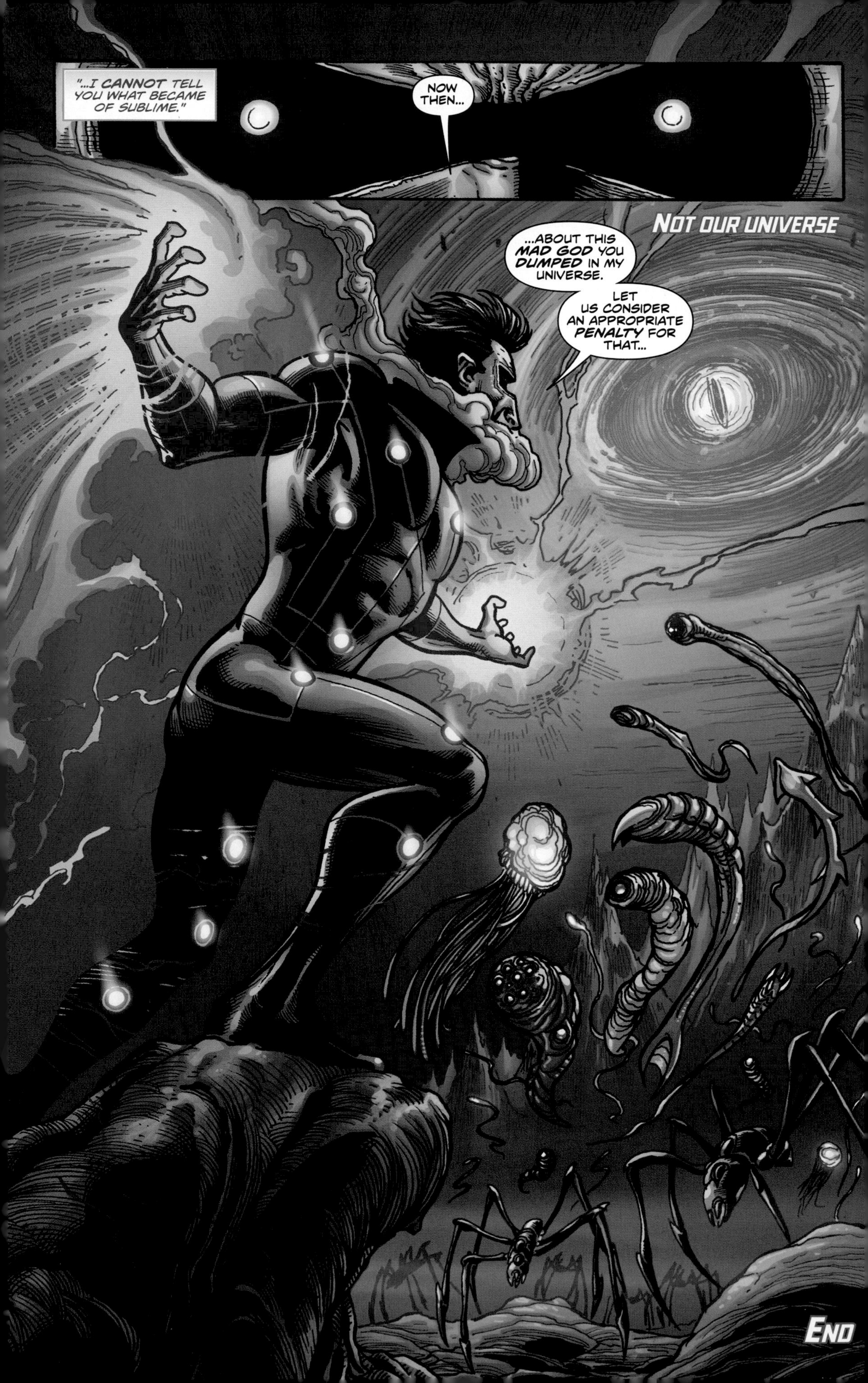
"...I CANNOT TELL YOU WHAT BECAME OF SUBLIME."
NOW THEN...
NOT OUR UNIVERSE
...ABOUT THIS MAD GOD YOU DUMPED IN MY UNIVERSE.
LET US CONSIDER AN APPROPRIATE PENALTY FOR THAT...
END

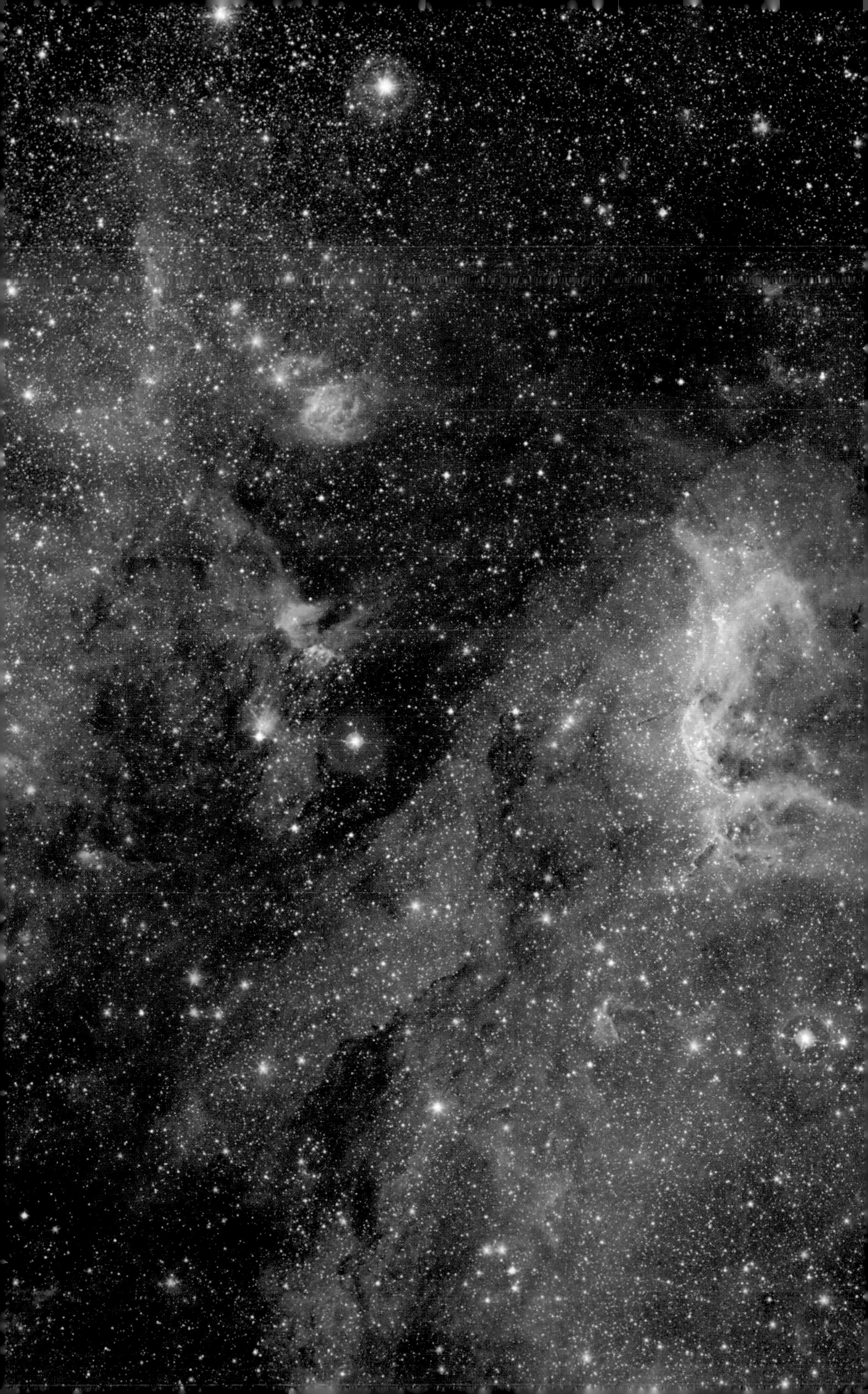

COVER GALLERY

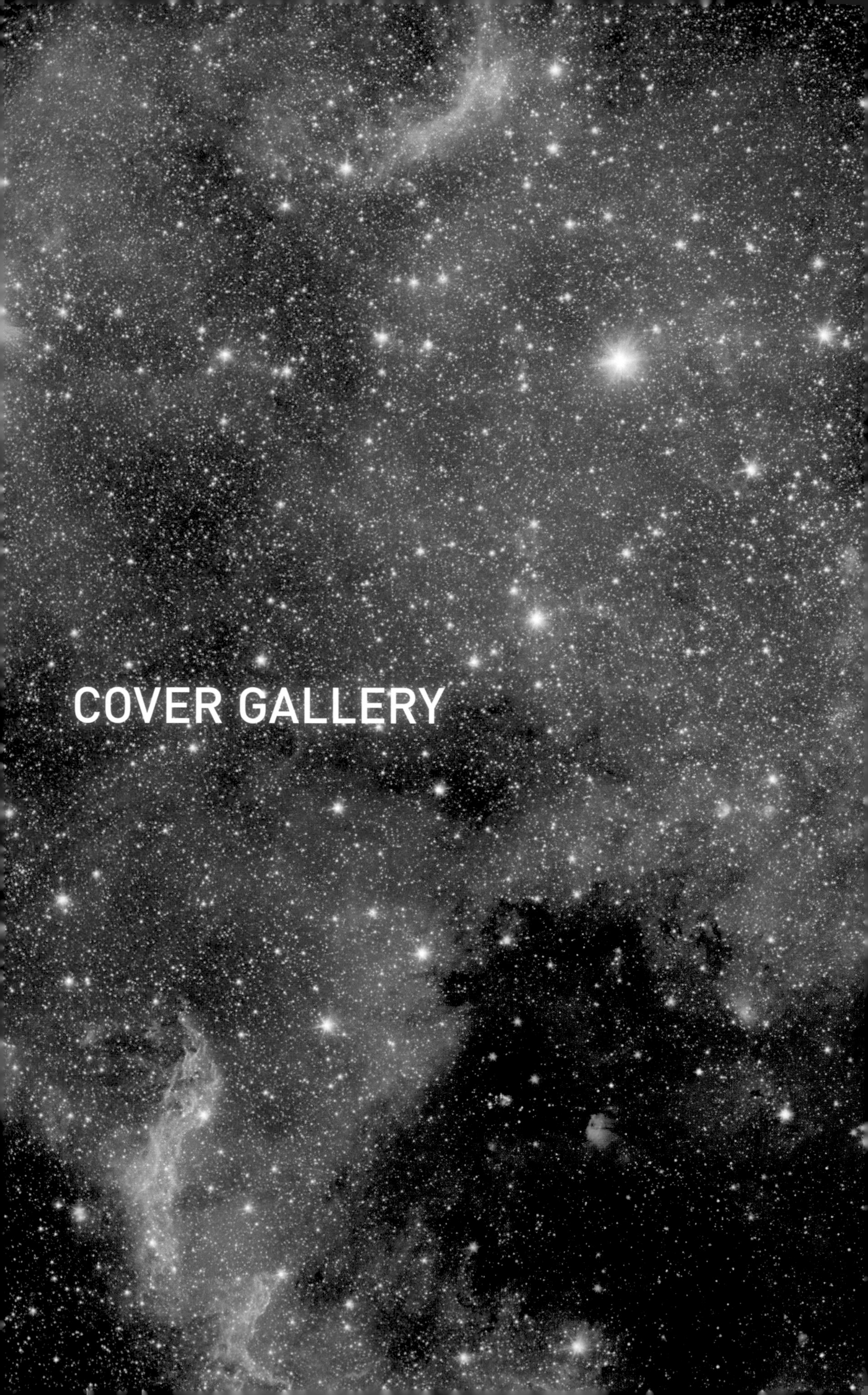

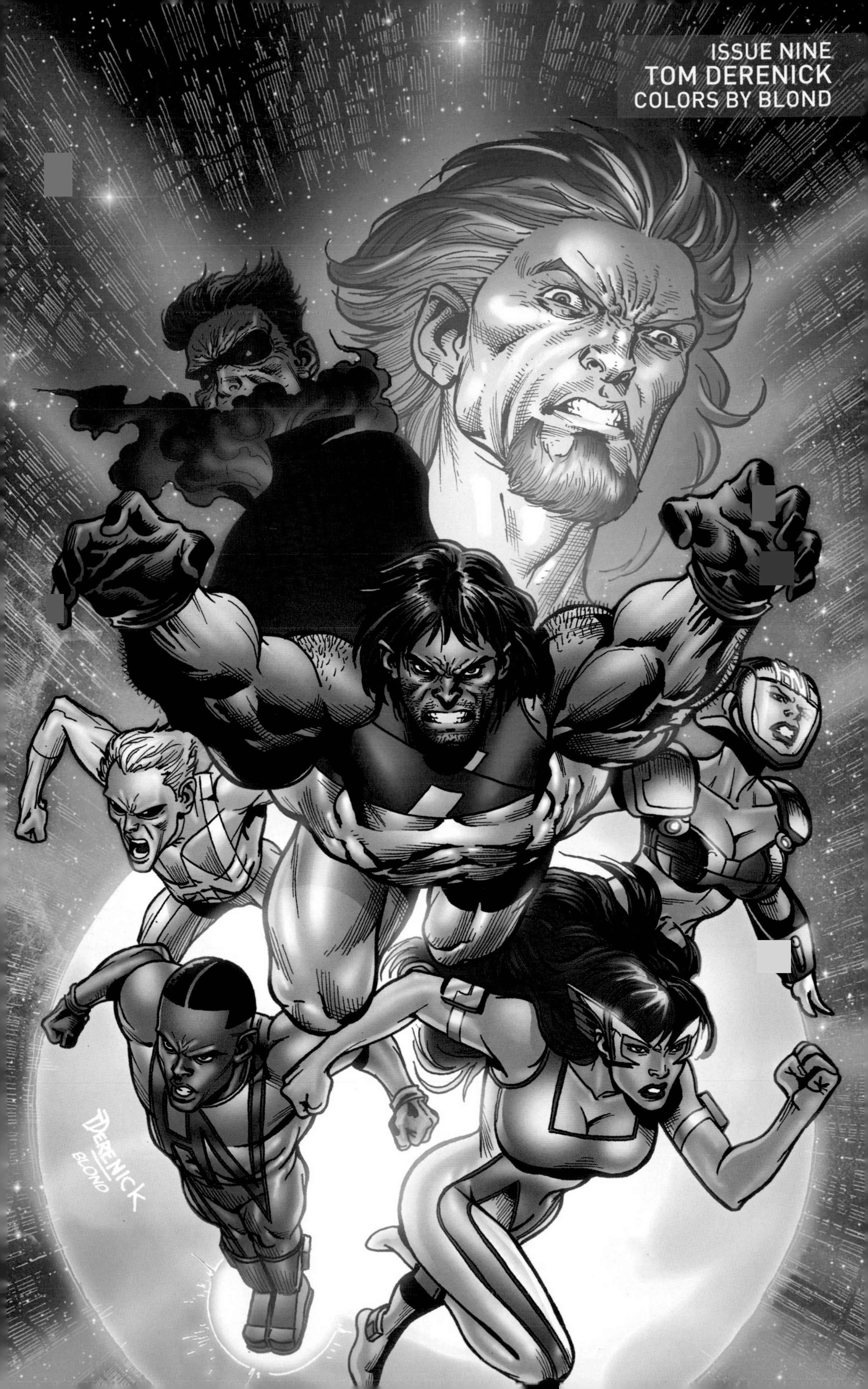
ISSUE NINE
TOM DERENICK
COLORS BY BLOND
DERENICK
BLOND

ISSUE NINE
KRIS ANKA

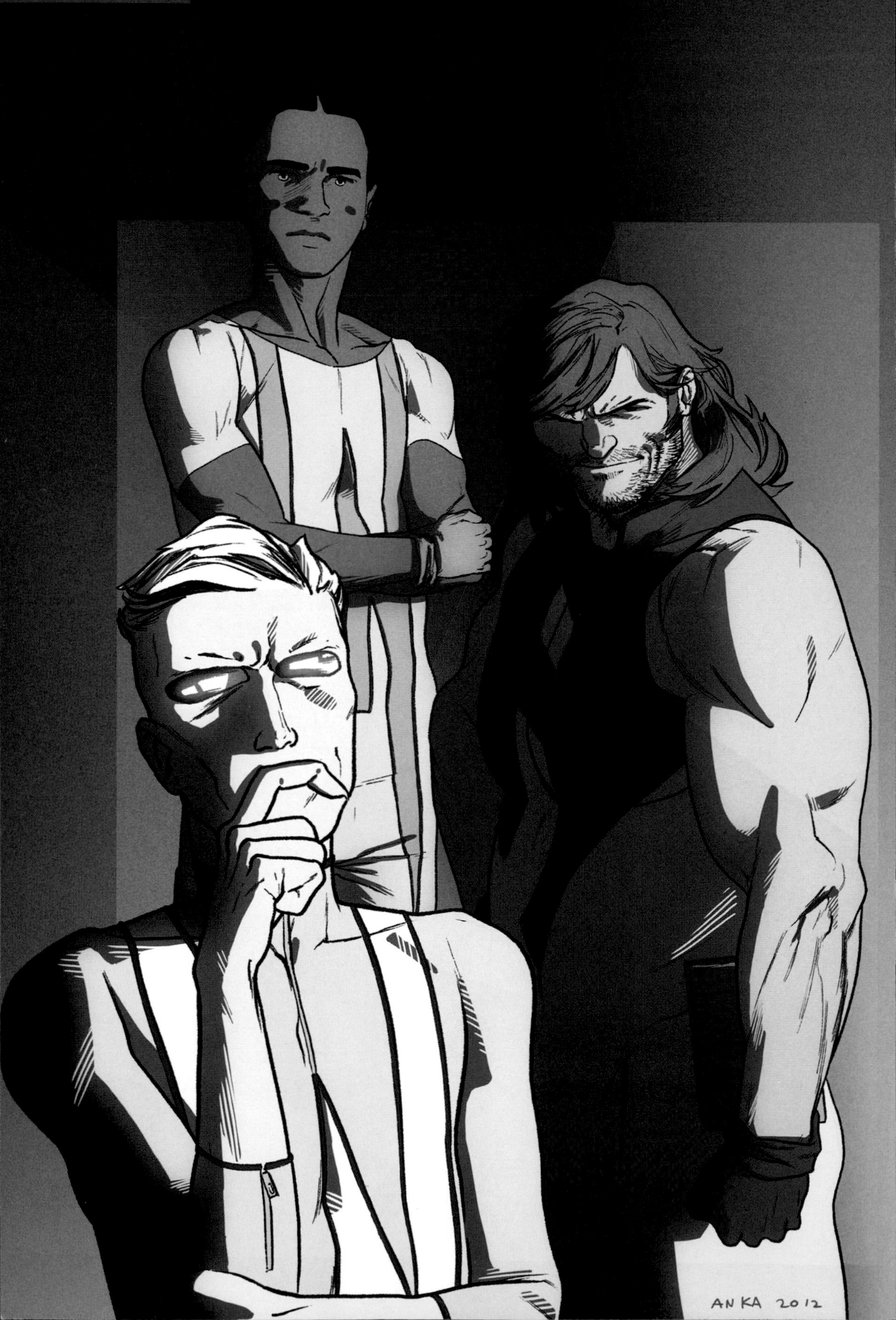
ANKA 2012

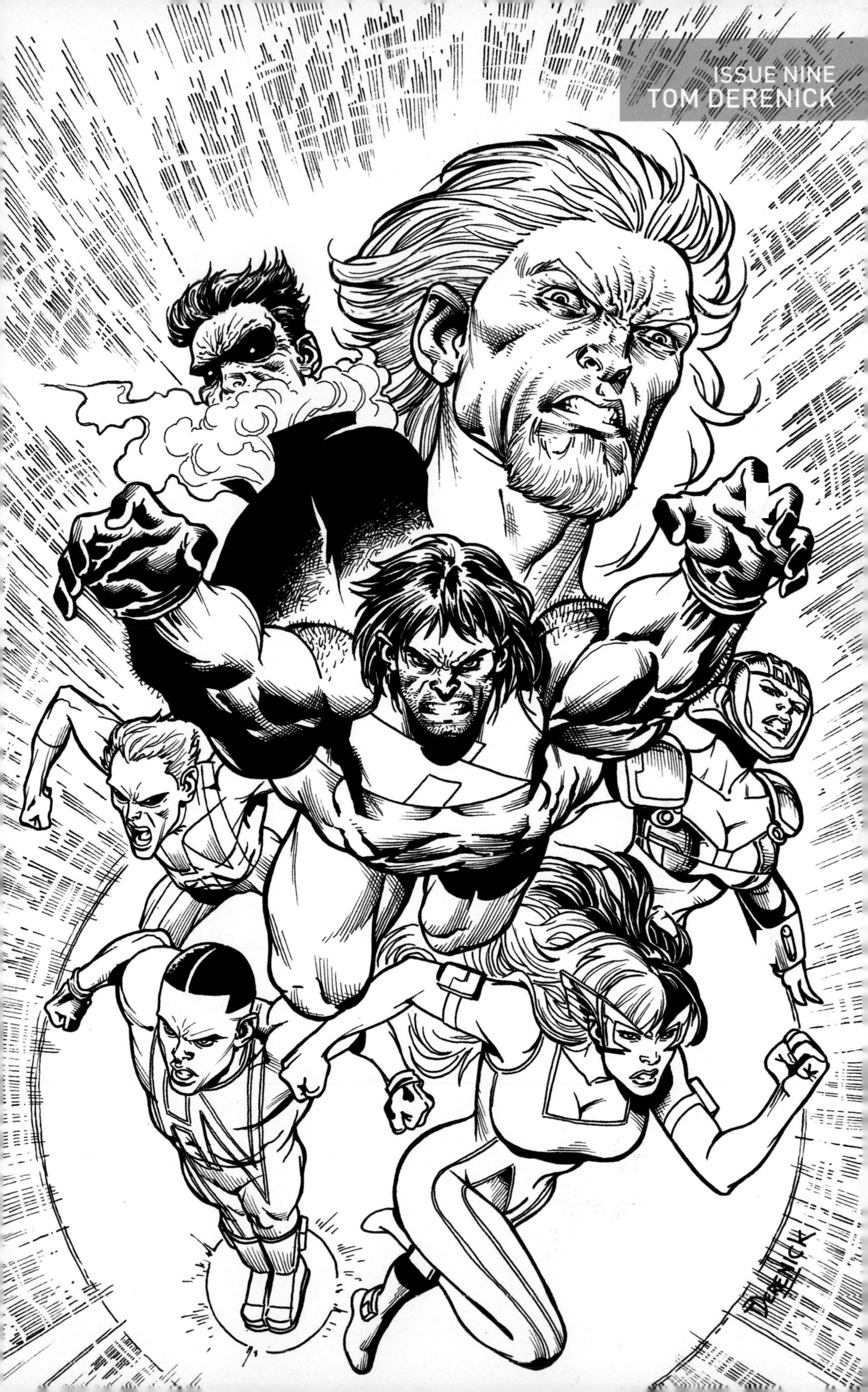
DERENICK

ISSUE NINE
TOM DERENICK

ISSUE TEN
TOM DERENICK
COLORS BY BLOND

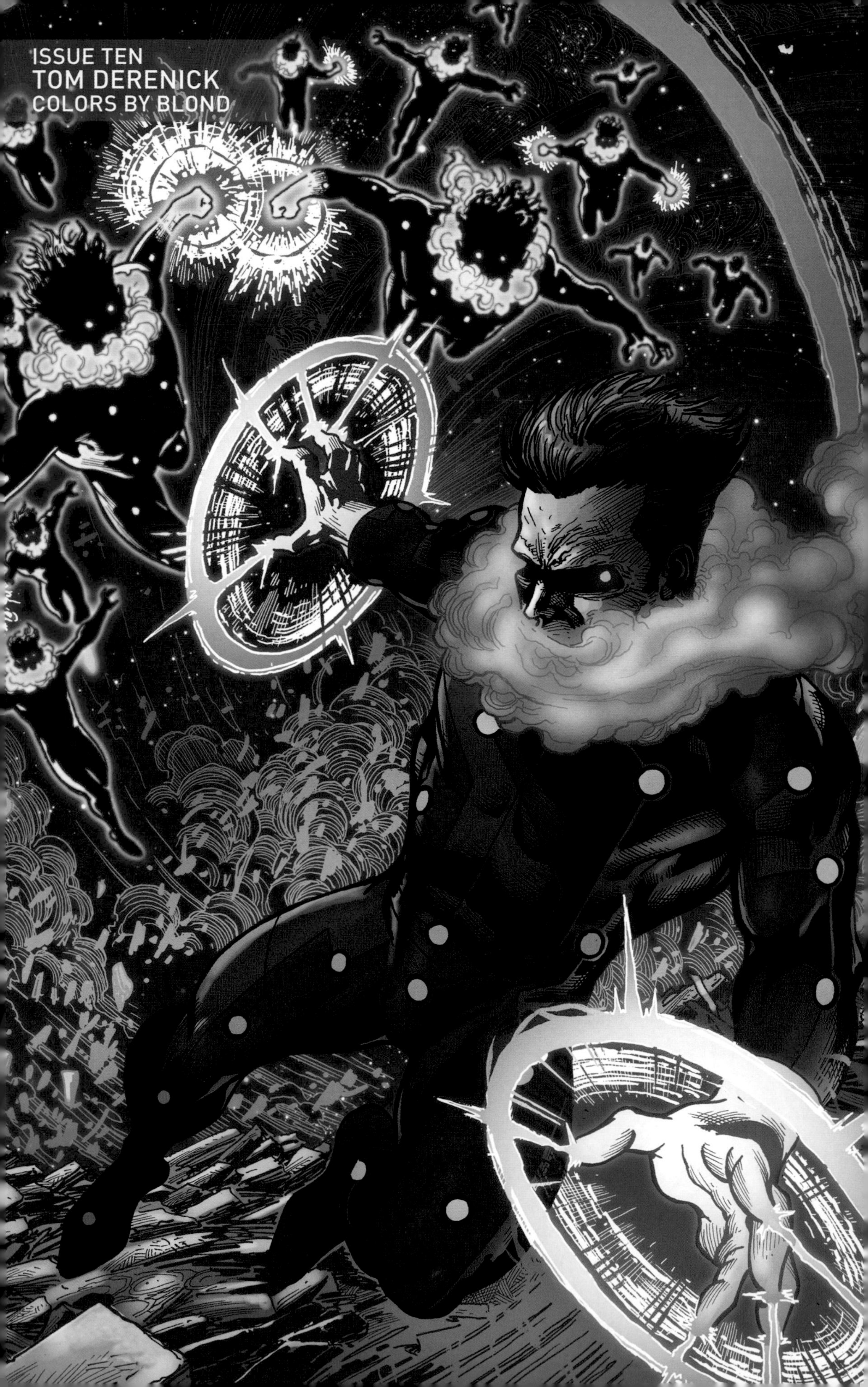

ISSUE ELEVEN
KRIS ANKA

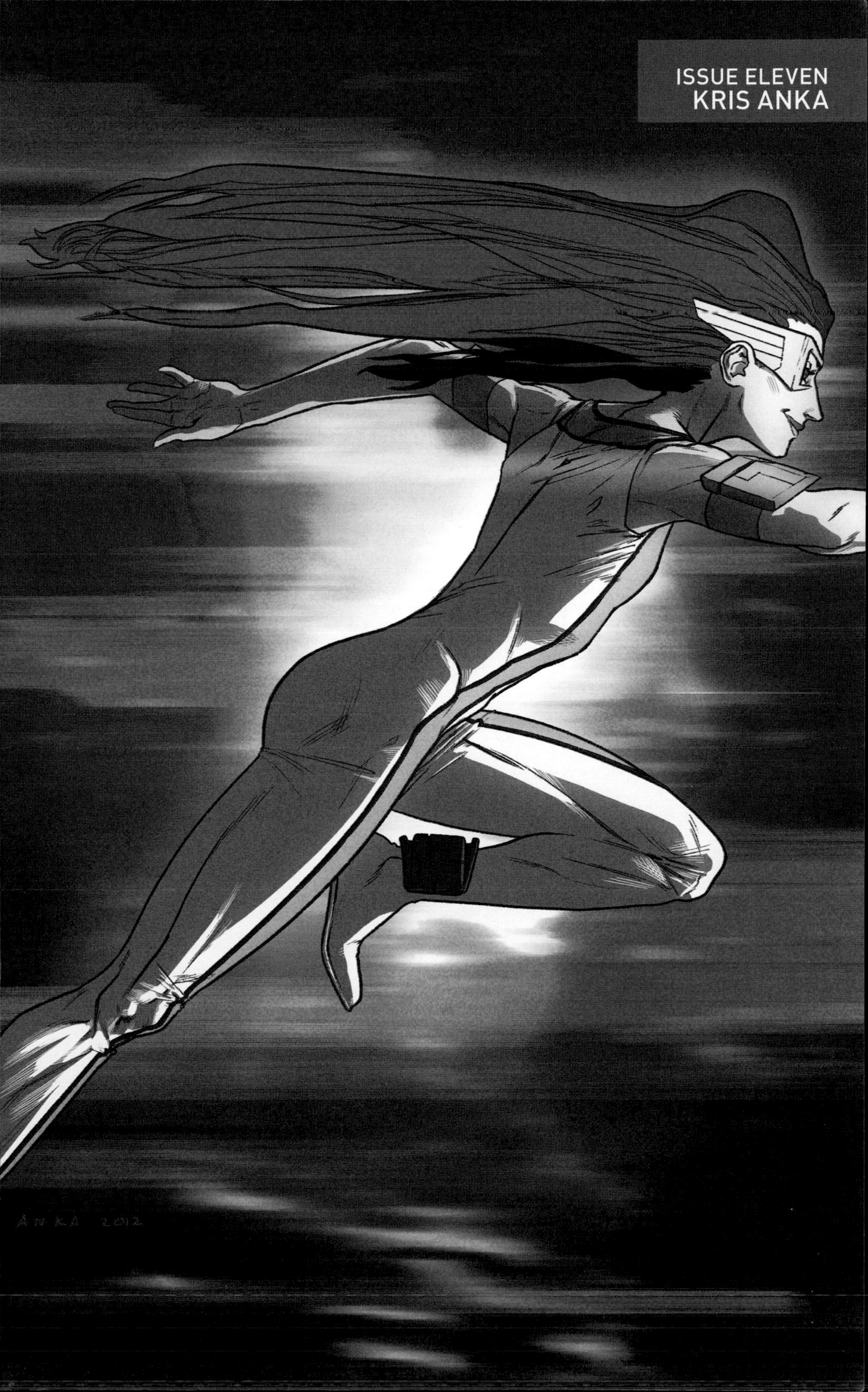
ANKA 2012

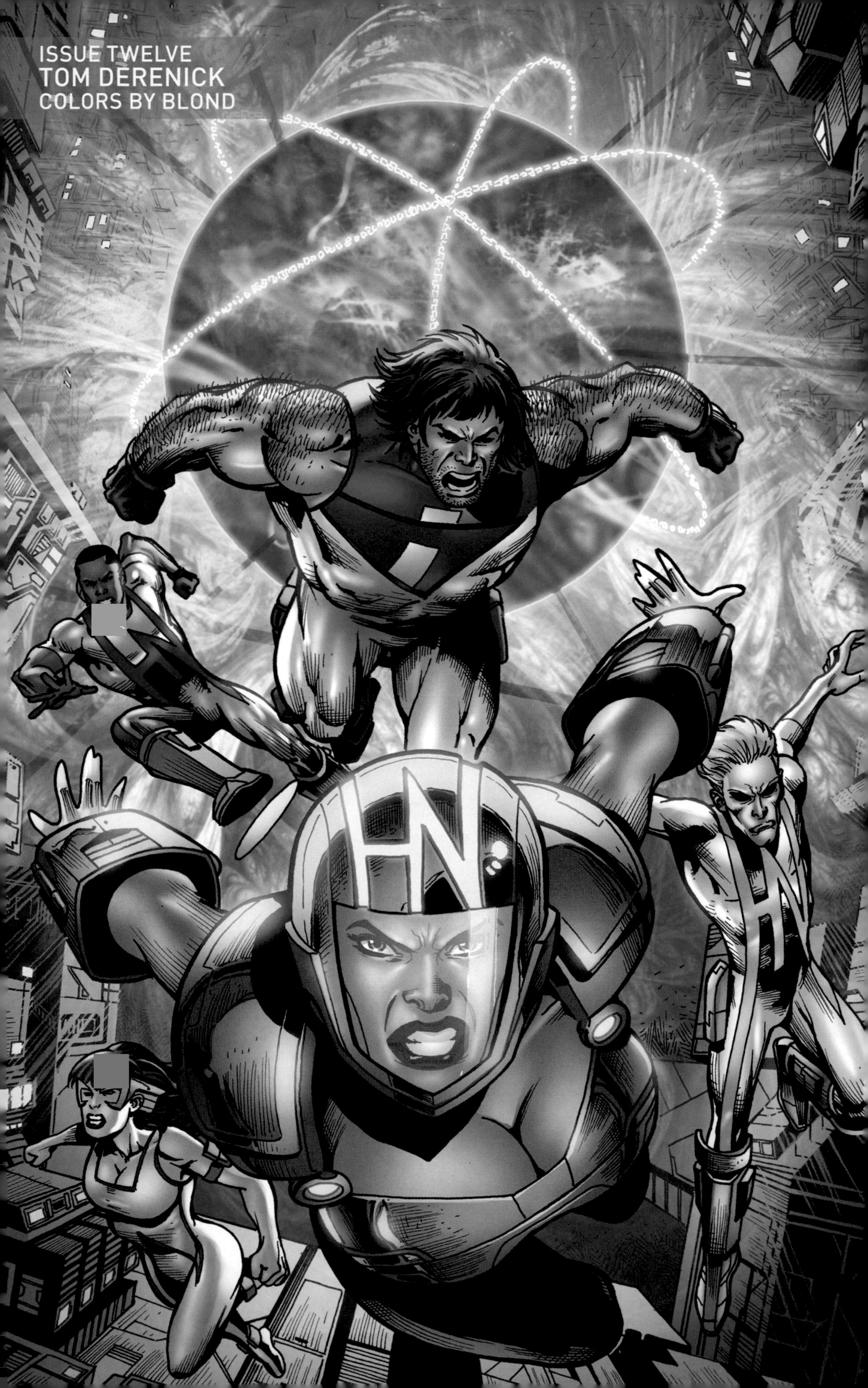
ISSUE TWELVE
TOM DERENICK
COLORS BY BLOND

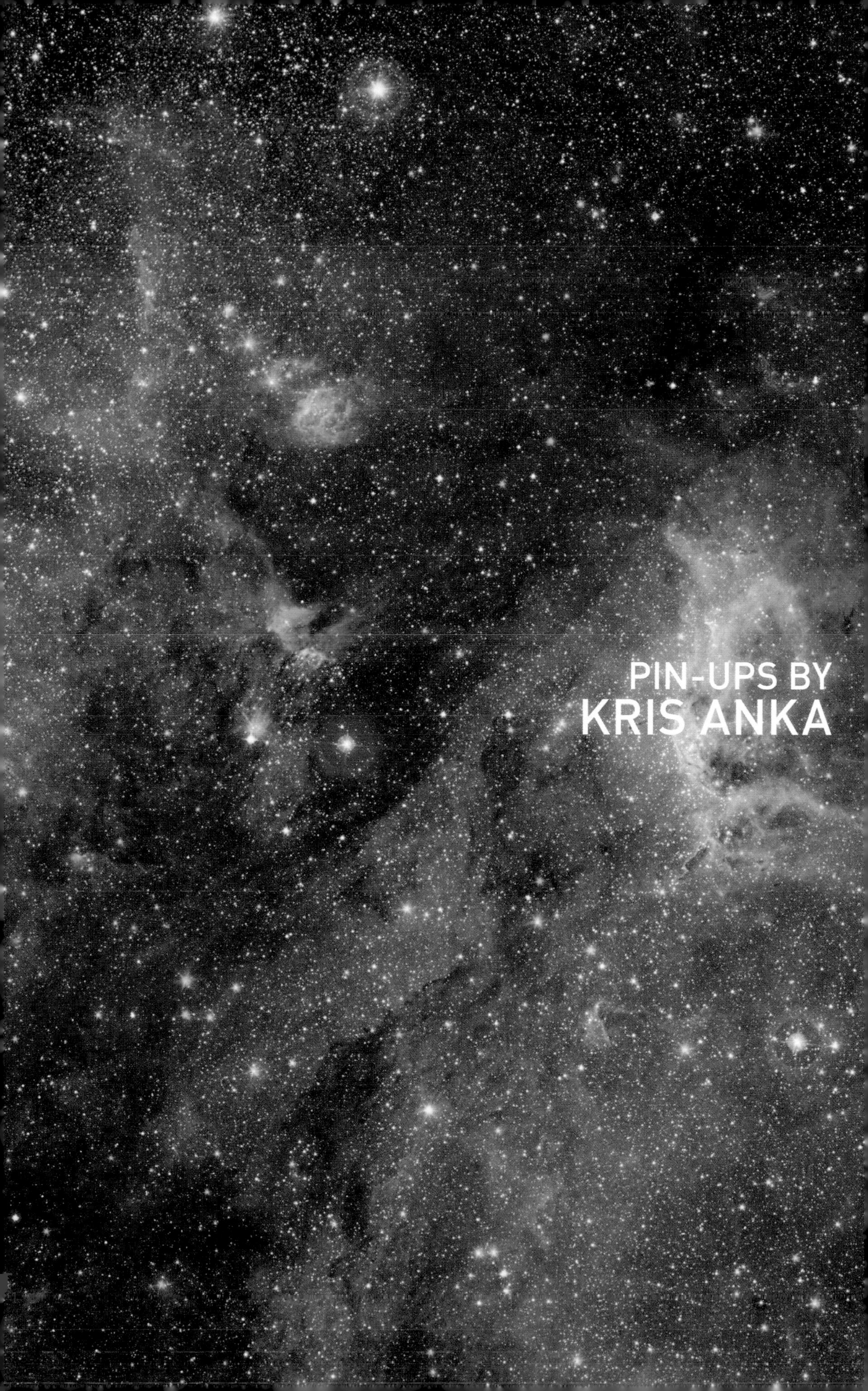
PIN-UPS BY
KRIS ANKA

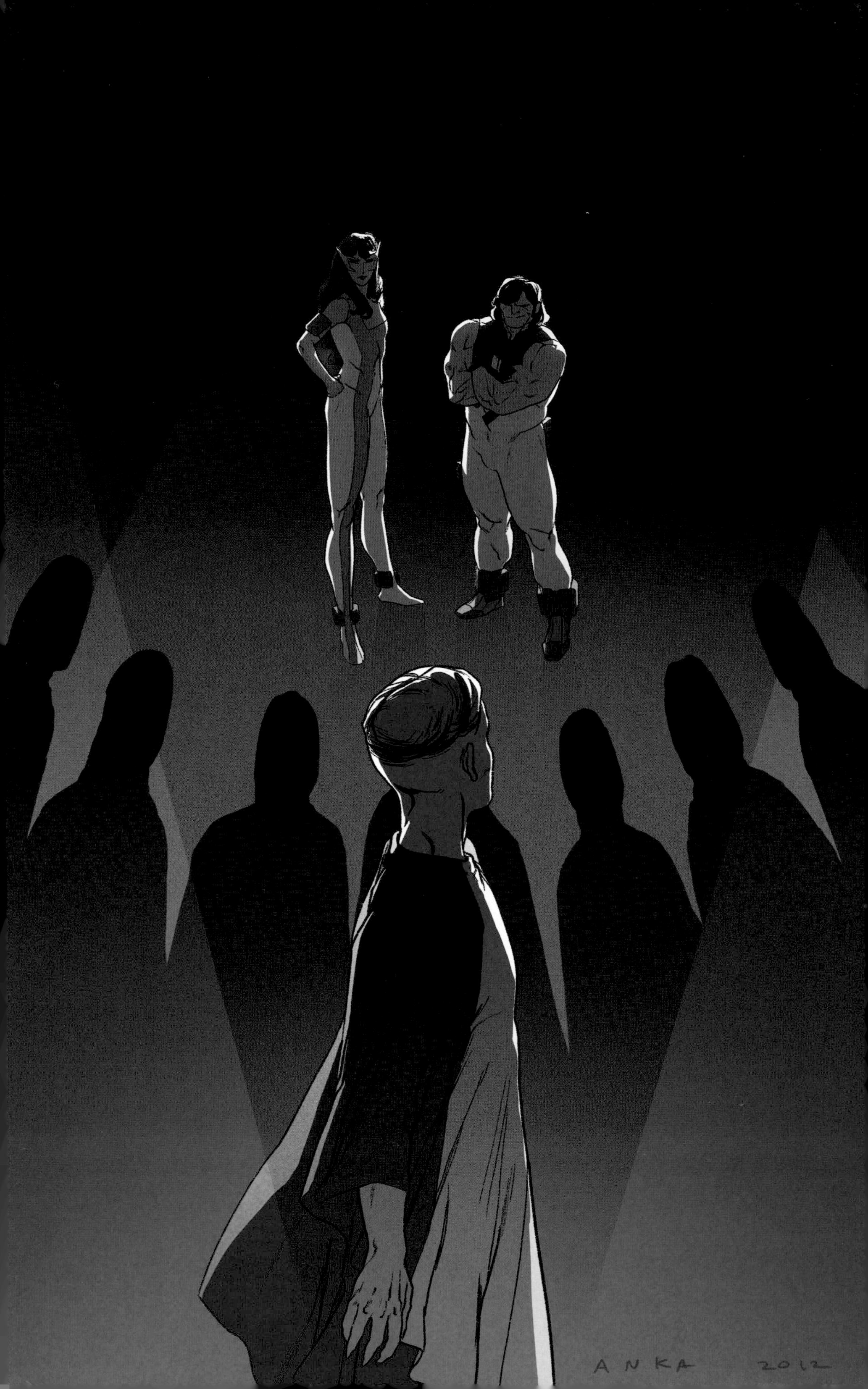
ANKA 2012

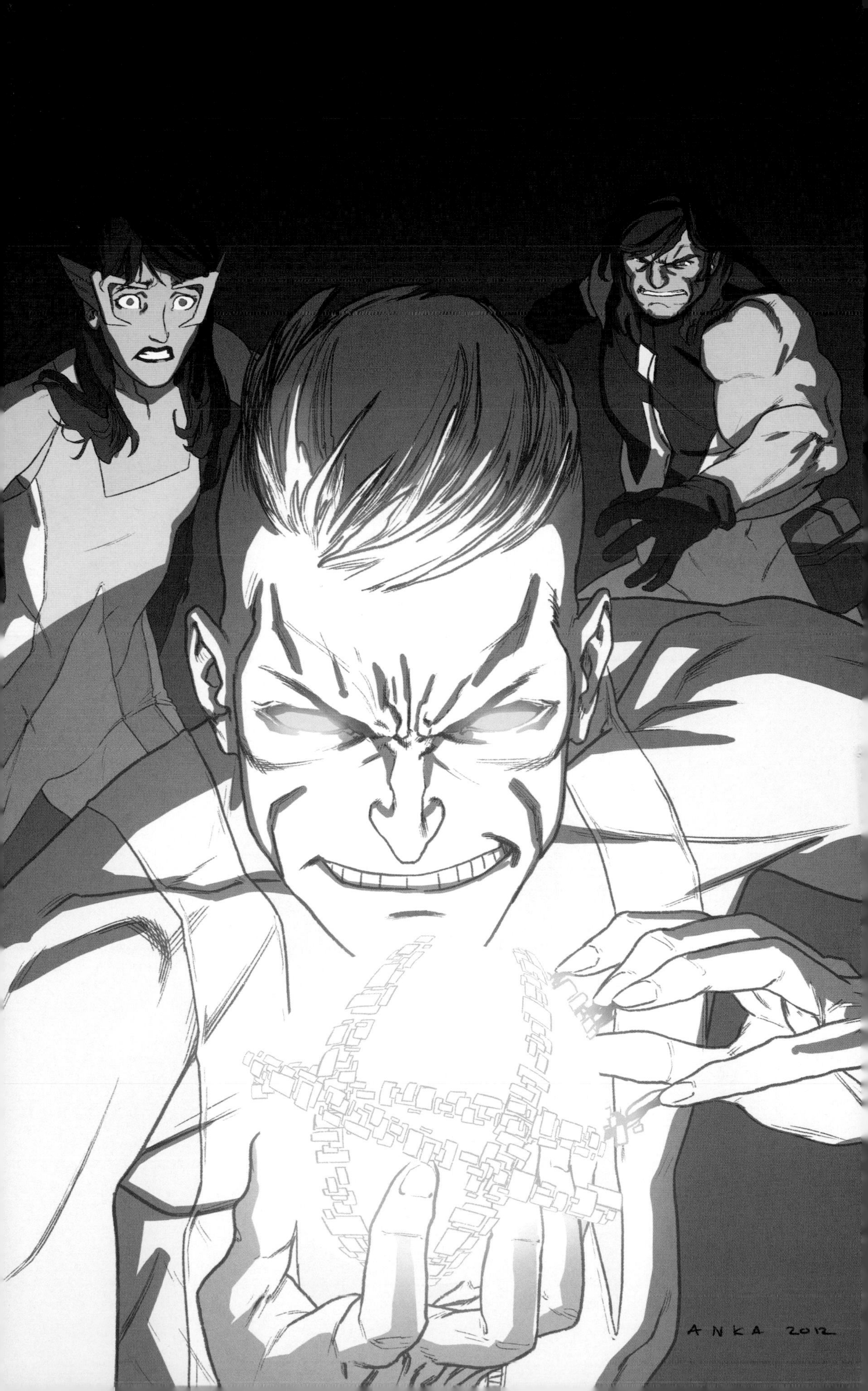
ANKA 2012

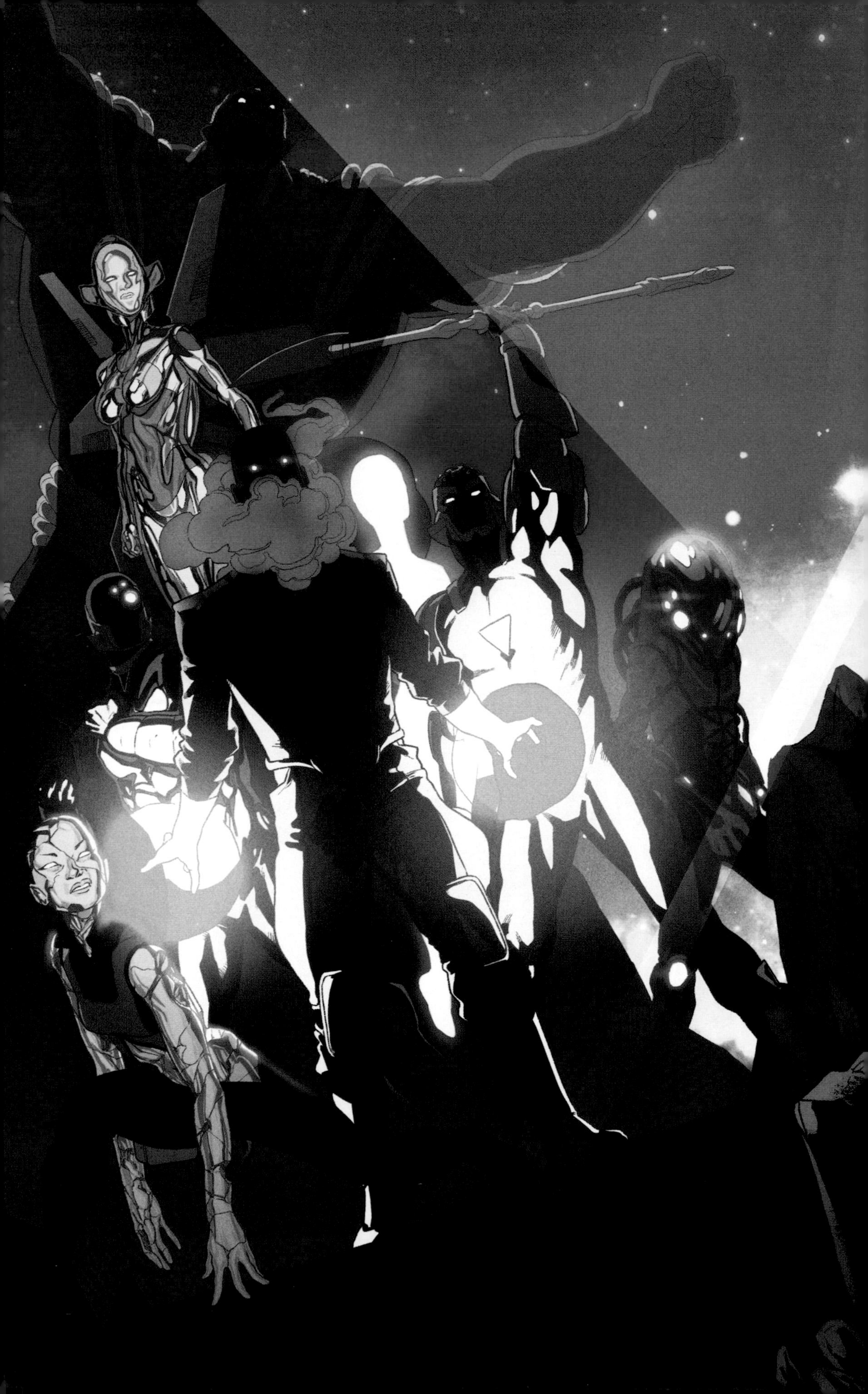

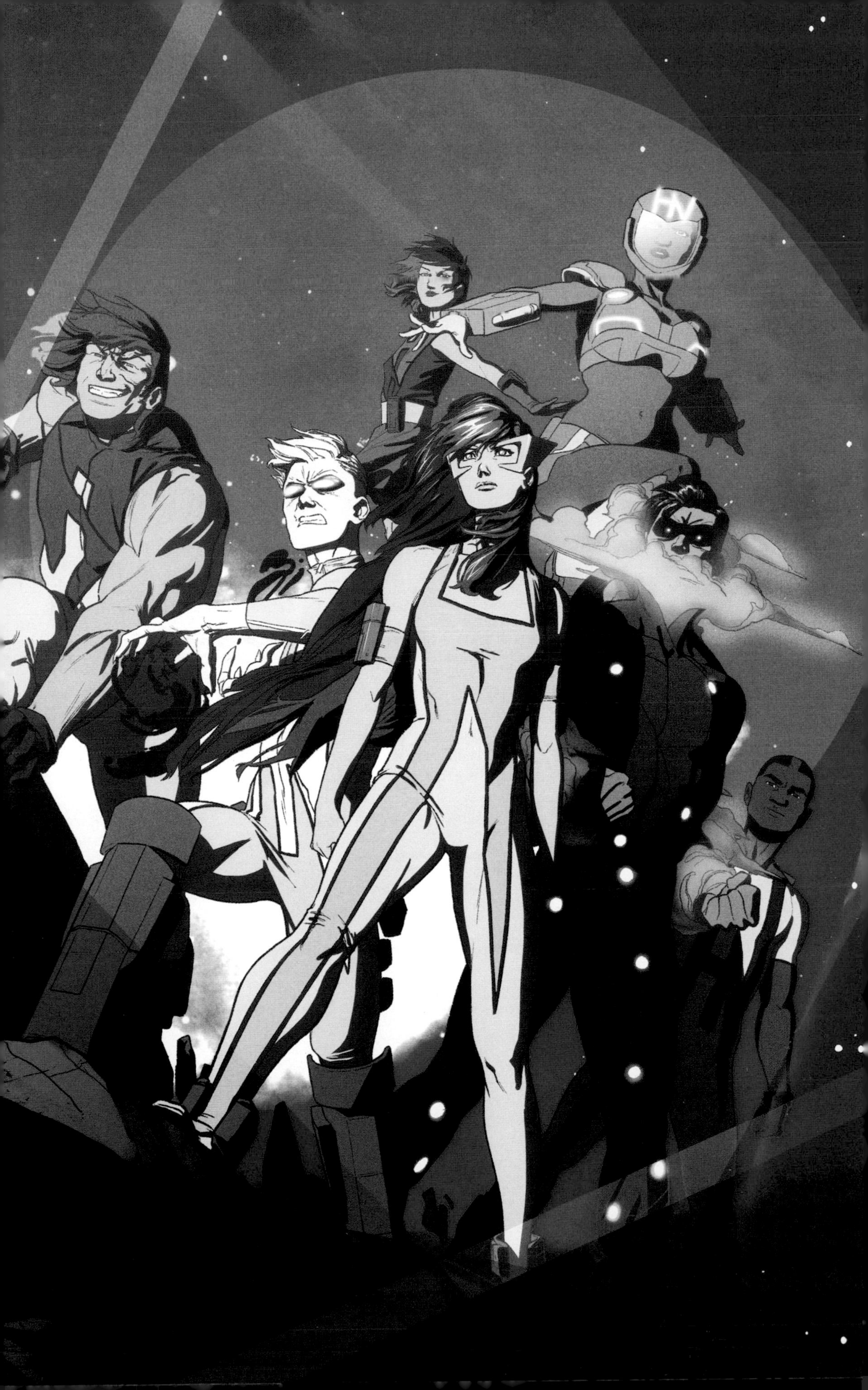